Stepping
lightly

Stepping *lightly*

Simplicity
for people
and the planet

Mark A. Burch

NEW SOCIETY PUBLISHERS

Cataloguing in Publication Data:
A catalog record for this publication is available from the National Library of Canada.

Cover design by Val Speidel.

Printed in Canada on acid-free, partially recycled (20 percent post-consumer) paper using soy-based inks by Transcontinental/Best Book Manufacturers.

New Society Publishers acknowledges the support of the Government of Canada through the Book Publishing Industry Development Program (BPIDP) for our publishing activities, and the assistance of the Province of British Columbia through the British Columbia Arts Council.

BRITISH
COLUMBIA
ARTS COUNCIL
Supported by the Province of British Columbia

Paperback ISBN: 0-86571-423-1

Inquiries regarding requests to reprint all or part of *Stepping Lightly* should be addressed to New Society Publishers at the address below.

To order directly from the publishers, please add $4.00 shipping to the price of the first copy, and $1.00 for each additional copy (plus GST in Canada).
Send check or money order to:
New Society Publishers
P.O. Box 189, Gabriola Island, BC V0R 1X0, Canada

New Society Publishers aims to publish books for fundamental social change through nonviolent action. We focus especially on sustainable living, progressive leadership, and educational and parenting resources. Our full list of books can be browsed on the worldwide web — see below.

NEW SOCIETY PUBLISHERS
Gabriola Island, B.C., Canada   **www.newsociety.com**

For Charlotte
who daily helps me remember
the goodness of simple things,
the value of slowing down, the
warmth of love, and the precious
gift of friendship.

Table of Contents

PART III

Acknowledgments

I would like to express my heart-felt appreciation to Maggie Paquet for her invaluable services in editing this manuscript as well as for her insightful and constructive suggestions on several key arguments in the text. I also appreciate the assistance, support, and encouragement from Christopher and Judith Plant of New Society Publishers in moving the book through all phases of the production process. Finally, I want to acknowledge the support and encouragement of my wife Charlotte, as well as the many questions, challenges, and suggestions offered by my students and friends that contributed in so many ways to my own learning process.

THE CHALLENGE
— AND THE JOY —
OF VOLUNTARY SIMPLICITY

This book has grown out of a long journey. Its beginnings certainly lie in the 1960s, when I was in full rebellion against what I perceived to be the materialistic values of my parents' generation and was surrounded by a very large number of like-minded peers. It was in this time that I fell in love with the idea of simple living, even though there have certainly been "seasons" in my practice of simplicity — including winters when it seemed to sleep under the snows of highly competitive full-time jobs, financial worries, and material aspirations as strong as any that motivated my parents. Nevertheless, whether it slept or whether it was awake and speaking to me, the love of simplicity has been a constant companion as well as a cherished ideal.

Through 30 years I have worked as a psychotherapist helping people make change in their personal lives, and later as an environmental educator trying to help people learn how to live in greater harmony with our planet. Mingled with both has been the conviction that the spiritual depths of human experience have a great deal to say to us, both in our individual journeys of growth and transformation and in our collective human experiment in community with each other and with the Earth. Overshadowing everything has been a pervasive sense that our future hangs by a thread, threatened since 1945 by nuclear annihilation, but more recently by the steady degradation of Earth's living systems.

The question that has been my most constant companion over the years is this: How can a person best live in order to be love, to be non-violence, and to be in harmony first with the inner spiritual realm and then with the outer realm of other people and the Earth? What I or others (whether or not of religious or scientific orthodoxy) believe is of less concern to me than that the form life takes is conducive to love and the further blossoming of life.

In 1994, I wrote a small book on voluntary simplicity in which I attempted to address this question as directly and simply as I could. The book was published in 1995 and then, as they say, one thing led to another. I started to workshop the book and developed several courses addressing ways in which the practice of voluntary simplicity might apply to different concerns, such as community well-being, environmental stewardship, spiritual growth, work, personal identity, and self-understanding. Eventually, a university in Canada invited me to develop a course on voluntary simplicity. This offered a further opportunity to explore the many areas of life in which simple living might have something to say to the experience of the millennium just ending, but especially to the millennium just beginning.

> *The question that has been my most constant companion over the years is this: How can a person best live in order to be love, to be non-violence, and to be in harmony first with the inner spiritual realm and then with the outer realm of other people and the Earth?*

One of the best things about teaching a course in something and then having bright young people ask very probing questions about it is that it offers a wonderful opportunity to learn more oneself and to think through the subject in far greater depth. The more pointed the challenges to what simple living has to say, the more convinced I became that it has a very great deal to say — not just to our contemporary very muddled, precarious, and almost hopelessly dangerous situation, but to every person of good will in every imaginable situation.

An additional motivation to learn more about the practice of simplicity was the fact that I was laid off from a comfortably remunerative position with a provincial government department in 1995. What up until then had been a potential life option turned into a pressing necessity. At first I lived with considerable anxiety and the belief that I needed to get myself right back into the same way of making a living that I had pursued very successfully for nearly 30 years. But there was another part of me that was healthy enough to be reluctant to reinsert my soul into the meat grinder of late-20th-century paid employment. Some deeper part of me kept calming and reassuring the anxious part and steadily steering a different course — in the direction of my love, not in the direction that would at first be recognized as "common sense."

Out of pressing necessity, my personal practice of simplicity found new reasons to move forward until it eventually became not a matter of necessity but of daily choice. In developing and teaching the course, I was able to explore the historic foundations of simplicity and its implications. To my delight, I've discovered that I'm not the only one interested in voluntary simplicity. We have a great deal to share and a great deal yet to explore and create. There are a lot of people more knowledgeable and experienced in living this than I am, many of whom will never write a word about it — to them I will always defer as my teachers and inspirations. Both my students and my mentors have taught me so much that I have wanted to bring it together somewhere so others can gain access to it. Hence this book.

The plan for the book is very simple, growing more or less out of the plan for the course. It is based on three questions: (a) What is voluntary simplicity? (b) Why would anyone adopt voluntary simplicity as a way of life? (c) How do people practice simplicity?

The first chapter explores the meaning of "voluntary simplicity," which turns out to be much richer and more complex than is at first apparent. The concept is linked to many other ideas, has a rich history, and is plagued by numerous confusions and stereotypes.

The next five chapters take up various aspects of the second question: Why would anyone adopt voluntary simplicity as a way of life? I explore this question from four perspectives: in respect of an individual's sense of self or personal identity, in respect of both personal and community relationships, in respect of our place in the ecosphere and our relationship to other beings, and finally in respect of the ultimate meanings and purposes of human existence, what we often call "the spiritual."

The remaining chapters of the book explore different dimensions of the practice of simple living, not so much as a "how-to manual" but as an exercise in developing mindfulness of life choices and options in each sphere. In turn, we take up the cultivation of mindfulness itself as a regular life practice, ways to discern and sustain sufficiency or "enoughness" in the practice of living, mindfulness of time and money, approaches to work and livelihood, and the larger spheres of action related to certain questions of economic and social equity. At last, we revisit the question of meaning and the ways in which all these aspects come to be drawn together in a perspective of human life that is as different from the dominant consumer value system that so pervades modern society as it is rooted in traditional values and time-tested customs for soulful living.

In no way does this volume attempt to be authoritative because "voluntary simpletons" are a characteristically feisty lot who tend to prefer their own anarchy to any "authoritative" statement on anything — unless they're looking for fodder for a good joke. But I feel privileged to have been able to explore this subject in this way since 1995 and want to share what I've found in case it may be of interest or use to someone else. I hope this book is comprehensive enough to answer many of the "yes, but!" questions that so plague those who are drawn to the ideas or imagery of simplicity but are terrified of trying it. And I hope that the book contains enough depth to compensate for some of the more superficial treatments of the subject that have appeared in the popular press since the most recent renaissance of interest in voluntary simplicity.

At the end of the day, however, I am convinced that no one takes up the practice of voluntary simplicity because they are intellectually convinced that it's a good idea. On the contrary, simplicity must first draw the heart, appealing to the soul in some mysterious way; only afterwards will the intellect follow along, filling in the details of how to organize life around this new passion and dreaming up rationales for curious friends. The attraction of simplicity is mysterious because it draws us in a completely opposite direction from where most of the world seems to be going: away from conspicuous display, accumulation, egoism, and public visibility — toward a life more silent, humble, and transparent than anything known to the extroverted culture of consumerism.

PART I

WHAT IS VOLUNTARY SIMPLICITY?

1

Voluntary Simplicity:
The "Middle Way" to Sustainability

Fashioning a New Culture

In his book *Ishmael*,[1] Daniel Quinn suggests that every society is an enactment of a story the people of that society tell themselves about the nature and purpose of their existence and of the world they live in. Quinn believes that modern societies, with all their triumphs and abuses, enact a story that claims human beings are the crown jewel of evolution and all the world's species and resources exist to satisfy human desires. By extension, the story of our "consumer society" tells us that the purpose of human existence is to find meaning, pleasure, and identity through consumption. In this story, the world exists for the sole purpose of satisfying human desires for things to consume. Technology is our instrument for making available new things to consume and economics measures our success in doing so. We have embraced the story of consumption but have forgotten that "to consume" means to eat, to use up, to waste and or to suffer destruction — and that "to be consumed by something" means to be obsessed by something.

No doubt many North Americans will protest that this assertion is too bold a generalization; that we cherish many non-material values; that our lives embrace more than just tripping back and forth to work and then shopping at the mall. As our churches, art galleries, public libraries, and parks fall into disrepair, as homeless people crowd our streets, as species disappear from our forests and the forests themselves dwindle, however, our protests sound more and more like lip-service to values which we may still cherish intellectually, but which we have lost sight of how to live out — how to *enact*.

While it is not widely advertised, there is much evidence to suggest that we are now writing the concluding chapters in the story of consumer society. Even as its technical advances exceed anything we have previously known, even as its business mergers surpass the scale and monetary value of the entire economies of many countries, even as its markets are jammed with more merchandise than ever before, and even as the promise of economic growth appears to be limitless,

7

the story of our society — the myth we tell ourselves about ourselves — is everywhere vitiated by contradiction, disillusionment, and emptiness.

Many people are beginning to understand that we
need to tell a new story if we are interested in sustaining
civilized human societies — a story that affirms higher
goals than the acquisition and consumption of material
things and that better measures human progress than the
yardstick of "economics" as we currently understand it.

The consumer culture of North America is spent, even though it continues to amass record profits. It never was socially sustainable. Now it is proving to be environ- mentally unsustainable, even toxic.

The consumer culture of North America is spent,
even though it continues to amass record profits. It never
was socially sustainable. Now it is also proving to be environmentally unsustainable, even toxic. It has no way to
account for its environmental deficits, and because of
those deficits, it will perish in an ocean of its own poi-
sonous wastes. It has few mechanisms for equitably dis-
tributing its material benefits, and that's another reason it will perish — whether
in an ocean of violence or with a sigh of indifference remains to be seen. The only
real question is which of these two deaths will happen first.

Fashioning a new culture is an immensely creative challenge. Its first crys-
tals have been seeded in the alembic of personal transformation. This new culture is emerging in human freedom as a voluntary choice and along a trajectory
quite different from that of the more-is-better consumer ethic with its Horatio
Alger myth of elitist competition for positions of hierarchical privilege. It is not
being foisted on people through media blitzes, nor is it being proclaimed as the
inevitable direction of a global market economy.

On the contrary, a new culture *is not* inevitable. The choice to live in equitable and sustainable relationships with other people and with the ecosphere is just
that: a *choice*. It is coming into existence through myriad small, quiet decisions
being made by individuals and small collectives, not in the grand councils of global international treaty-makers or in the boardrooms of transnational corporations.

Just as the roots of the consumer culture can be traced back to the values
and decisions of people who thought of themselves as "consumers," the roots of
the new culture are found in the ethos of *voluntary simplicity*. Voluntary simplicity offers an alternative story to that told by the consumer culture. The values
that underpin simple living express a different reason for living. The practices
that comprise voluntary simplicity, whether the people living it call it that or not,
are an alternative way of relating to other people and to the living world.

Voluntary simplicity is a social movement, a spiritual sensibility, an esthetic, a practice of livelihood — but is decidedly *not* a life-*style*. All sorts of people practice simplicity who might not call it by that name: environmentalists hungry to live more lightly on the land; artists, musicians, and scholars who live simply for the sake of their work; spiritual pilgrims who cannot truck clutter in the work of spiritual growth; people burned out and disillusioned by the frantic pace and empty promises of consumer hype; people in retreat from the dismal dangers of urban neighborhoods seeking friendlier communities and more caring relationships; people of wealth and social standing who hold themselves to a higher purpose than that of simply amassing more money or power over others; people fallen sick in mind or soul or body and thus forced to reconsider what really matters to them and then to find a way to live for it.

Voluntary simplicity isn't a fad cooked up by Madison Avenue to sell a new line of clothing or kitchen gadgets (although Madison Avenue is scrambling to co-opt the language of simplicity), nor has it sprung from academe as a philosophical system or research finding. In recent research conducted by Anthony Spina, voluntary simplicity is associated with the "successfully discontented," the "mainstream disillusioned," and the "cultural creatives."[2] In short, it is appearing in the lives of people who have sampled many of the rewards promised by consumerism and found them tasteless. Having gorged on food that does not satisfy, they are creating something different — something *profoundly* different — but not, paradoxically, something new.

Duane Elgin calls voluntary simplicity a "way of life which is outwardly simple and inwardly rich."[3] It involves directing progressively more time and energy toward pursuing non-material aspirations while providing for material needs as simply, directly, and efficiently as possible. It measures personal and social progress by increases in the qualitative richness of daily living, the cultivation of relationships, and the development of personal and spiritual potentials. Simple living does not denigrate the material aspects of life but rather, by attending to quality, it values material things *more* highly than a society that merely consumes them.

The term "voluntary simplicity" was first coined by Richard Gregg, a follower of Mahatma Gandhi. Gregg described it as follows:

> Voluntary simplicity involves both inner and outer condition. It means singleness of purpose, sincerity and honesty within, as well as avoidance of exterior clutter, of many possessions irrelevant to the chief purpose of life. It means an ordering and guiding of our energy and our desires, a partial restraint in some directions in order to secure greater abundance of

life in other directions. It involves a deliberate organization of life for a purpose.[4]

Gregg's description nicely captures several aspects of voluntary simplicity: that it involves many different "layers" of experience and that it includes stripping away whatever is extraneous to the central purposes of life. These are essentially *positive* things to do because we do so in service of things we value more than what is stripped away. Living simply is about the "deliberate organization of life for a purpose."

Voluntary simplicity begins in *personal action*. It has little meaning apart from how it configures individual lives. Anyone can understand it. Anyone can practice it in some way, regardless of income, cultural background, or educational attainment. Practicing simplicity requires no special training, expert advice, or official sanction.

> *Voluntary simplicity begins in personal action. It has little meaning apart from how it configures individual lives. Anyone can understand it. Anyone can practice it in some way, regardless of income, cultural background, or educational attainment. Practicing simplicity requires no special training, expert advice, or official sanction.*

The practice of simplicity begins with individuals and is well attuned to the humanistic outlook of modern society. It also reconnects a person with the traditional values of thrift, temperance, self-reliance, responsibility, and, where appropriate, spiritual asceticism. It immediately empowers people to make realistic, creative changes in understandable areas of their lives at no additional cost and at whatever pace is comfortable. Moreover, voluntary simplicity is highly "adjustable" since a person can simplify his or her life to any degree and in whatever way they find most congenial. It follows that how we practice simple living will change with each of life's seasons and situations.

One of the most encouraging aspects of voluntary simplicity is that there is no need to wait for one's neighbors to attain enlightenment, a federal election, an ascendance of principled politicians, a sea-change in social consciousness, new technology, global spiritual awakening, or a new political party before positive change can begin. Thus, simple living sidesteps the cynicism, delays, and dithering that come with large, complex institutions, policy discussions, government "procedures," or commercial ventures. For all these reasons, adopting simple living is a humble, personal endeavor and at the same time socially, economically, and politically radical.

While some colorful practitioners of voluntary simplicity have worked publicly to change social institutions, thousands of lovers of simplicity have practiced the art quietly and unobtrusively. They are creating patterns of livelihood that progressively free them from the obsessions and disquiet that so plague their neighbors. When asked, they happily share their discoveries. The very nature of their journey, however, shrinks their footprints on the world, making them progressively *less* visible to their neighbors. As this journey unfolds, one can actually fall in love with the esthetic of minimalism, with an image of the lightness of being and of the gracefulness that characterizes changing seasons, winds, and waves that leave no traces as well as beings who love without thought of recognition or reward. A feeling-sense emerges about one's proper role in the world that is the very opposite of needing to "leave one's mark" on it. In a sense, we might then say that the mature practice of voluntary simplicity is creative play leading toward practical invisibility.

Nine Characteristics of Voluntary Simplicity

One approach to understanding voluntary simplicity is to consider some of the *values* shared by those who practice it.

In 1997, I initiated a "delphi exercise"[5] involving some participants in an Internet-based discussion group on simple living. The delphi process is a method for developing consensus on an issue or question among a group of people knowledgeable about the subject. Everyone participating in the process had been practicing voluntary simplicity in their personal lives for some time, though none would claim to be an "expert." I asked participants what values they thought were *essential* to the meaning of voluntary simplicity. After four rounds of the delphi process, a consensus formed around the following values, or characteristics, of voluntary simplicity, though no priority should be inferred from the order in which I describe them here:

- **Sufficiency, minimalism; anti-consumerism; deliberate reduction of consumption, clutter, noise, social over-commitment, superfluous ornamentation, and scale.**

Practitioners of voluntary simplicity value living with few material possessions. Those they do have are deliberately and selectively chosen to reduce the "equipment" of life to its essentials without compromising esthetic values. This "esthetic and functional minimalism" is also carried into the realm of social relations, the organization of daily routines, and the attempt to cultivate a simplicity of outlook that is honest and unpretentious.

As implied in the definition provided by Richard Gregg, this preference for sufficiency has both an inner and outer aspect. Living simply obviously means reducing the number and variety of one's material possessions. It also implies an inner "house cleaning" with respect to attitudes, prejudices, pretensions, worries, and expectations.

Valuing minimalism has complicated roots in esthetic preferences for spaciousness, clarity, gracefulness, streamlining, and efficiency. It also contains echoes from more traditional values like frugality, thrift, common sense, and modesty. The rejection of consumerism is partly a reaction to the intrusiveness of consumer advertising and marketing, the pervasive transfer of public properties to private ownership, the commercialization of cultural events and public education, and especially the exploitation of children.

- **Self-reliance, socially responsible autonomy, personal authenticity, and wholeness.**

Practitioners of voluntary simplicity value personal integrity, which they express through striving to match their actions with their values (walking their talk) and maintain through balanced choices and the cultivation of healthy self-reliance. Healthy self-reliance implies cultivating the capacities to meet some of one's own needs within a social context of equity and cooperation rather than in disregard for the needs of one's neighbors or the ecosphere.

"Simplicity" implies a certain directness in managing the affairs of one's life, and directness, in turn, implies personal knowledge and involvement. Life is not delegated but *lived*. Meeting one's real needs through one's own activities eliminates the "middle men" who tend to clutter our lives with agendas other than our own. For example, some practitioners of simple living learn to grow some or all of their own food; maintain their personal health; create their own entertainment; and repair and maintain their homes, appliances, vehicles, etc. Of course, the degree of self-reliance is a matter of individual preference and aptitude. But there are clear links between developing self-reliance and a sense of empowerment, competence, and high self-esteem. The products and services of consumerism tend to dumb life down, remove risk, promote passivity, and create dependency.

Ideally, developing self-reliance leads to "healthy autonomy." Healthy autonomy does not mean living in defiance of the community (as might be the case for a survivalist or misanthrope) but rather living in society as a contributing member capable of making a constructive difference to the quality of community life. It is partly through developing the skills and capacities essential to self-reliance and healthy autonomy that we also lay the foundations for well-being and self-esteem.

• **Connection, interdependence; co-operation with the Earth, other beings, nature, and other people.**

Practitioners of voluntary simplicity value the capacity to experience connection with the ecosphere and with other people, who obviously comprise a part of the ecosphere. They strive to express this connection through co-operative interdependence in family and community relationships, as well as through activities that strengthen and deepen the quality of community life. The value of connection also finds expression in concern for equality, international justice, and compassion for oppressed people. Practitioners of voluntary simplicity value social and economic equity and strive to practice compassion toward all those suffering marginalization in any way.

For some, voluntary simplicity especially represents a way of living in greater harmony with other species and natural processes. The North American consumer lifestyle is destroying the Earth. Many people sense that consumerism cannot be sustained, but rich, rewarding alternatives seldom get "air time" in the consumer-dominated media.

Few doubt that the extraction of resources and the manufacture and consumption of material goods and services contribute to environmental damage. These activities may not be carried out with the *intention* of harming the ecosphere, but they often do cause harm. In fact, no imaginable technology designed to serve endless craving could do otherwise, except as a matter of *degree*, because no imaginable technology can sidestep the Laws of Thermodynamics or the Law of Conservation of Matter and Energy. We cannot *create* energy on planet Earth. The final limit on what we can consume is determined by the energy the planet receives from the sun as well as the energy stored in fossil fuels and fissionable elements. When fossil fuels are exhausted, even if this were possible without the Earth's climate undergoing a radical change, all living things and all industrial activities would necessarily be limited to the energy available to us from the sun. Since the amount of this energy is more or less fixed, the limit that it imposes will sooner or later constrain the production and consumption activities of human beings.

At the end of the day, reducing environmental damage implies creating a richly satisfying way of life while also reducing the consumption of resources and the production of wastes. Advocates of cleaner production technology say resource consumption and waste production can be reduced by increasing efficiency — which is true *to some degree*. But simpler living *halts* both resource consumption and waste production *at source, immediately*, for all those products and services that practitioners forgo. Increasing production efficiency alone cannot achieve sustainability if we continue to pursue a consumerist ideology of the good life while also failing to control human population growth. But if improving production efficiencies could be linked to effective population controls *and* a cultural ethos of simpler living, a sustainable livelihood might be in sight.

Voluntary simplicity suggests as the goal for technical development a *minimalist emphasis* rather than growth. In a demonstrably finite world, such a goal is inherently more sustainable. Moreover, voluntary simplicity emphasizes attention to *true development*, which is a qualitative improvement of life rather than a quantitative expansion of consumption as the measure of a good life. As people adopt simpler living, they may initially reduce the quantity of their material consumption, but eventually they increase the sophistication and efficiency of providing for their essential needs and of realizing their personal aspirations in life.

Finally, voluntary simplicity contributes directly to environmental sustainability because it engages a powerful "reverse multiplier" effect. Every pound of "product" we see at the retail level represents tens, or even hundreds, of pounds of resources and energy expended in the extraction, manufacturing, distribution, and retailing stages "upstream" in the lifecycle of the product. Individuals often feel as though their choices matter little in meeting the global challenge of environmental preservation. Yet, as individuals forgo excessive consumption, each such decision avoids all the "upstream" environmental costs incurred in bringing the product to market. Gradually we come to perceive each thing we might own as the visible "tip" of a less visible environmental "iceberg" lying just beneath the surface of the economy. For example, it is estimated that every American consumes about 32 pounds of resources (forest products, minerals, energy resources) per week, while over 2,000 pounds of waste are discarded to support that consumption.[6] Thus, each consumption decision matters a great deal and can have more or less dramatic effects, depending on the items purchased. For many people, this by itself is enough reason to simplify the material side of their lives.

- **Mindfulness, spirituality.**

Practitioners of voluntary simplicity value a mindful, unhurried, intentional (rather than impulsive), and appreciative approach to living. Some practitioners value *mindfulness* as a personal spiritual practice in its own right. They also see applying the insights they gain through cultivating a mindful approach to living as part of living with personal integrity. For many, this is synonymous with spiritual practice.

We will explore the cultivation of mindfulness in a chapter all its own. It is enough at this point to say that in order to live "voluntarily," to bring more consciousness about making choices into our lives, we must be awake and paying attention to our experiences here and now. Those who value simplicity also value taking responsibility for making life choices. This is the exact opposite of allowing yourself to be just another automaton at the conveyor belt of consumer culture, of being narcotized by advertising, hypnotized by marketing imagery, or manipulated by flimflam artists. Mindfulness is the means of maintaining connection with our experience — another one of the values essential to simple living. By cultivating mindfulness, we also happily discover that it can become a pathway to our deepest spiritual intuitions.

You needn't be a devotee of simple living to share the values of mindfulness and spirituality. But to the degree that these values *are* shared and lived out, it seems that people who hold them gradually develop simpler ways of life as a consequence. Each of us has limited time and energy. We each decide how much we will give to nurturing relationships versus acquiring, maintaining, and protecting possessions. While the two focuses are not entirely exclusive of each other, they clearly represent different ways of being in the world. Similarly, many people find that cultivating the depth dimension of their experience calls for silence, solitude, time for reflection and appreciation, and energy for exploration and new learning. Pursuing these kinds of purposes usually takes you out of the consumer mainstream into quieter pools where the currents are slower and deeper and different forms of reflection become possible.

It would be misleading, however, to think of people who are attracted to voluntary simplicity as only fashioning a life based on practical applications of abstract values. Closer to the mark perhaps is to imagine myriad life experiments guided by a certain sensibility, an inner image of gracefulness and spaciousness that expresses itself first through a *practice* of livelihood that only later reveals its values. Values and practice become closely linked and strengthen each other. In the words of the Franciscan theologian Richard Rohr, "We don't think our way into a new life; we live our way into a new kind of thinking."[7]

The idea of "practice" is especially helpful because it links simple living with other practices, such as meditation, artistic development, scholarship, crafts and trades, farming, dancing, martial arts — in short, any human endeavor that allows one to be a *perpetual student*. Those who "practice" are always on the road, always learning, always developing and deepening their practice and understanding. This is the case no matter how skillful or adept they may become. Great pianists and dancers still practice. Practice requires openness and humility. It is the attitude of one who communicates and co-operates rather than of one who dominates and controls.

- **Deliberate reduction in the number of material possessions and the amount of consumption, reduction of clutter and unnecessary complexity, and a conscious re-direction of consumption decisions in favor of more environmentally sustainable forms of transportation, food production, housing, and entertainment.**

This characteristic of voluntary simplicity is more a cluster of practices that aim to apply the values of sufficiency and minimalism. The practices of reducing material possessions, consumables, and clutter, and of redirecting choices to more environmentally sustainable forms of transportation, diet, housing, and entertainment echo the "Golden Mean" or "Middle Way" espoused by philosophers and spiritual teachers. This cluster also entails reducing unnecessary complexity in the financial aspects of everyday living and developing financial responsibility, frugality, freedom from debt, and financial literacy. All these help provide for a more fully humane existence that is marked neither by conspicuous excess nor by deprivation.

Clearly, what might be "excess" to one person at one time in life may prove entirely necessary and appropriate in another situation with different personal or family responsibilities. But regardless of climate, geography, or social station, those who love simplicity are attracted to a leaner, more streamlined form of existence.

This process of "stripping down" is not something painful. Pejorative presentations of simplicity suggesting that it is driven by a grim commitment to moral principle make it hard to appreciate how joyous the material side of simple living can be. Picture a toddler stripping off clothes as he runs for the beach! What is happening *is* loss of a sort, but what is being gained in the process is a more intense connection with daily experience. Reducing excess baggage reveals more and more clearly the central purposes of our lives. Since these purposes are often beautiful and frequently go unlived in a consumer-oriented society, the simplification of material possessions becomes a form of personal liberation — as invigorating as a good skinny dip!

- **Practices that develop one's spiritual, intellectual, emotional, physical, interpersonal, and esthetic potentials.**

  These can take a diversity of forms, including meditation, music, fine and folk arts, martial arts, various forms of physical culture such as yoga, Qi-Gong, or sports that contribute to a sense of "flow," for instance long-distance running, cross-country skiing, and cycling. What is shared is an active commitment to wholistic personal growth.

  The practice of inner simplicity ... begins with cultivating the capacity to be conscious and mindful of ourselves, our relationships, and our moment-to-moment experience. It's that "simple."

  This cluster of practices is the enactment of the value of self-reliance and the cultivation of healthy autonomy. For some people, the inner aspect of voluntary simplicity serves as their starting point. The practice of inner simplicity, as we shall see later, begins with cultivating the capacity to be conscious and mindful of ourselves, our relationships, and our moment-to-moment experience. It's that "simple." From the cultivation of mindfulness there unfolds a whole array of other attitudes, emotions, insights, and habits that serve to express and embody a progressively clearer awareness of *who* we are, *what* we want our lives to be about, and just *how* we can express that most artfully.

  From the cultivation of mindfulness, a new center for personal identity is forged that spins itself into forms and actions in the world — a new pattern of activities and commitments that define a new way of living. We cease to pursue a life*style* and instead start fashioning a *life*. In this process, the organization of one's outer life comes to reflect and help sustain what is growing in one's inner life. The reduction of material clutter finds its psychological and spiritual counterpart in increasing mindfulness, integrity, heightened attention, deliberateness, focus, and clarity. We cultivate a way of life that is free of pretense, affectation, façade; in short, a life decidedly uninterested in *image* but passionately interested in *substance*. It matters less and less what one *has*, but more and more what sort of person one *is*.

  The consumer economy actively strives to divert individuals from realizing their inherent potential, unless it can be easily linked with selling goods and services. Advertising, marketing, manufacturing, a great part of the legal code, many financial enterprises, and the very physical shape of communities distract people from the knowledge and expression of their inherent potential, or else they strive to re-interpret and re-align personal aspirations to economic goals. Vanishingly few commercial ventures are launched with the goal of helping people come home to *themselves*. Rather, consumerism seeks to bring people to the *marketplace*.

Just living in a technically complex and increasingly populous society can divert our attention and energy from the inner life and direct them instead toward the activities necessary for physical subsistence and safety in urban centers that have become so fast, noisy, mechanical, and dangerous that a moment's lapse of attention can be lethal.

Voluntary simplicity is all about realizing our inherent potential. It involves "growth by subtraction," or paring away whatever distracts us or is extraneous or alien to what we believe are our central purposes in life. When we begin to practice self-reliance and healthy autonomy and learn not to succumb to the distractions on which the consumer economy depends, we learn to recognize our life purposes, the quality of their depth and mystery, and ways to best express and honor them in how we live.

- **Practices that build strong, intimate, non-violent, and compassionate relationships with people and with nature that contribute to the personal and common good.**

Nurturing interpersonal connections is important to practitioners of voluntary simplicity, especially through co-operative activities that serve one's family or community, including the wider international and natural communities. Many North Americans say they feel oppressed by stress, hurry, bureaucracy, debt, fear of violence, or fear of abandonment — in short, they feel disconnected and unsupported. As a result, their anxiety increases. The pace and direction of life in a consumer society can carry us away from connections and relationships that would nourish us and sustain our self-worth or heal our disappointments, while at the same time promising us that all its gadgets and services will give us more time to cultivate and enjoy relationships. Increasingly, we spend more time with technological devices (machines, computers, paperwork) and less time with people.

Fashioning a simpler way of life is part of fashioning a life that offers more opportunity to establish relationships and to then live within them. Those who practice simple living make building and sustaining relationships a conscious part of daily activity. (We will explore these themes in greater detail when we take up the discussion of simplicity and community.)

- **Development of a conscious, intentional approach to living rather than acting on unconscious impulses.**

Many practitioners of simple living actively develop awareness, knowledge of issues, and intellectual and emotional skills that support making responsible life choices. These may include participating in civic affairs and making sound purchasing decisions rather than being driven by momentary impulse, appetite, or urgent necessity.

The practice of cultivating and maintaining consciousness in making life choices, including purchasing decisions and being involved in issues of community concern, even in our approach to individual and work relationships, is simply seen as a mode of life appropriate to living simply

This cluster of practices grows out of the values placed on mindfulness in daily living and our capacity to exercise our freedom of choice in making life decisions. We have already seen how these are linked. The practice of cultivating and maintaining consciousness in making life choices, including purchasing decisions and being involved in issues of community concern, even in our approach to individual and work relationships, is simply seen as a mode of life appropriate to living simply. Developing a conscious, intentional approach to living affirms some of what is best about life, rather than focusing, as consumerism often does, on whatever will promote sales.

Related to this is the belief, implied by the practice of mindfulness, that our choices *matter*. They matter in how they contribute to our own quality of life, to the future we give our children, to the quality of life enjoyed by people elsewhere in the world, to the security of life enjoyed by other species, to the promotion of justice and wellness in our own communities, and to our spiritual growth. Since our choices and the quality of our daily experience matter, blundering through life purely on impulse, following appetite, chasing the ephemeral, accepting what amounts to lies are all betrayals of ourselves. In effect, they silently demonstrate that we don't value our own lives. Practicing a conscious, deliberate, attentive approach to living directly opposes the siren song of consumerism. What consumerism prefers in its customers is that they only be awake enough to "swipe the plastic."

- **Practices contributing to a wholistic approach to personal health.**

There are many examples of how people live out this general practice. For instance, adopting a vegetarian or vegan diet incurs lower environmental impact during food production, can (though not always) simplify food preparation, and, some people feel, represents a more compassionate way of meeting our nutritional needs than diets rich in animal products. A preference for organically produced foods further expresses the conviction that personal health cannot be cultivated in isolation from planetary health or be secured through the use of pesticides, fertilizers, and herbicides in food production. Healthy habits of rest and exercise, commitment to health maintenance practices, and activities that relieve stress and promote wellness are seen as primary foundations for personal health that prevent us from relying on disease-care services in the first place. Some practitioners of simple living also express a preference for alternative treatment approaches (e.g., homeopathy, nutrition, energy, massage) in time of illness, perhaps because many of these call for a greater level of involvement and control to be exercised by the "patient" during illness treatment than is the case with allopathic approaches to treating disease. Taking more responsibility for our health and also our treatment in times of illness is simply another expression of the values of mindfulness and self-reliance in living.

Attention to maintaining one's health is a logical outgrowth of self-reliance and the directness implied in simpler living. Increasingly, practitioners of simple living perceive a professionalized, impersonal, medical-pharmaceutical industry that promotes "consumerism" of its own products and services and is not necessarily interested in human health per se, despite its protestations to the contrary. Documented examples abound of the "over-medication" of North Americans, especially of vulnerable seniors and children; of the specialized and often arcane medical vocabularies that serve more to alienate than to connect people with their own bodies and wellness processes; of a readiness to prescribe rather than collaborate and advise; of disproportionate over-funding of disease-cure technology and services and concomitant under-funding of health and wellness promotion and education programs; of a general tendency to respond to illness by treating its effects rather than attending to its causes in environmental pollution, sanitation issues, and an inadequate general education.

These considerations and many others incline those practicing voluntary simplicity to the view that healthy food, knowledge of one's body and environment, wholesome exercise, and safe communities make a more direct and immediate contribution to personal health than sophisticated technology, exotic and expensive pharmaceuticals, and large medical service bureaucracies. Certainly people get sick and sometimes need invasive interventions. But what is of concern is the way priorities are established. It makes little sense to spend billions on cancer research while turning a blind eye to lifestyle and environmental factors that clearly cause cancer. Promoting wellness is far less expensive and far more pleasant than curing disease.

Perspectives from History and for Today

As David Shi illustrated in his book *The Simple Life*,[8] simple living has a long history in American culture, reaching back to the Puritan and Quaker religious movements in Europe and their subsequent settlements in North America. Perhaps because simple living has periodically gained a high profile in North American history, it has also accumulated a number of stereotypes and given rise to nostalgic fantasies. For this reason, another useful perspective on voluntary simplicity is to consider what it is *not*.

First, voluntary simplicity is *not* new. Those who portray it as some radically new social innovation overlook its deep roots in traditional values and virtues. Thrift, temperance, co-operative self-reliance, community interdependence, harmony with nature, and the pre-eminence of spiritual and interpersonal values over material and consumer values have a far older heritage in our culture than the more recent messages to spend, consume, compete, and radically isolate oneself through the "in-your-face" behavior celebrated by consumerism. Voluntary simplicity reaffirms values that have a much more established track record in contributing to survival and human well-being than anything emerging from the muddy dreams of advertising agencies.

Simplicity has an ancient pedigree. The Chinese philosopher Lao Tzu left a career in the Mandarin civil service to live simply as a mountain-dwelling hermit, during which time he wrote one of the classic texts of Taoism, the *Tao-Te-Ching*. The Greek philosopher Diogenes was said to live in a tub in the agora of Athens, where he walked the streets and questioned passersby in search of one honest person. Siddhartha Gautama, himself the heir to a throne in ancient India, forsook the pleasures and power of a kingdom to search for enlightenment. Eventually attaining it as the Buddha, he taught that attachment to material things was simply one of many impediments to liberation from suffering. Jesus of Nazareth embraced simplicity in solidarity with society's outcasts and in order to set his heart first of all on his Heavenly Father's kingdom. St. Francis of Assisi, innumerable desert recluses and hermits, and thousands of people entering religious orders that include vows of religious poverty, embraced simplicity in imitation of Christ. The same is true for millions of the followers of Buddhism, Taoism, Islam, Hasidic Judaism, Sufism, and Hinduism. Thus, simplicity has drawn its enthusiasts from both the high- and low-born and has included intellectuals and spiritual leaders as well as legions of ordinary folk.

In more recent times, the Russian literary giant Leo Tolstoy sang the praises of simple living, while North America has seen a long line of people who lived simply as part of their religious practice (Puritans, Shakers, Amish, Quakers, and Mennonites, among others) or because of their philosophical convictions (Henry David Thoreau and the New England Transcendentalists, for example).

The birth of modern India in 1948 was sparked by the forceful simplicity of one of its most charismatic leaders, Mahatma Gandhi. Partly inspired by his example, a whole generation of youth in North America and Europe, at least for a time, took their ideological leave from the materialism of the 1950s in a variety of counterculture "back-to-the-land" experiments during the 1960s and 70s.

While the love of simple living, and even occasional extremes of material asceticism, can, as described above, claim some lofty figures among its proponents there have been periods during which very large numbers of ordinary people have adopted simplicity to some degree and for a variety of reasons. Usually people embrace simplicity because it is either a pathway to or an expression of values that they believe are more meaningful and rewarding than the material benefits they forgo. Sometimes, as Shi points out, people embrace simplicity to assist with a war effort or some other national crisis, only to revert again to whatever is the historical equivalent of consumerism. But in any case, the concept of simple living is certainly not an invention of the 1990s.

Given its venerable history, some people are surprised to discover that voluntary simplicity is *not* about going back to anything. There is deep nostalgia within our society for what we suppose were the "simpler" values of North America's aboriginal or rural agrarian past. Many people (including myself) who participated in the "back-to-the-land" spin-off of the 1960s counterculture discovered that rural living using 19th century technology is anything but simple! For some, this experiment has been deeply satisfying. For others, it was a stepping stone that helped disentangle sentimental illusions about nature, rural living, and earlier periods of history from the realities of living a physically more demanding, direct, and rooted way of life. We have come away from these experiences with the awareness that simple living is indeed rewarding and that one can live simply in *any* century and in *both* rural and urban settings. The essence of simplicity is not about living in a certain historical period or at a certain level of technical development. It definitely is not about returning to the "Little House on the Prairie" or reconstructing tube-powered radios as if integrated circuits didn't represent an immense advance in the quality of life with a simultaneous reduction in the intensity of its energy and resource use. While the ranks of those living simply probably include some "technophobes," voluntary simplicity is a *forward-looking* cultural development aimed at higher states of focus, attention, mindfulness, awareness, and conscious purpose. Technology, however advanced it may be, must serve these values. Technology is not the enemy. It can very much be a part of living simply versus being, as it is currently presented, a rationale for "consumerism."

Simplicity, on the other hand, is all about knowing how much consumption is *enough* and then setting aside efforts to further expand consumption in favor of pursuing other goals. Simplicity is what a healthy culture develops toward if it escapes getting caught in the *growth* trap. Our society is fixated on expanding the scale and volume of everything it does. Consumer economies, and the political interests that serve them, depend on economic growth to generate increasing profits and shareholder dividends. The practice of voluntary simplicity shifts focus onto the quality and meaning of life and away from its scale and quantity.

In his original essay on voluntary simplicity, Richard Gregg refers to the work of historian Arnold Toynbee, who argued that the essence of civilization consists in a progressive "etherealization of culture." That is, mature civilizations, after having sufficiently provided the necessities of life, turn their energies to other goals: spiritual development, learning, art, the promotion of justice and peace, cultural development. Any society that simply goes on to produce more and more of what it already has is stuck in a kind of perpetual cultural immaturity, never ripening to full maturity. Thus, on both the personal and the societal level, the movement toward voluntary simplicity is a sign of personal and cultural maturation, not merely a nostalgic indulgence, a throw-back that may have sentimental appeal but no relevance to modern life.

> *Simplicity is what a healthy culture develops toward if it escapes getting caught in the growth trap.*

Voluntary simplicity is not necessarily anti-technological or anti-modern. Instead, it calls for the re-orientation of technology as a means of achieving economic growth for its own sake to being a means of developing sufficiency and equity in society. The goal is to recognize that human well-being can never be achieved solely by maximizing production and profit. In fact, the opposite is closer to the truth: we should be striving to maximize human and ecological well-being on the *minimum of production*. This is a post-modern goal, not an exercise in nostalgia.

Despite its venerable history and association with many spiritual traditions, voluntary simplicity is *not* a religion. Its close relationship with spiritual practice is both instrumental and essential. There is no "creed of simplicity" that binds all its practitioners. Simple living is trans-denominational and has its proponents in all major spiritual traditions. It has also been practiced by secular humanists, atheistic philosophers, and some followers of schools of spiritual thinking, such as Henry David Thoreau, a New England Transcendentalist.[9]

There are also people who embrace simplicity for financial reasons, to find relief from stress, because the Zen-like esthetics of simplicity appeal to the, or because it's a practical response to the demands of a particularly compelling life work, such as the completion of an art work or saving money to put a child through university.

Simple living, therefore, is purely a *means*. It is not a creed but a *practice*, not a destination but a *vehicle*. Its value rests in what it helps us achieve: more time, peace, solitude, gracefulness, mindfulness, justice, ecological sustainability, equity, sufficiency, silence, gratitude, generosity, interdependence, spiritual intuition, humility. That the lovers of simplicity share certain values or configure their lives in similar ways in no sense requires that they hold the same opinions on religious matters, or that they subscribe to any religion at all.

Simplicity and Clearing away Distractions

Simplicity by itself does not automatically improve human character. It merely "clears the decks" so that something new can grow according to the aspirations of the person concerned. If a person happens to be narcissistic or selfish, he or she can live simply and still be narcissistic and selfish.

It is important to recognize that voluntary simplicity is *not* poverty, puritanical self-denial, or negative asceticism. Those advocating simplicity are *not* saying that poverty is noble, a good thing, or a way of life that should be adopted. Rather, simple living is practiced for the values it conserves, many of which are antithetical to any philosophy that espouses the denial of pleasure for the sake of denial.

Poverty often arises from uncontrollable circumstances (such as chronic or catastrophic illness, unemployment, natural disaster) or results from systemic injustice (such as discrimination, existing inequitable patterns of privilege and want that exist in many places today). Poverty is usually not voluntary. Extreme poverty can result in destitution, a condition of material, psychological, and sometimes even spiritual impoverishment in which choice and mindfulness are not options. Negative asceticism and some other self-denial philosophies view consumption and the enjoyment of material things as morally suspect. None of this has anything to do with simple living.

Today, in North America, poverty and destitution are spreading like cancers. A whole generation of young people is being cut off from education and employment opportunities while their elders are being forced into "early retirement." All alike are exposed to the same daily drone of messages from advertisers that promote an idea of a good life that fewer and fewer people can afford.

Both the affluent *and* the poor are enmeshed in the same destructive system. Consumerism exploits the poor and the affluent at the same time as it lies to both. While the poor suffer the pain of deprivation, the affluent suffer the pain of disillusionment when all they have to show for their affluence is a lot of "stuff," but spiritual emptiness. Consumerism as a way of life destroys people and communities as a whole, even those people who suppose they are in control of it.

Simple living speaks directly to the moral, social, spiritual, and ecological costs of affluence. It enables the freedom of choice open to the affluent to conserve their communities, the planet's ecosystems, and their own opportunity to find meaning in life. The message of simple living can heighten awareness among the affluent of the ever-increasing stresses and costs that attend the ever-diminishing rewards of an acquisitive lifestyle. Finally, voluntary simplicity can underline the truth that, beyond what is needed for sufficiency, looking for meaning in life through consumption is futile.

Advocates of simplicity have never idealised destitution. Death by starvation is agony. Homelessness, illness, inadequate clothing, loneliness — all these are not only personally calamitous, they are socially degrading. The fact that our social systems don't remedy or prevent them offends our principles of decency. The only appropriate response to conditions such as these is to do what many of the great philosophers and spiritual teachers of history have always taught: Feed the hungry, clothe the naked, house the homeless, care for the sick, educate the ignorant, visit the lonely, welcome the stranger, look after the orphan, comfort the afflicted — in a word, *love* each other.

Yet when we have *enough,* and there are very many of us who do, what then? Could it be that some of the discontent associated with a modest income is caused by the ceaseless din of advertising messages that one can be happier by earning or owning more? And could it be that if we were less open to these messages, our minds and hearts would be more open to those aspects of living that cannot be bought and sold? Could it be that some of the pain of unemployment (apart from the very real and legitimate fear of starvation and homelessness) comes from the loss of a sense of personal identity that consumer societies find only in working and earning and owning? In truth, is this an appropriate basis for personal identity in any case? If the answer to any of these questions is "yes," then simplicity has something to say to nearly everyone.

Closely related to the misconception that simple living celebrates poverty is the idea that it celebrates *cheapness*. Practicing simplicity doesn't mean surrounding oneself with junk, regardless of its price. Neither does it require always purchasing used items, such as clothing or cars, or always riding a bicycle for transportation.

On the contrary, there is a strong esthetic element in simple living. Moreover, it seems to imply a love and stewardship of material things, which in turn implies that they be beautiful and well-crafted. Consumer society, for all its supposed emphasis on "materialism," is often deeply hostile to the material world, to the senses, and to the care and love of material things. It expresses this hostility by converting almost everything it touches to *waste* that can neither be cherished nor used for long, nor passed along as a heritage. Consumerism hurries its worshipers through life with little time to linger or enjoy or feel anything.

Simplicity, by contrast, seeks reduction of the material items used to provide for life's basic needs, but insists that they be beautiful, sturdy, and functional celebrations of the Earth and the human intelligence that fashioned them. There is certainly scope within simple living for works of art that celebrate creativity and beauty as values in their own right. In her book *Frugal Luxuries*,[10] Tracy McBride nicely expresses this sensibility, which makes it possible to experience great reward in simple pleasures.

Should voluntary simplicity become the cultural mainstream in North America, I imagine people living not cheaply or meanly or with any sort of barren austerity. Rather, homes and communities would reflect elegant design (in the sense of intelligent — rather than fashionable — design) and a deep respect for the laws of physical and biological nature. Our inventions would work with efficiency and directness. "Quality" would encompass beauty as well as durability, utility, and price. I imagine people living in smaller homes that are less cluttered with "technology" but of unique design, jewels expressing the taste and life of their owners. Our homes and communities would communicate the sense that people living there actually intended to have grandchildren, to be around for a while, to sustain their culture, and to leave behind things to be admired and enjoyed for a long time.

Simplicity involves centering thinking and action upon what is most essential and central to our humanity. Precisely because of this, simplicity also tends to a healthy kind of "materialism." By this I mean a deep respect for the material, or physical, world for the resources it provides us, for the responsibility and power we have to be the co-creators either of beauty, utility, and lasting value, or of ugliness, futility, and waste. Doing this may involve living inexpensively, although not always. It will certainly involve applying human ingenuity to existing materials and wastes to bring out of them something better than we have now. But in both cases, the goal is not just to minimise spending or to maximise recycling. The goal is to build our lives around *different values*.

Simplicity and Financial Freedom

Frugality concerns economics, whereas simplicity relates to one's outlook on the whole of life. In his classic book *Small Is Beautiful*[11], the economist E.F. Schumacher wrote that the goal of any sane economy should not be to maximize wealth measured in money, but to meet real human needs ever more efficiently with less and less investment of labor, time, and resources. The goal of a sane economy would be to *free* people to do more important things than make more money or consume more goods. A humane economy certainly would not place people on a treadmill of frustration or avarice by manufacturing and marketing an ever-changing and expanding menu of distractions and unfulfillable desires.

The goal of a sane economy would be to free people to do more important things than make more money or consume more goods.

Amazingly, in its most recent incarnation, voluntary simplicity has been confused with being independently wealthy! Voluntary simplicity is *not* essentially a financial management system for the wealthy, nor is it the rigorous practice of living cheaply.[12]

Those who live simply must manage their finances well and make thoughtful purchasing decisions. The simplest, most environmentally sustainable and socially responsible way of meeting one's needs may not always be achieved by purchasing the cheapest items available. In addition, simple living encourages people to focus attention on those life goals and activities that bring them lasting reward. These will be different for different people, and for some activities may imply significant expense.

A popular book in the United States, *Your Money or Your Life* by Joe Dominguez and Vicki Robin,[13] has been described as the "bible" of the recent renaissance in simple living. The book contains a great deal of valuable information and insightful analysis, much of which is directly pertinent to simpler living, especially when it helps readers develop more mindfulness (awareness and choicefulness) regarding their use of money. Calling it a "bible" was unfortunate, however, because I don't think Dominguez and Robin ever set out to write scripture, and they certainly did not intend to become the focus of quasi-religious commentary. The popularity of the book has helped contribute to the idea that voluntary simplicity is mainly for those affluent enough to need financial planning assistance and fortunate enough to contemplate a day when they might receive an income without working for it. Linking the practice of simple living to financial independence inclines people to the misleading conclusion that the latter is somehow the prerequisite of the former — a notion that Jesus, Gandhi, St. Francis,

Gautama, and Thoreau would have found utterly laughable. Voluntary simplicity can be practiced *immediately*, by *anyone*, in any area of life where there is room for choice. It has little to do with money, and one certainly doesn't have to be financially independent (or even interested in becoming so) before being able to take up simple living.

Again, while I don't believe this was the intent of Dominguez and Robin, the popularity of their message fits logically with the dominance of the pecuniary spirit in North America. Money is seen as prerequisite to almost everything else, the axis around which the North American mind turns. This may be partly due to our deep-seated delusion that possessing money confers freedom. It's not money that many people say they want, so much as the "freedom" they think money will give them to do as they like, when they wish, wherever they want — as if any imaginable constraint in any of these directions somehow negates our capacity for happiness or meaning.

Freedom gained through money, just like beauty, love, sexual attractiveness, or power gained through buying the "right stuff," represents a "supply-side" approach to living: To increase freedom, increase the supply of money. But it's an insecure freedom since it depends upon the security and constancy of the supply of money. Interrupt or take away the money, and you also take away the freedom. Moreover, the focus is on the "freedom to" (e.g., the freedom *to* indulge one's impulses and appetites without thought for, or much involvement with, others), with little attention paid to the "freedom from" (e.g., the freedom *from* loneliness, violence, insecurity, distraction, injustice, a polluted environment).

Since the "freedom" offered by consumerism depends on wealth, from this single contingency flows a great deal of uproar and unpleasantness. People compete with each other for new supplies of wealth or are tempted to exploit others to increase their wealth. They may build defences and amass hoards to keep their wealth secure. Paradoxically, as the hoard of money increases, so can the anxiety about losing it and the frenzy to conserve and protect it. As the financial capacity to consume grows, decisions on how, when, and what to consume gradually come to occupy more and more time and attention. Since monetary wealth, and hence consumerism's understanding of freedom, depends on the continuation of the existing order of things that supplies the wealth, extreme conservatism is inevitable. How can we permit change when change may reduce the supply of money that we think assures our freedom?

Another feature of "supply-side" freedom is that it emphasises scarcity rather than abundance. It simply won't do for everyone to print his own supply of money, although this is a natural spin-off from supply-side freedom. Indeed, promising business ventures are sometimes referred to as "a licence to print money." But when people actually do this, we call it counterfeiting and prosecute them. Only governments can print money, which means that they also control the supply. But if the supply is limited, it is also likely to be scarce, and unless very special social and economic arrangements are put in place, some people will have more and others less of it.

When the measure of freedom is monetary and someone else controls the supply of money, then someone else controls our freedom. This can never be a secure freedom.

Another way of thinking about freedom grows from the practice of simplicity. Simplicity is a "demand-side" pathway to freedom. It is freedom gained through reducing and redirecting *desires*. It grows from the insight that *satisfying desire does not produce happiness or contentment*. In fact, seeking happiness through the satisfaction of desires leads to suffering and conflict. To construct an entire social and economic system on the cyclical and deliberate generation of *artificial* desires, their temporary satisfaction and then re-stimulation, is, in a word, lunacy. Yet this is the "miracle" of consumerism.

To increase freedom, contentment, and happiness, we must instead *reduce* artificial wants and desires. This approach to securing freedom is within the reach of everyone at no charge. There is no way to make money from this recommendation, corner the market on it, or really convince other people who understand the idea that you have it and they can't unless they buy something from you. It's not about scarcity.

Unlike the steps taken to become wealthier, each step into simplicity *increases* rather than reduces security. Simplicity is always secure since it doesn't depend on anything outside ourselves, and certainly not on divine providence. Nothing has to be hoarded (or can be). Nothing has to be defended because the freedom conferred by simplicity doesn't require a secure or expanded supply of anything except mindfulness. Once a small measure of simplicity is attempted, the door is opened a crack to provide time to develop deeper mindfulness. Mindfulness is delightful. This can cause people to search for additional ways to simplify their lives so that they can feel more secure and have more time to grow in mindfulness and the delight in living that it brings. A self-stoking cycle is set in motion that runs entirely opposite to received wisdom about where freedom comes from, how it can be "secured" and enlarged, and what exactly contributes to feelings of reward and contentment in life.

Yet another aspect of thinking of freedom in terms of financial wealth is that having conspicuously more than our neighbours can undermine relationships. Indeed, it *must*, since the false freedom and false security promised by money tend to become an enclosed, isolated, defiant, and self-absorbed condition.

Often wealth can elicit jealousy, envy, suspicion, distrust, and sometimes even violence from other people. The "freedom" brought by consumerism comes at the price of continually looking over one's shoulder and living in "private compounds" and "exclusive" clubs that witness as much to fear as they do to privilege. What sort of freedom is that? Why would anyone aspire to it?

The freedom of simplicity is found in *relationship* and *social solidarity*. For those who live simply, freedom of choice and action grow up through social influence and community connections. Pleasure and security in living are enlarged not through consumption but through social co-operation, sharing, and interdependence. Unlike the "security" offered by bank accounts and alarm systems, the security of simplicity is achieved by embedding our lives in the affections and shared debts of love that make up community. The "price" we pay for this sort of life, for this kind of access to such a variety of freedom, is reduced "freedom" to consume. It remains for each person to decide how important, compared to other kinds of freedom, the freedom to consume without restraint actually is. Simple living is most joyful for people who have discovered something they love more than just "stuff."

> *It remains for each person to decide how important, compared to other kinds of freedom, the freedom to consume without restraint actually is. Simple living is most joyful for people who have discovered something they love more than "stuff."*

Despite the rangy tone in Thoreau's *Walden*, voluntary simplicity is *not* necessarily about rugged individualism or a survivalist brand of self-reliance. As Duane Elgin has described it,[14] simpler living is usually about living more *directly* and with greater depth of *personal involvement* in the daily tasks of meeting one's needs, but this isn't the same thing as antisocial individualism. Simple living seeks a healthy integration of self-reliance (doing what one can and appropriately should do for oneself) and community interdependence (sharing goods, resources, and time toward the common goal of a healthy community). Achieving this integration is, of course, an endlessly creative process.

People who interpret simple living as *autonomous* living have found that meeting all of their personal and family needs on a strictly self-sufficient basis is not simple! Historically, those lifestyles that optimize the personal practice of simplicity are usually *communitarian*, e.g., lifestyles found in tribal villages, monastic communities practicing vows of poverty, fraternities and sororities, kibbutzim, and cohousing co-operatives. When applied to an appropriate degree, the specialization and division of labor that is possible in communities can contribute to the common welfare and reduce the complexity of life for individual members, at least as far as meeting basic material needs is concerned. By sharing those tools, appliances, and other material possessions that can be shared, individuals can transfer "ownership" of such things to the community and hence be free of them. It is a matter of historical record that the growth of individualism in society has paralleled the growth of commercially driven consumerism. And from a commercial perspective, the most profitable society imaginable would be one of fully "cocooned" individuals, terrified of their neighbors and deeply possessive of their "things." In such a society, every person must have his or her "own" collection of possessions to support their life, numb their boredom, and, of course, protect them from all the other intensely lonely and envious individuals who might steal what is "theirs" rather than simply borrow things from a shared inventory, use them, and return them! By contrast, simpler living has more to do with "going it together" than with "going it alone."

It is often for the sake of family and community that individuals choose simpler living in the first place. It may be through re-establishing relationships of community interdependence that individuals find ways for developing their own practice of simplicity.

For example, by consciously reducing the material complexity of their lives, practitioners of voluntary simplicity liberate time, money, and emotional energy for deeper involvement with others. To the degree that simpler living brings with it a greater measure of inner peace, financial security, and relief from the stresses associated with the competitive pursuit of consumerism, it helps people become more emotionally and psychologically available to others. It also frees up resources for creative contributions to one's household and community as well as time and energy for creative efforts to build up the cultural richness of one's neighbourhood or town. Survey after survey of the determinates of life satisfaction reveals that people find spending time with each other consistently more rewarding than spending time with things.

Similarly, it is through deepening interpersonal bonds that people develop mutual commitments to shared values. Strengthening relationships also helps develop a sense of connection and interdependence within one's community. A person with time *for* others finds that bonds begin to develop that place one in solidarity *with* others. This in turn makes it emotionally possible to substitute collective sharing for personal ownership. Thus at one and the same moment a much wider range of material "riches" becomes available to the individual at no additional personal burden of ownership. For example, communities whose members can muster strong collective support for parks reduce everyone's individual need to maintain a private yard at great savings of land, environmental impact, and personal cost. Moreover, the shared space of a park provides another opportunity to nurture community rather than isolation. In this way, community can be both a value that is strengthened through the practice of simplicity and also a *means* to a simpler life.

やる

Voluntary simplicity is *not* about "dumbing down" our lives. Voluntary simplicity is built on paradox — the paradox that less can be more, that growth can be deadly, that affluence destroys happiness, that making life more "difficult" can make it easier, and that simplicity enfolds complexity. The practice of simplicity consists in the voluntary removal of *extraneous complexity* so that more mental, emotional, and physical energy is available to engage *meaningful complexity*.

> *The practice of simplicity consists in the voluntary removal of extraneous complexity so that more mental, emotional, and physical energy is available to engage meaningful complexity.*

For example, meditation is an outwardly simple but inwardly extremely complex and active process. Music consists of simple, straightforward conventions, yet musical compositions can be very rich and intricate. The individual movements included in T'ai-chi are very simple, but the choreography of their linkages and the mental and physical effects they produce are anything but simple. Simplifying life in service of pursuing some of these other activities is the exact opposite of dumbing down. It is consumerism, in fact, that in its search for the lowest common denominator in the marketplace dumbs life down. Simplicity, by contrast, requires that we smarten up.

やる

Finally, there is a great hunger in the media for the next new "miracle" development that will solve all the world's problems — the silver bullet that kills all bad guys. Unfortunately, voluntary simplicity is *not* a panacea. As mentioned above, simple living is purely a *means* that is especially accessible to individuals. It clears the way for some fresh thinking, perhaps for some alternative institutional innovations, and certainly for higher levels of cultural and political involvement by ordinary people. Voluntary simplicity is not an automatic antidote to all of the systemic and structural problems of society. This, however, in no way detracts from its value.

Voluntary simplicity points in a constructive direction toward the evolution of an environmentally sustainable and socially equitable society. Because it is an individual practice, it circumvents the delays and rigidities we encounter in organizing larger-scale social reform movements; the directness of simpler living achieves immediate "results." It is not a preparation for something else that will achieve results, nor does it displace responsibility for action onto someone or something else. To conserve energy, governments write new legislation, business awaits new technology, economists fiddle with monetary policy, academics do research projects — but practitioners of voluntary simplicity just step up and turn off the lights.

Voluntary simplicity doesn't necessarily demand instant, radical changes in our lives. Of course, there may be some people who are ready to attempt major changes, but many people come to simplicity as a *practice* that they develop over a long period of time and through many shifting seasons and experiments. Simple living can be adopted at any pace, rapidly if desired, but normally in an organic and gradual way. In my view, slowly diffusing simplicity into one's life grounds it more solidly in daily routines than does giving way to impulsiveness, as if simplicity were just another fad. The practice of simplicity takes different forms in the lives of young people, the newly married, young families, more mature families, "empty nesters," and among elders. In the words of a Chinese proverb: "Be not afraid of growing slowly; be afraid only of standing still."

The Question of Values

Proposing voluntary simplicity as a more sustainable way to live is no more, nor any less, value-laden than traditional technological or economic recipes for the good life. It is most definitely *not* about indoctrinating people with a particular set of values. The values we mentioned above, as interesting as they are for discussion purposes, don't form a creed to which a person must subscribe in order to practice simplicity. They merely reflect a consensus among a small group of people currently doing so.

In fact, it is consumerism that attempts to systematically configure North American values to its own ends through the incessant efforts of its multi-billion dollar marketing and advertising industries.

It can be observed that as people develop a conscious awareness and recollection of their personal experiences of value in life, most of these experiences are not associated particularly strongly with consumption, ownership, or possession of material things. From this perspective, the consumer culture of North America is actually an organized distraction system that attempts to superimpose the values and imagery of consumerism onto those of the individual.

One of the key findings of a study done by the Merck Family Foundation[15] of US-American views on consumption, materialism, and the environment revealed what its authors describe as a deep "ambivalence" about modern culture.

On the one hand, Americans enjoy material things. They can be induced to purchase them and have been taught to associate material affluence with security and personal well-being. They believe what they have been taught — almost. On the other hand, they feel they have lost touch with, time for, and energy to pursue other more important and fundamental activities associated with family, community, and personal well-being. They are also deeply concerned about how their consumption affects the environment.

The Merck study describes these findings in terms of "ambivalence." But another interpretation that can be offered for the data is that they reflect a society in deep *value conflict*, specifically between what respondents know they value (e.g., identity and affiliation values) versus what they have been taught to want through the culturally pervasive activities of commercial advertisers. Had the Merck study included questions that asked people to rank their values or to identify values that they believed were more or less authentically their own, ambivalence might have been more readily identifiable as conflict. Readiness to entertain voluntary simplicity as a life choice increases as this conflict becomes more acute.

Anthony Spina has conducted research on people practicing simple living and likens their life changes to "tuning" a radio so that static (noise) is reduced and signal (music, meaningful words) is increased. He attributes "noise" in modern society to the clatter and clutter of "system" messages, i.e., "data smog" representing the views of governments, commercial retailers, and organized institutions. The "signal" that most people find rewarding in their lives is connections with their "Lifeworld" — a sense of personal meaning, goodness, and vitality that is contained in ordinary human relationships, sensuous contact with the world of nature, and experiences of face-to-face community. As "signal" from the Lifeworld becomes increasingly lost in the data smog generated by large corporate and government systems, we become increasingly lost and disoriented and feel cut off from our sources of meaning and reward in life. People practicing voluntary simplicity do so, Spina argues, because it has proven to be an effective means for them to reconnect with the "signals" coming from their Lifeworld.[16]

Simpler living begins when people become conscious of their values and live congruently with them, *whatever they may be*. This, in itself, is a value which is significantly different from those of the consumer culture.

Practitioners of voluntary simplicity begin from *questions* such as these: What do I value in life? How can I align my practice of daily living so that it brings me more into the presence of my values or expresses them more clearly? What in my life distracts me from this task or clutters my expression of these values, and how can I rid myself of it?

Consumerism, on the other hand, asks no questions; it *advertises imperatives*. If you want to be happy, sexy, socially influential, odor-free, nice, financially successful, etc., buy this.

The challenge of sustainability cannot be met without addressing the relationship between consumption and values. This subject is no less "realistic," "objective," or "practical" than are technical and economic matters. Some spokespeople for science and economics seem to believe that their pronouncements emanate from an "objective" realm that has irrefutable validity and stands above, or outside, more "subjective" matters like human values. But contemporary science, particularly physics and mathematics, have long since departed from such a view.[17] Every assertion of "fact" and every act of "observation" is also at the same time necessarily an assertion of value and an act of subjective creativity. No system of thinking, including economics, can claim to stand outside a relativistic universe. Therefore, discussion of values is just as essential to the future of society as discussion of observational methods is essential to the progress of science. And many of the most important things in life cannot be measured or observed at all.

The Push-Me-Pull-You of Voluntary Simplicity

From the perspective of a consumer-dominated culture, the idea that simple living might be widely adopted can seem far-fetched. But there are already signs of both a "push" and a "pull" toward simpler living.

The factors that will "push" the societies of developed countries toward simpler living have already been mentioned above as the challenges to environmental and social sustainability. Simpler living will be a key characteristic of any imaginable *civilized* future for the mass of humanity. The critical decision before us is whether we voluntarily embrace the practice of simplicity now or see it involuntarily imposed by circumstances which, through neglect or denial, become self-stoking transnational emergencies that no longer allow for choice, for conservation of civil and political liberties, or perhaps even for the survival of democracy. Despite the scoffing ridicule directed toward simpler living by the captains of commerce, an inescapable challenge must be addressed: If voluntary simplicity were adopted by all the world's people, it would at least be plausible to foresee a sustainable, healthy, and reasonably peaceable future for all humanity. If, however, everyone on Earth adopted the North American "standard" of consumerism, could we honestly foresee a similar future?

There are also increasing indications that traditional values surrounding work and compensation for work through material reward are buckling under the strains of exploitation inherent in a growth-oriented consumer economy. Studies conducted in 1997 by the Angus Reid polling organization and Statistics Canada clearly reveal the increasing strain on individuals and families from the need to work more hours and often multiple jobs in order to maintain the same or often-times diminishing material benefits. Two million Canadians (about 20 percent of the workforce) now work 25 percent or more overtime hours per week, much of it unpaid. Use of employee assistance counseling programs to help workers cope with personal and family stress has nearly doubled since 1995, and enrolments in "time management" classes are exploding.[18] People are coming increasingly to understand that the system doesn't deliver what it promises. Diligence and hard work are not delivering a better life. The consumer system is delivering a less secure, more stressful and driven life. For increasing numbers, it's time for a change.

There are also many factors at work on the "pull" side of voluntary sim-plicity — early indicators of its attractiveness at the close of the millennium. In her new book *Circle of Simplicity*, Cecile Andrews notes that when she first offered a workshop on voluntary simplicity in Seattle in 1989, only four people attend-ed. In 1993, when she offered another workshop, 175 people came. During the intervening years, over 100 "study circles" on voluntary simplicity have formed in neighborhoods, community centers, churches, and workplaces across the United States.[19]

Since 1993, many new books and resources, too numerous to mention here, have started to appear on the subject of simpler living. Key among them are a second edition of Duane Elgin's ground-breaking book *Voluntary Simplicity*, orig-inally published in 1981 and then re-released in 1993; Joe Dominguez and Vicki Robin's best-selling *Your Money or Your Life*, released in 1992; Sarah Ban Breathnach's very successful bestseller *Simple Abundance: A Daybook of Comfort and Joy*[20]; and a plethora of other books that range from personal accounts of experi-ences with simpler living to entertaining and provocative appeals to explore alter-native approaches to paid employment, as well as formation of intentional com-munities and even the processes of psychological transformation necessary to make the transition from consumptive living to voluntary simplicity.[21]

Building on an already established and lengthy history of activities aimed at promoting social justice and peace, the Mennonite Central Committees in Canada and the USA have launched their *Trek: Venture Into a World of Enough* pro-gram, which consists of a series of stories, prayers, and reflections intended to help people of the Mennonite community think about the relationship between their Christian faith and their patterns of consumption.[22] Similarly, the Seattle-based Earth Ministry has launched a resource package of discussion questions, reflections, meditations, and readings that also present voluntary simplicity from a Christian perspective.[23] Even prior to this, the Northwest Earth Institute, also a Pacific Northwest-based organization, had been offering its introductory course on voluntary simplicity by means of workplace seminars and discussion group presentations — an adjunct to its existing course on deep ecology. Over 4,000 people have participated in these programs.

There has also been steadily growing activity related to voluntary simplicity on the Internet. There are Internet discussion groups dealing specifically with simpler living, such as the "positive-futures" discussion list, which supports nearly 200 participants, and several other lists of closely associated interest, such as the frugal living list, the frugal education list, the "Maxlife" list (devoted to discussions on increasing the quality of life), etc. An important focus of Internet activity is the Simple Living Network (SLN) website (http://www.slnet.com/), which contains an extensive set of web pages and an on-line magazine. SLN includes books and resources with descriptions, reviews, and ordering capabilities, information on study circles in all 52 US states and territories and all 11 Canadian provinces and territories except for Newfoundland/Labrador. SLN also includes a great deal of information about products and services that may be of interest to people seeking a simpler life, including periodicals and links to other websites.

The Pierce Simplicity Study website was originally set up by Jim and Linda Pierce as a vehicle for conducting an online survey of people embracing voluntary simplicity in preparation for a book of anecdotes and biographies that describe people's motivations for and discoveries with embracing voluntary simplicity. The site has been expanded to include resource lists, book reviews, study circle information, and a variety of resources and links to other Internet sites. It's on the internet at http://www.gallagherpress.com/pierce/index.htm.

Similarly, Tom Gray has established the massive Frugal Education website (http://www.igc.apc.org/frugal/index.html), which includes dozens of articles, resources, book reviews and website links.

The Context Institute (http://www.context.org/), headquartered in Seattle, Washington, maintains an extensive website generally devoted to more sustainable living but with a strong emphasis on voluntary simplicity. They publish an on-line version of the formerly print-based *In Context* magazine, an excellent resource of positive and constructive articles aimed at tracking the emergence of a new, more sustainable culture.

Yes! A Journal of Positive Futures is the print-based successor to *In Context* and is published by the Positive Futures Network, also based in Seattle and also devoted to sustainable living generally, with a specific interest in voluntary simplicity. Its inaugural issue in 1996 was entirely devoted to voluntary simplicity.

Subsequent issues have taken up various themes touched on in this book, such as local currencies and participatory community decision-making. While these sites have been created by individuals or small groups, they nevertheless reflect an expanding public interest in voluntary simplicity as they record the growing lists of books, articles, conferences, public seminars, courses, study circles, and meetings that are all signs of vibrant creative and developmental activities.

There are some indications that the marketing juggernaut of the 1980s and '90s that sought to offer consumers an ever wider range of choices and options has simply reached a saturation level, with consumers themselves being on "choice overload." Some consumers seem ready to trade more options in the products and services they purchase for a greater measure of comprehensibility, which can only come through simplification. In Canada, for example, following the deregulation of long distance telephone services, competition between long distance service providers became intense. An explosion of advertisements during prime time TV offered a tangle of competing discount plans, time-of-day savings plans, day-of-the-week "specials," etc. When Sprint Canada offered long distance service "anywhere, anytime" for a flat rate per minute, suddenly people could comprehend and actually know ahead of time what a long distance telephone call would cost. The transparency and simplicity of this approach was a sales windfall for Sprint Canada. Now a number of advertisements feature references to how this or that product or service will "simplify" the purchaser's life — even if it won't. The encouraging sign in all this is that it provides indirect evidence that advertisers with big research budgets have discovered that simplicity matters to more and more people and are including it in their sales pitches, even if they don't know what it means.

By now one of the central paradoxes of voluntary simplicity should be clear. The meaning and practice of simplicity are simple: finding a "middle way" in life that minimizes material and non-material clutter, except for what is essential to our chief purposes in living. The implications and connections arising from this way of living are complex and numerous. In the discussion that follows, we will explore the question of *why* one might take up the practice of voluntary simplicity.

PART II

WHY PRACTICE
VOLUNTARY SIMPLICITY?

2

Simplicity and Self

If you look for Truth outside yourself, it gets further and further away.
— Tung-Shen

We begin exploring the question, "Why practice voluntary simplicity?" by focusing on the self — on one's individual life and subjective experience; in short, on one's *identity*.

Early in our development, we view the world and all that happens in it entirely through the window of subjective experience. The perspective that our own consciousness forms the center and source of everything that is important is "normal." Should consciousness wink out of existence, it would, regardless of how the world goes on without us, be no longer of any significance *to us*. Eventually, we learn that this idea is mistaken. Until we do, it is natural to think: "Well, this simplicity stuff is sort of interesting, but what exactly does it have to offer *me*?" Thus, answering the question "Why adopt a simpler way of life?" requires showing how it benefits us personally.

People take up simpler living for a variety of reasons: stress is driving them to migraines or manias; there is no time in their lives for spouse or children; there is no energy for pleasure after meeting the demands of work; there is no opportunity to make a contribution to the community; personal health is being threatened by a lifestyle of perpetual motion; financial stress and oppressive debts haunt every waking moment.

In 1995, The Harwood Group undertook a national survey[1] in the United States at the behest of the Merck Family Fund and discovered some startling things:

- Americans believe their own priorities are out of whack; materialism, greed, and selfishness increasingly dominate American life and crowd out more meaningful values centered on family, responsibility, and community.

- Americans are alarmed about the future and feel the material side of the American Dream is spinning out of control and is increasingly unhealthy and destructive.

- Americans are uncertain about what to do. They want financial security and material comfort, but their deepest aspirations are non-material ones.

People take up simpler living for a variety of reasons: stress is driving them to migraines or manias; there is no time in their lives for spouse or children; there is no energy for pleasure after meeting the demands of work; there is no opportunity to make a contribution to the community; personal health is being threatened by a lifestyle of perpetual motion; financial stress and oppressive debts haunt every waking moment.

- 85 percent of Americans rate responsibility, family values, and friendship as key guiding principles for their lives, well behind prosperity and wealth (37 percent).

- Despite advertising messages supposedly "responding" to what Americans "need," 66 percent wanted more time with family and friends, 56 percent wanted less stress in their lives, and nearly half (47 percent) wanted to contribute more to their community.

These findings, and many others cited in the survey, are not consistent with the projection of happy people enjoying security, material bounty, and spiritual peace. Rather, they reflect a sense of deep inner disorientation — an important clue that the culture of consumerism seldom delivers what it advertises. But since many works on simple living already address personal issues, such as stress and financial solvency, it isn't necessary to repeat these discussions here.

More pressing is the question of how the culture of consumerism affects the soul, the self, the very identity of a person trying to live out its values.

❧

I mentioned Daniel Quinn's suggestion that every society and its customs, behaviors, and beliefs can be understood as the enactment of a story the people of that society tell themselves about the nature of things. Similarly, the forms and activities that give shape to the life of individuals can also be understood as the acting out of stories the individuals tell themselves about what sort of being they are, why they are here, where they are bound, what is and isn't worth doing. Of course, the stories we live are not stories we make up on our own; they are first absorbed from the society that rears us. Because they are conveyed in so many different forms and assimilated in such an uncritical way at such a tender age, most of us are never consciously aware that we're learning a story.

Consumer societies enact the story most recently proposed by the French philosopher René Descartes, with some help from England's John Locke. According to Locke, we are born as blank slates *(tabula rasa)* that get filled up with experiences coming to us through our senses. Sense experience is the only reliable source of knowledge about anything. These experiences make us what we are. Thus, what we are, our *identity*, is something we *acquire* from outside, from teachers, parents, friends, and, in our own society, most notably from advertisers. It may be too much of an inferential leap to suggest that, in a manner of speaking, our identities are built up out of what we *consume*. We do not consume sense impressions or information in the same way we consume food or clothing. Yet the Lockean view of human psychology conveys a clear sense of the inner world of subjectivity being empty and passive apart from what enters it from the outer world, and of the events transpiring in the outer world determining the texture of consciousness and the psychological content of the self-concept. Apart from the sense impressions that originate outside us, there is no psychological content that might form part of our personal identity.

One unhappy consequence of this story of human nature is that we can come to believe we are helpless victims of what has been put in us from outside, with all the disempowerment and sense of displaced responsibility and anger that can accompany such an idea. Equally tragic can be the fact that this concept of human nature robs people of self-determination and of the possibility of developing enough self-confidence to make meaningful life choices.

The Cartesian story also has a chapter about the natural world, what today we would call the ecosphere. This story says that the planet is made up of dead resources. Animals, plants, and even our own bodies are biomechanical "systems" devoid of spiritual significance, subjective consciousness, or emotional capacity. While Decartes did not assert as much, consumer culture seems to conclude from this that all the material attributes of the planet and all of its species exist primarily as raw materials for satisfying human desires. Science is the method of inquiry that determines the properties and describes the behavior of the natural world. Technology is an instrument for manipulating the natural world to enrich human entrepreneurs and to maximize pleasure and consumption for everyone.

If Locke has it right and we really are born empty and incomplete, then maybe consumer culture also has it right and we really have no identity apart from what we acquire. *Having* more then *makes* us more. Marketing people and advertising firms are totally at liberty to impose whatever they might dream up as being important products that contribute to our identity since we don't believe there is really any other *inner* agenda present in human beings. Because both Descartes' assertion that mind and body are radically separate and Locke's idea that the mind has no innate capacity for understanding or knowledge have become so deeply plowed into consumer culture that we become susceptible to believing we are whatever the market tells us we are, e.g., body odor in need of perfuming, yellow teeth in need of whitening, profoundly insecure beings in search of power, security, and social acceptance. Paradoxically, the captains of consumerism are just as enmeshed in this story as everyone else.

If there really is more to us than our physical bodies and what they can be taught to want, then the marketing motor that keeps consumerism's cage spinning is really an *assault* on the self. It is a planned, forcible campaign launched on us from the moment of birth, not to "offer choices and inform about products," but to hijack consciousness and focus it instead on the market. Whenever it succeeds, the price we pay is the connection with our own souls.

One of the most pernicious aspects of the consumer mythology is the idea that the chief goal of human existence is to achieve *wholeness*. To say that "wholeness" is the goal of human existence implies that human beings are *born defective* or incomplete and that we need something — something that someone else may have or make or give us for a price — to "achieve" wholeness. When our inner connection with our own souls is severed, this is in fact how we *feel*. Moreover, this myth tends to portray wholeness as an *achievement* (either a personal achievement or a vicarious participation in the achievement of a cultural hero or icon), something that the ego can use to aggrandize itself once it is achieved, and yet at the same time making the ego vulnerable to all sorts of appeals to power, fear, envy, and so on — all eminently useful in designing marketing campaigns and exercising social control.

From this perspective, consumerism and its breeder reactor, advertising, take on a different character. There can be little doubt that there is much brokenness and sorrow in the human situation. But it is highly equivocal whether we are *born* incomplete and all our trouble arises from this incompleteness, or whether our suffering arises instead from the *contest* between whole human souls and their natural tendency to develop toward higher states of wholeness and those interests in society who profit mightily from breaking them. Broken people buy stuff. Happy people tend not to.

Fortunately, the Cartesian story about human nature is not the only possible story, nor is it necessarily the whole story. At best, it is a partial and limited "model" in the same sense in which the Newtonian description of the universe has its area of application but breaks down under certain conditions. As any marketing representative will testify, people are nowhere near as pliable as Locke would like us to believe — suggesting that there is something more to human nature than can be measured or than meets the eye. Any scientist versed in the most recent developments of mathematics and quantum physics would say that the natural world, especially its living components, are far more mysterious and interdependent than either Locke or Descartes could ever have dreamed.

So, it may be that the Lockean concept of human nature is mistaken. It may be that we are not really "blank slates," that there really *is* something more that makes us who we are than simply the messages we receive from our social environment. It may be that because we are living beings, life itself as it courses through us has a few ideas of its own about what it is and what it's here to do. Moreover, it may be that we are also spiritual beings and the nature of this being, which is not limited by our physical bodies or a single lifetime, also has something to do with our identity. And it may be that how we come to know these things and how we act once we know them has profound implications for the "story" we tell ourselves and how we live it out in the world.

$$\mathscr{P}\!\partial$$

A different sort of story than that offered by Descartes and Locke about human nature and the possibilities open to human societies is being woven by people like Margaret Wheatley and Myron Kellner-Rogers[2], whose work displays strong resonances with earlier contributions of people like Arthur Koestler[3], Gregory Bateson, Fritjof Capra[4], Ira Progoff[5], and earlier still, Jan Christian Smuts[6] and Edmund Sinnott.[7]

Wheatley and Kellner-Rogers suggest that rather than thinking of living things (including people) as complicated bags of chemicals devoid of soul or psyche, modern science sees life as complex, spontaneously self-organizing "systems" or, psychologically speaking, *selves*. Every "self" organizes itself around an *identity* that, for human beings, is a set of beliefs about ourselves and our world. We are seldom completely conscious of all of these beliefs or the ways they work in the background of consciousness to select what we think is important and valuable from the full range of experience potentially available to us. But the nature of complex self-organizing systems is that they spin themselves into form by dynamically re-organizing the world of "outside" experience according to the identity that defines the self. So we are not blank slates at all, but active *creators* of our own identities, and we select from and organize the raw material of personal experience to build this identity, reinforce it, and protect it. Thus, the link between simplicity and personal identity is important because identity is the organizing center from which we spin our lives into forms and activities in the world.

In linking voluntary simplicity and personal identity, we adopt the position that we *do* have an inner consciousness and that the elements of identity do actually spontaneously spring from inside us. In fact, the elements of identity form the most durable and deeply rooted touchstones for knowing who we are, where we come from, where we are going, and why we are here. These elements also provide the most immediate and reliable guidance on how we can live well in relation to ourselves, to each other, and to our planet.

According to Wheatley and Kellner-Rogers, one of the most important characteristics of human beings is that we are "meaning seeking." As an identity spins itself into form in the world, what it creates in the process is meaning, and what it realizes through the recognition of its meaning is its *purpose*, its reason for being. Recall that Richard Gregg described voluntary simplicity as the "deliberate organization of life for a purpose". Choosing to seek meaning through the discovery and development of identity and trying to *acquire* an identity through material consumption are two very different ways of life.

There are dozens of modern self-help books using "purpose" as a noun instead of a verb. According to these sources, life purpose is something we *have* by setting goals. Purpose is a *possession* of the ego, since it is the thinking, willing part of the person who sets goals, assigns priorities to them, and then consciously organizes activities to attain them. In this way, our society confuses purpose with achievement.

Purpose can also mean the *end* or *finality* of human existence. It is the answer to the question "What is my life for?" Modern society says that the goal of human life is achievement and, through the rewards we garner for achievement, the acquisition of possessions. Material possessions are the visible evidence of achievement. It follows then that the lives of people who, for whatever reason, fail to produce a publicly recognized achievement of some kind (together with its visible proof in a large pile of material possessions) must have also failed of their purpose.

Such an approach appeals to our egos because it seems so reasonable, so thoroughly grounded in common sense. In this view, we are captains of our own fortunes with all the corresponding potential for inflation and despair. It would be even more appealing if only it were true!

Telling ourselves a different story about the origin and meaning of our lives, however, might help us begin to see some things differently. Indeed, life does have a purpose, but it is the purpose of my life that *lives me*, not something my ego possesses and that I consciously cause to happen by thinking about it. Goals, decisions, and thinking itself are all by-products of a much deeper process of dreaming, imagining, feeling, and longing. In this process, personal decisions and actions *are* important, but *no* less important than the dreaming, intuitive, soulful side of being. If we come to see ourselves as essentially mysterious, self-organizing but meaning-seeking beings, life purpose, and with it personal identity, becomes something that is both *achieved* through choices and actions and *received* as a discovery, an emerging mystery, a surprise to the conscious part of the self.

Living on purpose means living life *with* purpose. To live life with purpose means living in *relationship* with it, not in control of it. It also means to live with consciousness. Some spiritual teachers call this "staying awake." Their lives and teachings often urge cultivating an inwardly unified consciousness marked by clarity of purpose (the Christian "purity of heart" or the Buddhist "one pointed mind"). The way to singleness of purpose has everything to do with *self-surrender* and almost nothing to do with self-control. To become conscious of one's life purpose, to wake up, is not the same thing at all as sustaining the illusion that the ego can, or even ought to, control the depth and mystery of one's life.

Cultivating singleness of purpose both requires and produces simplicity. As we become more clearly conscious of our life purpose, the practice of living simply evolves by itself and reduces distractions from that central purpose. Simplicity also helps us express our life purpose because it clears away whatever is extraneous. *Serenity is the fruit of a simple life lived in fidelity to its authentic purpose, not a life that is merely well-managed and devoid of surprises.*

To live with purpose does not mean to live aggressively, to be stubborn, to be narrowly fixated on one's own point of view, or to be selfish, although all of these characteristics can be found in the company of those who are striving to achieve goals. On the contrary, purpose in life is both *chosen* and *discovered*; it is both made and found. Awareness of it grows between and within our experiences of motion and stillness, action and reflection, activity and passivity. To live with a fully human sense of purpose requires cultivating a fine sense of just when to seek and when to remain still so that what we seek can *find* us.

It is this second voice, the voice of our souls, that is almost totally silenced by the extroversion, aggressiveness, and materialism of modern life. Somehow, with the best of intentions, we have fashioned a way of life so fast, dangerous, and demanding that it leaves almost no time, silence, or emotional energy to relate to the deeper currents inside us that reveal our life purpose. We must think so hard, we forget how to feel. We must run so fast, we forget to sit still. We are under such pressure to produce, we scarcely remember how to receive.

> *It is this second voice, the voice of our souls, that is almost totally silenced by the extroversion, aggressiveness, and materialism of modern life.*

The serenity that is based on achievement is only as secure as this moment's achievement. The serenity that is based on controlling outer events must fail as our health may fail, our comprehension of change may fail, and ultimately, our youth fails. The serenity that is founded on our ability to plan and control change is on shaky ground.

There is another way to serenity. It begins with letting go, not hanging on. It grows in silence and stillness, not through achievement or striving, but through trust and surrender. It thrives in simplicity and expresses itself through the clean lines of quiet movement. Looking within, we feel the movement of something much deeper than anything we could consciously imagine or control. It moves there in the silence, mysterious and wonderful. It is indeed *us* but at the same time *more*. Little by little, we learn that serenity grows not by extending control over others, not by amassing achievements or possessions, but by *trusting* the arms in which we are carried.

Another instructive way of thinking about identity and simplicity can be gleaned from the work of Ira Progoff, a 20th century psychologist in the tradition of C.G. Jung and Otto Rank. Progoff described every person as being born with an inner psychological "seed potential," the unfolding of which provides both the structure of the fully developed personality and its highest meaning and fulfillment. Quite different from Locke who postulated that we are born "empty," Progoff believed that people are born "whole" and "well" and in a sense already "know" everything (at least in germ, as a seed) necessary for the full flowering of their personalities and for health and well-being. The development of personality is a process, not of achieving wholeness, but of *unfolding* wholeness from within itself toward higher and higher levels of organization, complexity, and integration. Pain, conflict, and a sense of inner fragmentation (even some psychoses) arise not because of the persistence of an innate defect or lack, but because the development of the personality toward higher states of organization and complexity has been frustrated. There is never a time when we are not "whole," although there may be times when both emotions and behavior become distorted because the "wholeness" of the seed potential cannot find a way to manifest and live out its potential.

The frustration of the innate power of the self to grow is extremely painful, since it is essentially the frustration of life's own striving to fulfill its purpose — its agenda for its own development. This innate thrusting of life toward its own actualization is expressed in every individual being, human and non-human. It is something that profoundly connects humans and every other species striving to live out its "birdness" or "fishness" or "horseness." It is not always easy to match up the dynamics of a growing soul (that which serves the unfolding potential of the person) with sales of products (that which serves corporate growth). In fact, when people become more conscious of their own seed potential, when they become conscious of the sorts of experiences and activities that most richly feed their souls, they seldom have much to do with shopping. Hence, what sustains and enriches the deepest life of the individual may not be something that can be engaged to enrich shareholders.

People can be enticed and coerced to abandon the inner project of nurturing the unfolding self by gradually having their attention trained to be focused outward by flashy advertising and a continually changing array of consumer novelties. We can also lose touch with the inner sources of identity by succumbing to appeals to fear, envy, lust for power, or sex. But the guaranteed cost of these short-term infatuations is a longer-term form of suffering that is bone-deep and inescapable. It arises from the abandonment of the inner side of one's most authentic self. The genius of consumerism is that it offers a continuous stream of products that anesthetize the suffering caused by the consumption of them. The ground is then fully prepared for the formation of a true addiction — a way of life in which the consumption of something becomes essential to be free of the pain that is experienced when it is withdrawn. It can be argued, I think, that it is just such an addictive process — one that anesthetizes North Americans from the pain of "loss of soul" — that sustains the consumer society as much as the rewards and delights claimed for the goods and services it offers for sale.

Since voluntary simplicity is the choice to live with fewer things, practicing it implies stepping out of the consumer culture to varying degrees. This is possible in a joyful and fulfilling way only *after* we find something we love more than what consumerism offers. We begin to discover this when we find some other basis for our personal identity than the vacuous promises of commercial advertising. As the famous Swiss psychologist C.G. Jung wrote to a man complaining that he felt lost and adrift in the shifting turmoil of modern life: "You will find yourself again only in the simple and forgotten things."9

It is very hard to kill the soul, though its subtle voice can easily be submerged under distracted attention, disrespect, and incessant advertising jingles. As long as we draw breath, the body continues to link us to the biological realities of life within the planetary ecosphere, no matter how hard we try to control them, ignore them, perfume them, or convince ourselves we have transcended them or "progressed" beyond them. Thus, connecting again with the "simple and forgotten things" that represent the voices of our deepest and truest selves is both as simple and as hard as *listening to them, respecting them, and honouring what they say.*

What I am suggesting here is not so much the tearing down of an old identity and the building up of a new one as a *turning aside*, if only temporarily at first, from all the clutter and racket of a consumer culture seeking to draw our attention away from what actually is our most original and authentic self. This turning aside is at the same time a *turning toward* all that we have ignored, undervalued, or simply haven't given time and attention in our lives. Like the toddler running naked over the beach, we do so when we truly believe that plunging in the sea is more real and more important to us than the labels on our clothes. Living simply with joy begins then, not in giving up, but in *coming home to who we are.*

ℰℴ

While this may be a somewhat lengthy preamble to answering the question "What's in voluntary simplicity for me?", it is, I think, an essential first step. The short answer is this : "A stronger connection with the inner sources of who you really are."

How, exactly, can we begin to reconnect with our most authentic identity and prize ourselves loose from the pervasive incursions of a culture dedicated to lulling us back to sleep? Clearly, one could begin by cleaning out drawers and closets or investing money in government bonds. Yet I think Margaret Wheatley and Myron Kellner-Rogers offer more useful suggestions:

> If we want to change what has come into form, we need to explore the self that has created what we see. All change — both individual and organizational — requires a change in the meaning that the system is enacting. It requires looking into the system's identity, the self through which it perceives and creates.
>
> A self changes when it changes its consciousness about itself. ... Thus, the source of change and growth for an organization or an individual is to develop increased awareness of who it is, now. If we take time to reflect together on who we are and who we could choose to become, we will be led into the territory where change originates. We will be led to explore our agreements of belonging, the principles and values we display in our behaviors, the purposes that have called us together, the worlds we've created.[10]

"Changing our consciousness about ourselves" can take practical form in two ways: first, by *remembering and honoring the reality* of who we most truly have been, i.e., how our "seed potential" has unfolded until now; and second, by *dreaming and honoring the dream* of who we aspire to be, i.e., what the seed potential is striving to become. Both of these acts require that we turn our attention toward the inner world, listen to it for a change and respect what it brings to our attention. This work often requires silence, time, solitude, and freedom from distraction — *simplicity.*

I know of no better summary of both the importance and the delicacy of this project than that offered by Mencius, a Confucian philosopher of the 5th century BC:

... And is there not a heart of love and righteousness in man, too? But how can that nature remain beautiful when it is hacked down every day, as the woodsman chops down the trees with his ax? To be sure, the nights and days do the healing and there is the nourishing air of the early dawn, which tends to keep him sound and normal, but this morning air is thin and is soon destroyed by what he does in the day. With this continuous hacking of the human spirit, the rest and recuperation obtained during the night are not sufficient to maintain its level, then the man degrades himself to a state not far from the beast's. People see that he acts like a beast and imagine that there was never any true character in him. But is this the true nature of man? Therefore with proper nourishment and care, everything grows, and without the proper nourishment and care, everything degenerates or decays. Confucius said, "Keep it carefully and you will have it, let it go and you will lose it. It appears and disappears from time to time in we do not know what direction." He was talking about the human soul.[11]

Mencius states the issue precisely for us. As individuals, we grow and develop by first identifying and then nurturing what is best in us, best in our souls. This partly involves removing from our lives whatever distracts us from this task or may cause us to cease to believe in it. How to go about nurturing the growth of one's own soul and how to construct families and communities that nurture the growth of soul will necessarily involve diverse activities and approaches. It is not an industrial or commercial activity. It is highly individualized and personal. It requires silence, tenderness, respect, personal attention, sensitivity to uniqueness. It requires conditions and attitudes that are almost diametrically opposed to those of a consumer society.

The Confucian philosopher also helps us understand that nurturing the soul is a delicate process. It is under "attack" from a variety of directions, and perhaps nowhere more so than in modern urban consumer societies. Failure to nurture the soul, he warns us, leaves us open to a condition in which everything human in us, everything that rightly distinguishes us from other species, can die out. Most tragically, if we allow this process to happen, we can come to a collective state of mind where we cease even to believe in its possibility. We cease to believe in the goodness of our own humanity and the goodness of others.

As individuals, this time in our history calls us to undertake a great work of *consciousness*. We begin this work by believing in its possibility and by reasserting its value. We begin this work by claiming time and space and resources to undertake it. In very practical terms, it means taking time to go to a place apart (sometimes literally, sometimes only figuratively) where we can ask ourselves some basic questions about what our life is for, what it is seeking to become, what value it has had in the past and how exactly we have experienced that value, what our life is like now and whether it seems to hold value for us, and how it needs to change, if that seems desirable.

By means of these simple but central questions, we can begin to bring back into consciousness what we *value*. We can learn to distinguish what we value from what we are enticed to want. We can then orient our use of time and money according to the subtle intimations, dreams, and leadings that issue from the seed potential seeking to grow and what we immediately apprehend to be life-affirming for ourselves and our families. Undertaking this "re-orientation" entrains many small practical decisions about what we shall own, discard, acquire, how we will make a living, how we will choose to relate to others, what goals will receive our attention and energy, and what things, activities, and social institutions will henceforth receive our allegiance.

As we come to orient our lives more accurately around our authentic identity rather than an acquired identity, our practice of living grows progressively simpler and progressively more sustainable.

As we come to orient our lives more accurately around our authentic identity rather than an acquired identity, our practice of living grows progressively simpler and progressively more sustainable. This is true because most experiences of value to humans are non-material in nature. In addition, it simply isn't possible to live in service of very many values at great depth. As we grow in our capacity to experience life with depth, that is, life with quality, with soul, the quantity of what we consume naturally moderates by itself. When we make this discovery, we cease the futile effort to construct a "lifestyle" dictated by advertising and fashion and begin living a definite *life* whose form grows organically as we enact the meanings that define our identity.

Paradoxically, it is from this very simple basis that a new "story" can be told concerning what society, the economy, technology, and institutions are *for*. Without a new story, these larger human enterprises will continue to function on behalf of the old story — the same old story, an unsustainable and self-destructive story. When a new story begins to emerge, first from the soil of meaningful individual lives, then a different pattern of meanings and intentions can be brought to our collective social project. Millions of people can then engage the full complexity of the transformation of that human project that now appears so incomprehensible and uncontrollable. No society can be great, or sustainable, unless its customs and institutions first spring from *great souls* who have each, in their own way, fashioned ways of living that are life-affirming.

But it is in our communities and our families that we can most directly exert influence over the quality and direction of community development and over the values it seeks to express. Voluntary simplicity will no doubt find expression in landscaping, architecture, community planning, social organizations, law, spiritual practice, the arts and sciences, and a variety of other human endeavors impossible to imagine at this writing. But it will do so with force and integrity only when the people involved in these endeavors establish simplicity within the compass of their own lives first, and then allow it to radiate from its personal center into all they do and make. Then we will be truly on our way to a more humane and sustainable society.

3

The Uses of Nothing

Thirty spokes unite around the nave;
From their not-being (loss of their individuality)
Arises the utility of the wheel.
Mold clay into a vessel;
From its not-being (in the vessel's hollow)
Arises the utility of the vessel.
Cut out doors and windows in the house (-wall),
From their not-being (empty space)
Arises the utility of the house.
Therefore by the existence of things we profit.
And by the non-existence of things we are served.[1]

— Lao-Tse
Tao-Te-Ching, Ch. 11

One of the most challenging aspects of voluntary simplicity is understanding that its most essential nature is not defined by cleaning closets or recycling juice can lids, but by a psychological transformation. Part of this transformation involves making the background of what we perceive become the foreground, or shifting attention from what is to what is not, or coming to value nothing as something. Lao-Tse captures this nicely in the above excerpt from the *Tao-Te-Ching,* — the general notion that "what is not" has as much utility as "what is" is a central tenet of Taoist philosophy as well as many other Eastern perspectives on living. "Nothing" has its uses. It is something the West would do well to learn.

One of the uses of nothing is that it can be a psychological "place" of inner spaciousness that offers a different perspective on our lives and values and behavior. In this sense, emptiness can be highly productive of insight and even wisdom.

During the course I teach on voluntary simplicity, class members are invited to participate in a simulation game we call "The Uses of Nothing." Most of us fear material loss so much that when we experience it through, say, a house fire or natural disaster, we are so traumatized that we scarcely have the emotional energy to listen to what the experience might have to teach us. But a simulation game provides an emotionally safe way for people to participate in an imaginary experiment of a similar sort of loss. Placing an imaginary toe in the imaginary water of nothingness can provide a sensory perception of what the actual "practice of stillness and emptiness" might hold.

Participants are asked to imagine a large tropical island with broad, sandy beaches, abundant edible fruits and vegetables, plenty of edible and harmless fish in the sea, lots of fresh water, dry caves for sleeping, and a total absence of dangerous predators, diseases, or threats to safety. They are not shipwrecked and awaiting rescue. In fact, they are the only people in the world and while there are other islands they may wish to explore, none is inhabited and none is as large and commodious as their own. There is no chance of rescue since there is no one else to rescue them. The only other caveat is that they find themselves on the island naked, with no tools or other artifacts of any kind. They have their own bodies and the companionship of each other on the island and that is all. From the perspective of the consumer society in which we have all been raised, the group has *nothing*.

One of the uses of nothing is that it can be a psychological "place" of inner spaciousness that offers a different perspective on our lives and values and behavior. In this sense, emptiness can be highly productive of insight and even wisdom.

Participants are then asked first to work alone and make a list of all the activities and experiences that they can, under the circumstances, imagine as being available to them as individuals and in relation to each others. After everyone has written down some ideas, participants form small groups, pool their ideas and challenge each other to think of more. (This phase of the work can become quite raucous!) Next, I ask the groups to select their four favorite activities from the group list and to discuss the environmental impacts of engaging in each of the four activities. Then I ask them to discuss the effects on themselves and their little community of engaging in the activities. Finally, I ask each group to describe the emotional atmosphere that pervaded the discussion. When all this is completed, each group presents its lists of ideas of what they might do, the environmental and social consequences, and the emotional tone of the discussion.

When this phase of the simulation is completed, without further comment, I re-cue the exercise exactly as before except that prior to finding themselves on the island, each class member has $1,000 with which to go shopping before going to the island. They are free to buy whatever they wish within the constraint that whatever they bring to the island cannot require a technical infrastructure for its operation; for instance, electrical appliances would be of no use because the island has no power stations. Participants are then asked first to work alone and make a list of all the things they would buy, then to work as groups to combine their lists and answer the following questions: What does having these material possessions on the island add to their lives? What environmental and social consequences follow from possessing these goods? What has been the emotional tone in the group?

At this writing I have facilitated this exercise perhaps 40 times with groups as diverse as high school students and senior corporate executives. The results have been as consistent as the equinoxes.

During the first phase of the exercise, some participants encounter some difficulty with even thinking about what is available to them when they have nothing material in their hands. Some people actually get "stuck" with a dazed expression on their faces. But others think for a moment and then start writing very quickly. When the group work starts, this process moves forward even faster, with many ideas being generated. Often, since people are imagining themselves naked on a tropical island, the discussion becomes highly eroticised at the same time that it is playful and child-like.

At the conclusion of the first phase of the exercise, groups usually have created long lists of activities that are strongly linked to their physical capacities to sense and enjoy the natural world, relate to each other in every way, and live a deep sensory and spiritual connectedness with the island and its other creatures. They walk, hike, swim, explore, sing, tell stories, create myths, collect shells and rocks, have sex, compose and recite oral histories and poetry, dance, create and perform plays, prepare and share food, etc. Participants are surprised at how long the lists can be, how little environmental impact accompanies enjoying these activities, and how strongly they serve to bond members of the group. The overall tone of these conversations is playful, humorous, erotic, spiritual, grounded, and carefree. Often group members volunteer to move to the island if I tell them where it is!

During the second phase many different things happen. As in a consumer society, participants make their purchasing decisions in isolation from each other, hence the group can wind up with surpluses of knives and scarcities of matches as each member pursues his or her "rational self-interest." Some people clearly intend to relate to the island as a source of resources in the future and they select "practical" items that will help them exploit the island by harvesting and transforming its materials: tools, matches, cookware, etc. Others seem to realize that the island already provides for all their basic needs and opt instead to purchase "luxuries" like candy, musical instruments, and art supplies. In any case, a large variety of items appears on the island and members discuss the assigned questions.

At the end of round two, participants discover, often to their surprise, that bringing material possessions to the island *does* increase the quality of life. But the tone of their relationship shifts, becoming more serious, more involved with establishing formal rules and agreements about how to share scarce resources and how to protect each other and the island environment from the misuse of potentially dangerous items. While these items add some options to life, they also bring with them more or less inescapable environmental impacts, usually negative ones. For the first time, non-biodegradable wastes appear on the island, "landfills" are necessary, and the possibility of environmental disaster (for example., as a result of having introduced non-biodegradable wastes like plastics, or toxic substances like paints) becomes an issue. Most telling perhaps is the discovery that while the presence of these objects do contribute to a higher quality of life, they don't contribute a *vast* increase over the first scenario, and actually hold much potential to contribute to social divisiveness.

The Uses of Nothing simulation game is just that — a game. It sets up a fairly artificial situation as a learning context. What this context provides is a psychological "space" within which participants discover something important: A very large measure of our capacity to enjoy life, to find meaning in it, to learn, to cherish others in relationships, to build community, to understand our planet, to express ourselves artistically and philosophically, to undertake spiritual quest, to immerse ourselves in sensory pleasure, to give expression to artistic impulses, to revel in physical exertion — all of this and much more is *innately available to every person all the time* in the very nature and capacities of our bodies, minds, emotions, language, and relationships. Put differently, we are inherently capable of living very rich lives once our basic needs for food, water, shelter, and safety are met.

... everything depends on developing a sense for how much is enough and when further acquisition becomes a source of harm. More is better only to a point. Consumerism tries to erase that "point," whereas voluntary simplicity tries to keep it in view and balance on it.

This realization helps one then place in context the question that consumer societies *never* ask: How much does the acquisition of this new thing add to my innate capacity to experience richness in life, and *at what costs* to the environment and to those I love and care for? Consumerism promotes the idea that more is *always* better and that no costs (other than the retail price) are incurred by each increment of consumption. The more we consume, the better our lives should be.

Voluntary simplicity, especially evident in the island exercise, says something different. Everything that is essential to a rich and meaningful human life is already available free or at very low cost, either as intrinsic capacity within our own nature, within human relationships and community, or from minor extractions from nature to meet our food and shelter needs. Adding to our material possessions (beyond what is essential for meeting basic needs in various climates) *may* increase our quality of life to some extent, but *everything* depends on developing a sense for how much is enough and when further acquisition becomes a source of harm. More is better only to a point. Consumerism tries to erase that "point," whereas voluntary simplicity tries to keep it in view and balance on it.

Going further, voluntary simplicity would also propose that the powers and capacities that are innate to humans are the most authentic and inalienable foundation of identity and are entirely apart from what we may later possess in a material sense. This is hardly a radically new insight, since all major religious traditions, as well as secular humanism, affirm the inherent value and dignity of the human person. I mention it merely to point out that this premise for the value of human life is prone to become lost in the maelstrom of advertising and commercial hyperactivity that typifies daily life in a consumer culture.

ᢞᢒ

Distinguishing between when something and when nothing (the *absence* of something) enhances our lives is a key way in which simple living differs from what is currently considered a more "usual" way of looking at life. Participants in the Uses of Nothing exercise discover that the absence of many things consumer culture sees as essential to a high standard of living can enhance the experience of playfulness, co-operation, and contact with nature that contributes directly to a sense of quality in life. For those practicing simple living, the capacity to notice and appreciate how the absence of something can contribute to quality in living gradually becomes a major source of reward.

We traditionally measure human progress in terms of tangible artefacts or changes. This is especially popular among the staunchest advocates of what E.F. Schumacher called "the forward stampede."[2] They believe in progress when they see something built or when some new gadget appears that promises a better life.

As a society, we don't seem to place much value on the *absence* of change, such as changes in the quality of our water and air or in the status of wild areas. We take for granted that air and water should be clean and pure and that wilderness areas will always be "out there" somewhere; in a consumer culture, they are merely background conditions. We need to recognize that by *not* allowing changes to these conditions — *by inaction* — we are achieving something positive; that by restraining ourselves and *not* exploiting something, we can value it. This allows us to confer value on conservation and preservation, rather than accept the mistaken notion that all change is progress. Valuing inaction runs counter to the messages inherent in the consumer culture.

We are only slightly better at recognizing the *disappearance* of some condition or thing as a sign of progress. Many would probably agree that the disappearance of slavery and smallpox is a positive development. We would celebrate even more if we could eradicate poverty, racism, war, injustice, illiteracy, etc. But arguably, many human "achievements" create as much evil as they redress and this is often because we assign little value to what is *not*. We seem obsessed with *filling* the void instead of simply *being* in it. Thus we have much to learn from cultural traditions that know the value of the absence of something.

In the consciousness of consumer culture simplicity appears to be "poverty", and reduction of desires appears to be "indigence." One who does nothing may be suspected of laziness. One who consumes little may be accused of leaving his or her talents undeveloped. One who lives lightly upon the Earth may be judged as lacking aspirations, ambition, or industry, all of which are traits beloved by "the forward stampede."

In addition to our wired-in psychological preferences for foreground conditions or the immediate, short-term, visible attributes of things, we have a lengthy cultural tradition that associates material affluence and accumulation with *security*. In consumer societies, we are all taught from a very young age to associate having lots of something — indeed, what we need and much more to spare — with feelings of *safety* and well-being. Superficially, this association has a certain credibility. One can die from starvation or exposure. Having food and shelter with fuel for warmth prevents starvation and exposure. Logically, having lots of food and fuel should prevent one starving or freezing for a very long time.

The cognitive psychologist Timothy Miller has suggested that virtually every organism on the planet, including human beings, survives because it evolved with no "enough" switch.[3] We are biologically programmed to continually amass food, territory, prestige within our group, and mates because these are the pre-requisites to reproductive success. Any species that at any time said to itself "I have *enough* territory, food, status, mates, so I'll relax now" would have been quickly out-bred by more energetically acquisitive competitors. The upshot of this theory, if true, is that humans, like all other organisms, are innately programmed to desire more and more, *even if that no longer is necessary to assure survival or may even jeopardize survival.*

But the human emotional need for security against suffering and death and our particular ways of allaying these anxieties through hyper-consumption and hoarding simply don't square up very well with environmental sustainability. The proposition that *the very things we do to provide for our long-term security are now undermining it.* may be intellectually interesting for many people but *emotionally* it is preposterous to them. It is incomprehensible to some people that emotional security has little to do with consumption *per se,* so tightly have we webbed together these two aspects of our experience. It is therefore a major psychological task (although not impossible) to deconstruct the notion that consumption (or the power to consume, e.g. wealth) equals security and to erect a new and different foundation for one's sense of security.

Similarly, it has been noted by others[4], that we also tightly associate the consumption of goods and services with our sense of identity, our status within society, and material evidence of our success and worthiness, i.e., self-esteem. The decision to embrace voluntary simplicity thus can represent a foray into a style of life in which we aren't sure, for a while anyway, who we are, what value we have in the eyes of others, or whether or not we are "succeeding" as a person. For many people, this "limbo state" between an old socially and materially validated identity and a new, self-constructed, and internally validated sense of self is simply unendurable. But for those who *can* make this transition and construct a less materialistic and less socially determined identity, the result is a more secure sense of self and vastly increased personal energy, strength, and healthy autonomy.

What is needed, then, is a transformation of consciousness and of self-awareness so we can see more clearly the wisdom of observing limits, of discerning when enough is enough, of knowing how to decide when to act to produce a change in the world and when to remain still and simply receive from the world's own plenitude. To properly value simplicity, we learn to prize non-action, non-violence, holding our peace, forgoing what may be within our power but not necessarily in the best interest of the whole. We look for what is admirable in the life of one who lives with joy, energy, love, and generosity, yet with few possessions. Often, we must listen for the music that abides in silence. We must learn to dance naked.

4

Simplicity, Family, and Community

There are "larger than personal" reasons why we might choose to voluntarily simplify our lives. We will be exploring community, broadly defined, from two angles: the family, our most intimate "community," and the neighborhood, village, or town where we live. Community is the circle of familiar people with whom we interact more or less often, with whom we share a definable *place*, a linguistic and cultural *heritage,* and some interest in the outcome of collective decisions, whether these arise in a workplace, a civic project or community concern, or circumstances that affect us collectively as well as individually.

Clearly there are many people today who live in situations that don't offer even these minimal defining characteristics of community. Especially in some large urban centers, linguistic and ethnic diversit, and a variety of personal and cultural histories deeply affect the extent of the commonality among the people living in them. Even in suburbia, where ethnic and linguistic similarity is much more common, individual families are so cocooned in their houses and so occupied with activities based on shared interests rather than geographical proximity that the role of "neighbor" is mostly a formality engaged only in times of dire emergency. Nevertheless, there are still significant numbers of North Americans who know the people living near them and certainly can relate to "community" as that group with whom they share employment, a civic pursuit, or the practice of a faith.

We also belong to other "communities" defined by our biological, psychological, and spiritual interdependence with our bioregion and the planetary ecosystem. These relationships are so important that we will be discussing them in sections of their own.

One of the reasons most frequently cited for living more simply concerns finding more time to nurture relationships with the immediate and the extended family, and to participate more actively in community life. A survey of U.S. citizens conducted in 1995 by the Harwood Group[1] at the request of the Merck Family Fund yielded the following findings:

- Despite advertising messages supposedly "responding" to what Americans "need," 66 percent wanted more time with family and friends, 56 percent wanted less stress in their lives, and nearly half (47 percent) wanted to contribute more to their community.

One of the reasons most frequently cited for living more simply concerns finding more time to nurture relationships with the immediate and the extended family, and to participate more actively in community life.

- 72 percent of the 40-49 age group wanted to simplify their lives, and 28 percent had voluntarily made life changes that resulted in making less money within the last 5 years.

- Of these "downshifters," 68 percent wanted greater life balance, 66 percent wanted more time, 63 percent wanted less stress, and 53 percent wanted more time with children. 87 percent of downshifters said they were happy with the change, and 35 percent said they didn't miss the lost income.

- 85 percent of Americans rate responsibility, family, and friendship as key guiding principles of their lives, well behind prosperity and wealth (37 percent).

Clearly, North Americans value family and community relationships highly. We find great sources of meaning and reward in them. However, the results of the Harwood Group study are not unique. They echo research findings over a number of decades in North America, and even studies across cultures and countries:

> ... most psychological data show that the main determinates of happiness in life are not related to consumption at all: prominent among them are satisfaction with family life, especially marriage, followed by satisfaction with work, leisure, and friendships. Indeed, in a comprehensive inquiry into the relationship between affluence and satisfaction, social commentator Jonathan Freedman notes, "Above the poverty level, the relationship between income and happiness is remarkably small."[2]

It may be that we value relationships highly, but during the 20th century it has been equally true that we seem to have difficulty finding time and energy for them. The result has often been pain, guilt, anxiety, and a diffuse sense of futility and emptiness. For many people, working long hours at jobs they find marginally rewarding in a personal sense can be justified only if they promise eventually to deliver more time with family (perhaps through the purchase of supposedly labour- and time-"saving" conveniences) or to increase the supposed "quality" of time spent with loved ones (measured in the only way a consumer society knows how to measure things: the cost of the gifts given, the holiday spots we travel to, the lessons and courses and personal enrichments we can afford). The choice to simplify can often begin by taking a hard, honest look at whether consumerism is or is not actually *delivering* what it advertises.

There has been no shortage of speculation on what's wrong with North American families and communities. I don't intend to refute or endorse any of this, but rather to suggest perhaps a "simple-minded" supplement to all the other views that have been offered.

There are only 24 hours in every day and no technical or material innovation can add or subtract any hours to this total. As individuals, we have only so much energy and we cannot be two places at once. In spite of the advertising, we *can't* really have it *all*.

A basic principle of time management is that no one really manages "time." Under normal conditions, time passes at the same rate regardless of what we do, and it cannot be multiplied, only subdivided. What we can do is exercise more consciousness and choice in how we spend the time we have. *The brutally "simple" fact is that if the quality of our family and community relationships has suffered, it's because we've chosen to do something else with our time.*

To be fair to ourselves, some of these "choices" have been made unconsciously or on impulse, within an economic and social system that strongly encourages impulsive and semi-conscious decision-making, especially decisions concerning how we will spend both time and money.

Some "choices" are driven by external factors, such as how the economy works (an economy that worships growth based on the creation of personal debt demands large commitments of future time to pay for present consumption), how settlements are built (urban centers designed for cars and individual houses demand far higher levels of consumption than alternative forms of transportation and housing), how economic benefits are shared in society (when economic benefit is distributed on the basis of competitive advantage, all members of society are under pressure to invest more and more time in earning their living), and how certain aspects of the legal and institutional governance are organized (building codes, zoning regulations, access to public services, and social safety nets are all biased in favor of those who "play the game"). It is probably impossible for individuals to change these latter conditions, but we can most certainly change them through collective action.

Some of our choices have been influenced by social forces, such as "peer pressure," "social comparison," or "keeping up (or fitting in) with the Joneses." Despite the mythology of a consumer society that idolizes the individualist, anyone who steps very far away from what is considered "normal" (full-time employment, retirement at 65, two weeks of summer vacation, house in 'burbs, minivan, two children, golf on Saturdays, etc.) is quickly marginalized. Fear of social marginalization is often enough to keep people "normal."

Finally, some "choices" have been imposed through fear, intimidation, and threat of violence, as when a family feels it must spend a significant share of its income on personal and home security measures as precautions against an increasingly threatening situation of community decay. This form of pressure to consume is reaching new heights in "gated communities" with extensive security perimeters, significant regulation of the lifestyles of residents, and severe restrictions on who may enter, even to visit.

Nevertheless, all of these *are* decisions, even though they may have been semi-conscious, taken under duress, or made with an incomplete understanding of their long-term consequences. *The good news about choices is that increasing mindfulness of their consequences empowers a person to make difference choices.* It may take some time to free ourselves from the consequences of our past decisions, but we can set out in a new direction.

In his essay "Does Community Have Value?"[3], the American farmer/philosopher Wendell Berry describes a community that existed in rural Tennessee in the 1930s and that is still present to some degree among the contemporary Amish. This "community" for Berry was defined by *people* (not technology) linked through ties of friendship and kinship, who shared well-defined patterns of work and pleasure, who shared a history, who lived in an identifiable *place* (not "cyberspace"), who amused, consoled and educated themselves, and who shared both onerous work and celebrations. This community included nearly self-sufficient households that also cooperated in collective tasks, and in which the community and the economy were profoundly interdependent. In short, the community was a group of people who depended on each other both practically and socially, at the same time that households were far more self-reliant in meeting their own needs than any modern urban household of the twentieth century.

While this sort of community bears little resemblance to the diverse assortment of nearly anonymous, apparently economically autonomous, and self-interested strangers who populate most present-day urban and suburban neighborhoods, it does harken back to the sort of "community" many find appealing and a few can still remember. The interest in each other's lives that grows from real personal and economic involvement is something many people hanker to renew. But Berry is the first to admit that communities such as the one he describes, together with the strong fabric of family ties that thrived within them, no longer exist. What happened to them?

In a word, at least in part, *we traded such communities for consumerism,* more or less on purpose, though probably not with a very clear awareness of what we were giving away and what we were going to wind up with when the deal was done. In doing this, of course, we had help from those who benefit from the promotion of consumerism. In Wendell Berry's words,

> ... another fact that we must now reckon with is that this community did not change by improving itself. It changed by turning away from itself, from its place, from its own possibility. Somehow the periphery exhausted and broke the center. This community, like thousands of similar ones, was not changed by anything that *it* thought of, nor by anything thought of by anybody who believed that community had a practical or an economic value. It was changed, partly to its own blame, by forces, originating outside itself, that did not consider, much less desire, the welfare or the existence of such communities. This community, like any other, had to change and needed to change, but what if its own life, its own good, had been the standard by which it changed, rather than the profit of distant entrepreneurs and corporations?[4]

A century ago, the market economy was "peripheral" to family and community values, which most of us still consider to be more central. From this peripheral position, the consumer economy has gradually insinuated itself into our lives to such a degree that, little by little, we traded what is most central in our lives for what used to be marginal, or peripheral. We've traded our hearts for "nice" clothes and hair.

Because this process has gone on for some time and its values and worldview have been deeply plowed into our institutions, laws, settlement patterns, and life habits, disengaging consumerism's hold on our families and communities won't be easy. But the practice of voluntary simplicity can be one of our most potent weapons.

߆ઙ

The connections between the practice of voluntary simplicity and nurturing our family and community relationships can manifest themselves in at least three ways:

First, those choosing to live more simply reduce their consumption of things that, in order to be purchased and maintained, require high incomes, excessive overtime, and time away from family and community. Also, living in a smaller home and having fewer possessions places lower demands on us to look after all this "stuff." At the same time, we are freed to look after people — our partners, children, extended family — instead. Of course, material consumption is required to do this *to some degree*, but often not to the degree so strongly promoted by advertisers and marketing interests. We are urged to purchase this or that labor-saving gadget so we will have more time for our families in total disregard of the fact that *more labor*, more shared work on tasks that are obviously productive and essential to the life of the family, is one very important crucible in which love, relationship, and social maturity develop.

Another of the myths strongly promoted by the consumer economy is that "quality time" with family consists of consuming passive entertainment together. If we accept this idea, it's very good for the "leisure industry" because many hours will be invested to save money in order to purchase leisure entertainments. But the whole idea that a family might enjoy time together that is spent in *productive activity* rather than in consumptive activity gets little air time. Gardening, food preserving, making clothes, building or doing home repairs or yard work together, volunteering as a family on various community projects, making art, music, literature, hospitality — all of these are becoming increasingly marginalized to visiting theme parks, taking expensive trips, or having every member of the family gazing at his or her private television.

What our partners, children, and relatives often want from us is *ourselves*, our time, attention, respect, affirmation, esteem, trust, confidence, our stories, our help. What we often lose sight of is that buying them something, sending them somewhere, providing in no way substitutes for the gift of ourselves in relationships. "Saying it with flowers" just doesn't say it as well as we ourselves can. We are especially traumatized by cases of children committing acts of violence who come from homes that seem to "have" everything. It may be that such homes have an abundance of everything that is peripheral to the human soul but lack what is essential.

Second, some of those who choose simple living may decide to invest the time and energy "dividend" from this way of life in community activities, perhaps balancing family and community commitments or else emphasizing one or the other at different times in their lives. The same ways in which simpler living can strengthen family relationships apply to the community as well. Larger than personal projects naturally require money, but they also require leadership, volunteer participation, and commitment over the long term. In our increasingly monetarized and consumer-oriented society, some of the activities that bring the most value to our lives but which are difficult to turn into "paying propositions" are exactly the ones that become marginalized and are therefore most in need of our energies and time. Community theater, symphonies or other musical events, environmental restoration work, development of both fine and folk arts, sports, education and charitable social activities, seasonal programs for youth, elders, and the marginalized — few of these represent "profit centers" for commercial ventures, yet they are vital activities in maintaining the social fabric of communities.

There is an unfortunate misconception abroad that these sorts of activities are options for us only after we retire or have become "financially independent." If this were true, it would be socially disastrous. The fact is that for many generations those who have chosen to live simply have created ways to contribute both to their families and their communities, and they do this all along their life journey, not just on condition that they have banked their first half million or are comfortably pensioned off.

Practicing simple living necessarily implies a major reduction and redirection of our participation in the consumer economy, and further, a practical withdrawal of support for the *commercialization* of public life. The commercialization and privatization of public space (as when corporate logos and advertising appear in formerly strictly public spaces such as parks, auditoriums, art galleries, etc.), and of civic life in general, became a highly visible trend toward the end of the 20th century. The trend is fueled partly by the power of corporate funding, but mostly by the indifference and passive compliance of communities. It serves the agenda of consumerism that private spaces (whether corporate or personal) should gradually become more attractive, safer, and more interesting than public spaces like town squares, streets, parks, and civic facilities like theaters, galleries and libraries. If we can be enticed to support this shift either by patronizing corporate-sponsored events or by "cocooning" in our own houses, we will be spending and consuming in either case, and corporate consumerism will have won the day. But if we've simplified our individual lives and consciously chosen *relationship in community* as the starting point for nurturing wellness and beauty in society, then we've laid the foundation for fewer billboards, fewer "private" clubs and admission-only theme parks, fewer "exclusive" events. We're committing ourselves instead to beautiful, safe, and open communities where all people can enjoy the values that we can secure for each other through cooperation and sharing.

As part of a recent documentary on consumerism produced for the Canadian Broadcasting Corporation in 1999, the German economist Wolfgang Sachs noted a key difference between North American cities and many European cities.[5] In North America, he said, the most attractive spaces in cities are mostly privately owned or becoming increasingly so. In Europe, however, the grandest buildings, plazas, gardens, and monuments are mostly public spaces. This means that even the poorest members of the community can be surrounded, to some degree, by beautiful structures, art, and historic architecture. Sachs believes this tends to have an overall humanizing influence on the community since everyone can enjoy the fruits of cultural and artistic refinement. By contrast, public spaces in North American cities are becoming increasingly ugly, dangerous, and unhealthy oceans surrounding "islands" of privately owned and scrupulously guarded beauty. We are only left to wonder which approach to community brings the greatest good to the greatest number.

Third, there is another extremely important way in which voluntary simplicity can empower and enrich our participation in community that literally relates to maintaining democratic institutions and civil and legal rights. How might the widespread adoption of simpler living influence governance? Anyone who has ever become personally involved in a political or public issue quickly learns that the world has become a complicated place managed by large corporate and public sector bureaucracies. To be a well-informed and active citizen requires considerable time to learn about issues and considerable energy and persistence to pursue these issues along their labyrinthine pathways toward resolution. It also helps to have a minimum of financial and material "entanglements" so that one is free to pursue the work at hand and be relatively free of the vulnerabilities that can sometimes be used by unscrupulous opponents to influence the outcome of contentious issues. There have been some particularly odious examples of this kind of coercion where "whistle-blowers" within corporations or governments experience job loss or professional discreditation for actions they felt were ethically necessary.

... there is another extremely important way in which voluntary simplicity can empower and enrich our participation in community that literally relates to maintaining democratic institutions and civil and legal rights.

Democratic institutions require time, energy, commitment, and participation from their citizens. Any way of life that locks its people into burdensome debt, exhausting hours of work, primarily occupation-focused "education," totally commercialized uses of the media, family and community values subordinated to those of the market place, and a pace of life so hurried and mindless that people have no chance to consider *anything* beyond their next purchasing decision is destined to lose its democracy — and its people will lose their freedoms.

It is well to recall the birth of democracy in ancient Athens, a city of a few thousand people, most of whom probably knew each other. Pericles' famous oration on the nature of Athenian society made it clear that democracy was never designed for a society that was incapable of even the most rudimentary commitment: voting. Democracy assumes a continuous involvement of large numbers of people over prolonged periods of time, engaging in issues at considerable depth. Any form of government that assumes its people are sovereign also requires that they exercise that sovereignty as a regular part of community life, not just by casting votes in elections and then forever after delegating their sovereign role to elected representatives with no further involvement until the next election.

Decisions affecting our collective life *will* be made; they *must* be made. The question is: *Who will make them?* In democratic societies, if they are not taken by the sovereign people, they will be made by others, by default if not by design. In our own time, corporations stand ready in the wings — if they are not already on center-stage — to make decisions to implement a vision of the future they say is "inevitable," the future of a globalized economy under corporate rather than democratic rule. Once again, we stand at a historical crossroads where we may unconsciously allow the "periphery to exhaust and break the center." Or we may grow in mindfulness, exercise our power of conscious choice, re-dedicate ourselves to our families and communities, and maintain our democratic traditions and institutions.

These issues naturally lead to a consideration of governance as a particular aspect of community life that can intimately affect the quality of both family and neighborhood relationships. If we've made the case that voluntary simplicity describes one way to promote healthy communities, then might simpler living be something that enlightened governments would want to support and perhaps even nurture?

Such support might be plausible because, while simpler living can definitely set a new agenda for social and cultural development, its technical and economic expressions necessarily move in directions that reduce environmental damage and social inequity. Shifting the focus of development from "quantity of income" to "quality of life" will imply many changes to technology, production techniques, and product marketing that could make major contributions to sustaining communities and healthy ecosystems.

A highly relevant aspect of voluntary simplicity is that it could mark an important shift in how we think about social and cultural change. While governments and business now acknowledge we must change how we use resources because continuing as we have is unsustainable, they do not say how we should make this change. However it comes about, it will be strongly affected by how we view the world, nature, people, and governance.

Margaret Wheatley and Myron Kellner-Rogers[6] have observed that most contemporary organizations (governments, businesses, etc.) and most approaches to organizational change are based on a "Newtonian" view of the world, after the British physicist and mathematician who developed some of our culture's first unifying sets of scientific "laws" describing how nature works. To paraphrase the Newtonian view of the world: Both people and communities are seen as discrete, separate entities. They are passive, like blobs of matter that will not move or change unless "pushed" or "caused" to change by some external force. In the case of individuals, or even whole communities, it is the coercive authority of governments or the market forces of advertising, pricing, or competition that cause change. When change is being "managed," it is the actions of governments (e.g., adjusting tax rates, enacting regulations, raising and lowering interest rates, or modifying foreign exchange rates) that cause other things to happen in communities. In this worldview, change starts from "on high." It is planned by specially trained experts working for central governments and then implemented by the rank and file of society.

There are, of course, "Newtonian" businesses as well. They shape their operations around "control" systems that rely heavily on measurement, feedback, performance assessment, and a continual process of strategic planning to anticipate, and preferably manipulate and control, markets for their products and services. Employees are interchangeable units who must be "motivated" from outside by rewards and threats of job loss to "perform" according to formal rules, guidelines, procedures, and policies. The process of management involves continual efforts to maintain clarity, measurability, and order *within* the organization amid a continually changing and more or less threatening external environment of competition, shifting market preferences, changing government regulations, and volatile shareholder decisions regarding where to invest capital.

In general, the "Newtonian" approach to both business and public governance sees the responsibility for community development as resting with a minority of people holding positions of formal authority. Wheatley and Kellner-Rogers' argument is that, despite all the energy and resources we expend trying to force real world communities to conform to our outdated ideas of the universe, the Newtonian approach to understanding the world doesn't match the way things actually work and that consequently, many of our best-intentioned efforts to promote healthy communities fail miserably.

They suggest that in order to more effectively meet the challenges of the future, we need to think less about central management based on control and coercion and more about organic systems of creative innovation based on trust and support. This way of understanding communities is adapted from recent thinking in what is being called the "New Science" (relativity theory, systems theory, information theory, and quantum mechanics). This is justified, they maintain, because life itself consists of many hierarchically interdependent *self-organizing systems*. While rocks or billiard balls must indeed be pushed and pulled from one place to another in order to cause change, this is a "special case" situation. The larger world of which we and our communities are a part is a hugely complex but self-organizing and self-managing *system*. No part (manager, politician, economist) can ever hope to understand or control the whole. To try that is a waste of energy and resources.

Letting go of the outmoded Newtonian world view allows community leaders to take new approaches to promoting healthy communities that are more consistent with the nature of living systems as we are coming to understand them. In a world of complex, sometimes chaotic, and self-organizing systems, leadership consists in provoking, enticing, challenging, and midwifing the appearance of new sets of *goals and purposes* that constitute the *identity* of a community. Both public and private sector leaders work not to constrain and control every detail of community behavior (which is impossible in any case) but to continually articulate and challenge ideas about *what the community is and what it hopes to accomplish*. As the *identity* of a community becomes clear and coherent, the community can be trusted to organize itself to express and enact that identity through how it behaves and what it creates.

Voluntary simplicity fits very well with this approach because it requires that our collective response to the challenge of building healthy communities moves away from the policies and technologies controlled by centralized authorities back to the messier and far more creative arena of individual lifestyle choices. In place of government and business control, voluntary simplicity proposes a re-creation of personal identity based on mindfulness of one's values. This encourages more diversity and creativity in community development than is possible simply by implementing the directives of institutional leaders.

It may be that the challenge of building healthy communities may be too complex a task for the sluggish and paranoid dynamics of existing institutions to manage. It may be that rejigging an economic policy here or introducing a new business there will not really engage the full range of changes required for healthy community development. It may be that only millions of self-organizing and self-managing individuals applying themselves creatively and actively in the unique details and situations of their own lives will have the capacity to meet this challenge. But what we need is a new *identity*. We need to hear from many different directions, even perhaps from institutional leaders, that we are not *consumers* but *human beings*. And many of us will need help, support, and validation for the process of asking the basic questions needed to reshape our personal as well as our community identities.

Finally, since voluntary simplicity is essentially a *social innovation,* it can diffuse through society as a *message* rather than as a product or policy. Hence, it can move quickly. Over-reliance on technology to solve the challenge of community wellness implies relying on all the machinery (and the inevitable delays) in scientific discovery, technical development, product development, marketing, and, finally, adoption and diffusion of a new product or service. While this can be very helpful, it is inevitably a lengthy process. Even supposing a majority of North Americans decided that, say, more "environmentally friendly" technology was a good thing, it would take years to manufacture, deliver, and install the infrastructure necessary to achieve this goal. The adoption of voluntary simplicity, however, can occur immediately.

In promoting community wellness, governments must depart from their traditional collaboration with business and industry in a "command and control" approach to community development. This model of governance was plausible as long as society was less populous, less dynamic, and less diverse and exerted fewer environmental impacts than today. At present, however, governments neither understand nor control community change, nor can they. Their attempts to do so usually represent *obstacles* to community health rather than supports to it.

This is not to say, however, that government has *no* role to play, but that the definition and enactment of this role must change.

First, governments can re-own their *guardian* role in communities by fashioning regulations that encourage health in communities. Governments must not allow economic development that is known to compromise human or environmental health. They must also re-own their role as a progressive influence to promote social equity, protect the vulnerable, assure the rights and security of minorities, and set standards for health, work, and general welfare that respect the authentic needs and dignity of citizens.

Governments should see themselves as *participants* in community development through the collection, verification, and dissemination of information critical to assuring healthy communities. Governments certainly have a role in maintaining social order and regulating destructive or prejudicial behavior in society. But extending their vision of this role to one of leadership in social and economic development is vain. Both society and the ecosphere are too complex to be "managed" in the traditional sense of the term. Governments can act in ways that challenge, perturb, or inform the larger systems of society and nature that surround them, but they cannot effectively *direct* these systems. Rather, participating as provocateurs in community development, and especially using their large resources for collecting and sharing information, are roles completely consistent with our new understanding of how leadership can be realistically exercised.

Governments can use their taxation authority to *progressively* tax higher consumption rather than continuing to offer tax incentives for high consumption. Taxation should discourage consumption of services and products that are most environmentally harmful or that jeopardize human health (e.g., higher taxes on automotive fuels than on bus fares[7]). Both William Rees[8] and Paul Hawken[9], among others, have described how tax systems can provide incentives to commercial enterprises to design their operations in ways that support and restore rather than undermine communities and the ecosphere.

Finally, governments should become active participants in an on-going dialogue that explores the value of simpler living in meeting fundamental human needs, strengthening communities and families, and supporting human and environmental health, especially when these bear no logical or natural relationship to the consumption of material things. This is not to suggest that democratic governments necessarily *advocate* simple living, even though today they strongly advocate economic growth and consumptive living! Rather, governments certainly have a role to play in, and resources to contribute to, community dialogues on the meaning and implications of simpler living as a developmental goal for public institutions and the management of public assets. If governments can moderate debates on economic development priorities, the role of the public sector in regulating and stimulating business, or the values that guide the use of public lands, for instance, why not promote debate on voluntary simplicity?

5

Simplicity and the Environment

Consumerism is a system that links the desires of those without awareness to the actions of those without scruples to produce destruction without precedent.[1]

It is probably natural to think of "community" as a purely human reality, but I prefer to expand the definition. Each of us also belongs to a very real "community of life" — Earth's ecosphere. We live in a "neighbourhood," our *bioregion*. Each bioregion is a community of living things in its own right and the assemblage of bioregions that makes up the ecosphere bears all the marks of community as we have been discussing it so far.

As human beings in the community of All Life, we share the history of biological evolution with other creatures. We live in an identifiable *place*. Our lives (as a species) are so intertwined within this community, i.e. the ecosphere, that we cannot survive apart from the whole community — though the ecosphere can certainly survive without *us*. The community of All Life continually surrounds, sustains, and nourishes us, whether or not we are aware of it. I certainly don't want to ascribe pantheistic or mystical significance to the ecosphere, but the relationship of interdependence between ourselves and the ecosphere is a scientifically demonstrable *fact*.

For centuries, people have advocated simple living for personal reasons: to find some peace, to advance a work important in their lives, to reduce their debts. People have practiced simplicity for reasons of family and community — to free time for important relationships, care for the sick, tend the lonely, contribute to community projects. People have lived simply to nurture their spiritual development or live out their spiritual vision — as we shall see in the next section. All these reasons for voluntary simplicity are as valid today as they were a thousand years ago.

Since the 1960s, however, there has appeared another pressing reason why we might embrace voluntary simplicity — and why a number of people are doing so: Consumerism is threatening the community of All Life by destroying species, consuming resources, and altering the climate that sustains life on Earth.

This is a comparatively recent and, on a global scale, historically unprecedented situation. Humans have always exploited the environment to the limits of our ability and technology. Even the arrival of paleo-Indians in North America 10,000 to 20,000 years ago was followed by mass extinctions of New World camels, mastodons, horses, ground sloths, and lions and major reductions in the numbers of other species. Ancient civilizations turned the fertile areas of North Africa and the Middle East into deserts, and the classical civilizations of Greece and Rome denuded their respective peninsulas of tree cover. Until the Industrial Revolution, however, human numbers were comparatively small and our technology was relatively limited. While we often had high impacts on local or regional landscapes and on individual species, we were not yet producing chemical wastes or destroying habitats on scales sufficient to endanger entire classes of organisms or whole ecosystems, as is the case today.

> *Since the 1960s ... there has appeared another pressing reason why we might embrace voluntary simplicity — and why a number of people are doing so: Consumerism is threatening the community of All Life by destroying species, consuming resources, and altering the climate that sustains life on Earth.*

Since 1800, and especially since 1950, there has been an explosive growth in three key aspects of the human presence on Earth: (a) a growth in population such that we are now the most numerous large-bodied animals on the planet; (b) a development of technology such that the flows of energy and resources through our economic systems rival the resource and energy flows of natural systems themselves; (c) the rapid diffusion and near dominance of the culture of consumerism to all corners of the "developed" and "developing" worlds. These three trends tend to interact and reinforce each other, and their combined effects are proving to be absolutely toxic to the ecosphere. There is now an enormous body of evidence documenting these effects.

Working at the University of British Columbia with the assistance of colleagues, William Rees and Mathis Wackernagel[2] developed the ecological footprint concept, setting out to estimate how much productive land and ocean is required to support one person at the typical North American standard of living. This would include the land needed for growing food, fiber, and timber, of course, but also land for buildings, land to absorb wastes from manufacturing and energy consumption, and land for public areas like parks, shopping centers, and streets.

Rees estimated that about 17.75 acres of land and productive ocean are required to support each North American, land that is either allocated to these uses on the North American continent or "appropriated" from other continents through the importation of resources or the "export" of wastes. If we ask how much land area would be required to support *everyone* in the world at the North American standard — the standard to which many people in developing countries aspire — we discover a startling fact. Achieving this goal would require about 106.5 billion acres of land (6 billion people times 17.75 acres per person). The problem is, there are only 22.5 billion acres of productive land and ocean surface on the planet. Hence, to realize the goal of a typical North American consumer lifestyle for everyone on Earth would require four extra planets *at the present time.*

If we flip this around and ask how much land area would be available to each person if existing resources were shared fairly, we discover that it would be about 3.75 acres per person (22.5 billion acres divided among 6 billion people). Thus, to live in an equitable world with our current population and technology requires that North Americans learn to live on about 25 percent of the resources we are currently consuming.

The beauty of this "ecological footprint" analysis is that it leaves open for us the question of how we might resolve this unsustainable situation of 6 billion human beings thinking they "need" four planets in order to be happy. We could, for example, reduce our population, although this has been a contentious issue for two generations since the developing countries perceive developed countries to be preaching the virtues of family planning while themselves indulging their every consumerist fantasy. Moreover, at current consumption levels, one child born into a consumer society uses as much as 106 times the energy of a child born in some developing countries, clearly indicating that population growth in developed countries is far more of a problem for the ecosystem than the same amount of population growth in developing countries.[3] Nevertheless, reducing the total human population would reduce our global ecological footprint at least in the short run, but not in the long run, as long as we continue to think of the "good life" as defined by more and more consumption.

There is also the possibility that improvements in technology will help reduce our ecological footprint. If we can develop ways of delivering the same goods and services using less energy and resources, that is, doing it more efficiently, then logically the ecological impact of consumerism could be reduced — but again, probably only in the short run. For no matter how efficient we make technology, it can never be 100 percent efficient. Often, even the best technology is considerably less that 100 percent efficient. This means we will always be producing some waste and destruction of the ecosphere, depending *both* on how efficient our technology is *and* on how much stuff we're asking it to produce for us. If we insist on continuing to develop technologies that serve the goals of consumerism, in the long run we will simply be ensuring that we consume the planet with greater and greater efficiency. We buy time this way, but we don't change direction.

Clearly, neither technology nor population control alone can solve the sustainability dilemma, unless of course the population "collapses" or technical development "stalls" to such a degree that we may attain sustainability but at the price of our current notion of civilization. What is called for instead is a *cultural alternative to consumerism*. Many people are coming to see voluntary simplicity as part of that cultural alternative. These same people also see the need for this development to occur promptly because the ecological impacts of consumerism are already monumental.

In 1990, the Worldwatch Institute in Washington, DC, estimated the net global human population to be increasing at 94 million people per year. This figure has fallen somewhat in recent years to about 80 million people per year. But population growth still averages 2 to 3 percent annually, assuring that it will double in about 28 years, or one generation.[4] Moreover, the Organization for Economic Cooperation and Development, the club of the 17 most powerful world economies, has set an economic growth target of 2 to 3 percent per year, which promises to double the scale of the global economy in about 25 years, also the span of one generation. If these two events come to pass, there will be a need for an *additional* 16 "Earth's worth" of productive capacity over and above the four planets we already need to achieve North American living standards for everyone (i.e., four planets to achieve economic equity at present, plus four more to provide for double our current population, plus another eight to provide for doubling the scale of the economy).

More worrying still is the fact that we are systematically destroying the productive and regenerative capability of the one planet we have. It was estimated in 1986 that the human economy at that time was already appropriating 40 percent of the Net Primary Production (NPP) of the planet (the total annual production of all green plants on the Earth: 225 billion tons of fiber, grain, forest growth, etc.).[5] In the ensuing years, partly because of a growing population and partly due to an expanded economic activity, this fraction must have increased substantially, today leaving probably less than half of NPP for the consumption of all the other species that also depend on it for their livelihoods.

Global automobile use mushroomed eight-fold from 70 million vehicles in 1950 to 550 million in 1995, along with all attendant increases in air pollution, landfill space allocated to junked cars, loss of farmland to highways and parking lots, and the huge expenditure in energy and resources needed to build, maintain, and dispose of cars.[6]

Since 1800, with the beginning of the Industrial Revolution, burning fossil fuels has added about 225 billion tonnes (a 50 percent increase) of carbon dioxide to the atmosphere, which climate scientists now concur is changing Earth's climate, promising numerous unpredictable impacts on habitats, agricultural production, and human settlements around the world.[7]

During the decade of the 1990s, consumerism depleted the world's petroleum reserves at the rate of 23 billion barrels per year, while only an average of 7 billion barrels per year was discovered in new reserves — this promises to exhaust the thermodynamically recoverable reserves within one generation, or before 2025.[8] Once this threshold is reached, more energy will be required to extract a barrel of oil than is contained in the oil itself. Therefore, even though much oil will remain in the ground, it will make no sense to try to recover it.

Studies completed in 1998 by the US-based National Research Council showed that 80 percent of commercial fish species in the US and 70 percent of all fisheries in the world are being fished at or beyond capacity. Global fish catches in 1997 were 84 million tonnes, down from its 100 million tonne peak in 1989. Overfishing is blamed for declining fish populations due to overcapacity in the world fishing fleet, which is about 2.5 times larger than necessary to catch the available fish resources.[9]

Similar stories can be told about the depletion of forests,[10] the loss of topsoils due to desertification, urbanization, and erosion,[11] the loss of biodiversity at thousands of times the natural rate, dwindling per capita grain production,[12] dwindling per capita fresh water reserves,[13] depletions of the ozone layer protecting Earth's surface from harmful ultraviolet radiation[14] — the list goes on and on.

None of these effects are inevitable consequences of a human presence in the community of All Life on Earth. They are specific consequences of the culture of consumerism: growth without limits in the manufacture and consumption of material things as the definition of humanity's highest state of happiness and fulfillment.

The relevance of voluntary simplicity to addressing this situation is direct and obvious. To the extent that we choose to live more lightly on the Earth in a material sense, we greatly reduce resource depletion, energy use, and habitat destruction. The easiest and least expensive way to prevent pollution is to never create it in the first place. Voluntary simplicity is a very "simple," low-tech, individualized way of doing this. Anyone can understand it. Everyone can apply it. Its practice can be shaped and "sized" to fit each person's way of life, family responsibilities, and geographic location. It requires no new technological developments. It is equally accessible to all people. It costs nothing.

We might consider embracing some of the practices of simple living as a rational response to our desire that our children live in at least as safe and healthy a world as we ourselves have enjoyed. Given the obvious and pervasive threats posed by consumerism to the ecosphere, taking such steps would seem only to be consistent with our long-term self-interest.

The easiest and least expensive way to prevent pollution is to never create it in the first place. Voluntary simplicity is a very "simple," low-tech, individualized way of doing this. Anyone can understand it. Everyone can apply it. Its practice can be shaped and "sized" to fit each person's way of life, family responsibilities, and geographic location. It requires no new technological developments. It is equally accessible to all people. It costs nothing.

There are also people who feel a deep connection with other living things. Our concern reaches far beyond the future of humanity to the intrinsic value we find in the community of All Life, of which we sense ourselves very much to be citizens. As lovers of wilderness, indigenous people, Tree People, Rainbow Warriors, Sea Shepherds, and others, we experience an intense personal connection with other species, a sense of shared fate, of mutual concern, of emotional involvement. These provide additional reasons for embracing simplicity. This commitment grows up entirely apart from whatever economic or personal "value" may attach to the relationship in the future.

In thinking about how we live in relation to the natural world, we can discern at least two perspectives on the relationship. Recent (post-Cartesian) history has urged us to think of the ecosphere as not having any intrinsic value, but only a value derived from its usefulness to human beings. If part of the ecosphere can be mined, harvested, or manufactured into some other commodity we have taught ourselves to want, then it has economic value and we consider it important. Otherwise, it has no value; it is blasted waste, howling wilderness, etc. From this perspective, voluntary simplicity can hardly be justified since it represents a decidedly "extra-economic" approach to living.

Alternatively, the last few decades have witnessed the appearance of another perspective on our relationship with the ecosphere, a perspective that shares *some* elements with current aboriginal views of nature and that also contains some definitely post-modern, post-industrial elements. From this perspective, life itself has value, wilderness has value, and the human project finds its meaning by situating itself seamlessly *within* the community of All Life that inhabits the planet as a whole. The goal of human existence is not, as practiced by the culture of consumerism, simply to *expand* through physical growth until every nook and cranny of the Earth is filled with something made or discarded by humans. Rather, the goal of human existence is to *deepen consciousness* of our place in All Life and to develop a greater capacity for *love*, or *compassion*, or *holiness* — whatever word we wish to use to describe the realization of the transcendent possibilities of human existence within the context of our life within All Life.

From this latter perspective, it is not particularly important or inherently desirable that humanity be multitudinous since our numbers are no measure of the development of our consciousness (though they *are* a measure of the size of a market). Moreover, from what we already know about the conditions that are conducive to the deepening of consciousness (see Chapter 7), we would have many reasons for minimizing our impact on the natural world, living simply in relation to it, though not *primitively* as in the past. The key difference here is that while consumerism directs the development of technology toward the generation of further rounds of consumption and profit for their own sake, a culture that valued the deepening of consciousness would direct the development of technology toward those projects that promised to *liberate* the greatest number of people from lack of necessities and provide the peace and security that are conducive to the deepening of consciousness. Moreover, it would aim to do this on the *minimum* investment of time, energy, and resources. For this sort of "development," voluntary simplicity is an eminently skillful means.

$$\wp\partial$$

We can consider the practice of simplicity for the sake of our environment as taking at least three forms.

First, we can make the voluntary choice to *reduce waste*. This practice already has considerable currency, particularly in the popularity of waste recycling programs, but also with respect to efficiency improvements in our use of energy, triggered by the oil embargo of 1974.

In reducing waste, we attend to all the ways we use energy and resources and the degree to which they are expended to no useful purpose. The aim is to reduce what we waste, not what we use. Thus, a person who installs water conserving shower fixtures may shower just as often and just as long but with less waste of water flowing uselessly into the tub without having first washed the person. Or someone else installing energy-conserving lights may have just as many lights and operate them just as many hours as before, but with less energy wasted in heat and in the production of electricity.

Waste reduction can reach fairly deeply into our practice of livelihood, for example when people decide to grow part of their own food in a backyard organic garden. Such an arrangement delivers food to the family table while at the same time providing a way of diverting previously wasted kitchen garbage into a compost pile, reducing the need for the commercial production, processing, shipping, and retailing of food with all the attendant use of energy and resources, as well as reducing the need for persistent, toxic agri-chemicals. The family may eat just as much, and may not even change its eating habits, yet waste has been reduced in the food supply system.

If voluntary simplicity were to evolve beyond individuals changing their practice of livelihood to become instead a central set of values and practices that could guide technological development, then additional possibilities for waste reduction would be found. Reducing waste, in a technical sense, means increasing efficiency. Even a society whose members valued simple living would have an endless need for efficiency improvements in all forms of its technology. These improvements would be measured in terms of energy savings, resource conservation, time savings, and increased community and personal wellness, not simply by the expansion of profit.

Waste reduction, however, doesn't necessarily imply a fundamental change in consumption patterns or goals. It's possible to imagine a consumer society that still aims to reduce waste and improve industrial efficiencies. Indeed, our own society sees these goals as more or less "motherhood" issues, since each of them can also be associated with "profit centers", i.e., money can be made from waste reduction and efficiency improvements. They are in fact the linchpins of the late 20th century infatuation with "sustainable consumption initiatives" and "green consumerism," both of which are oxymorons, even though pursuing waste reduction and efficiency improvements remain worthwhile goals.

Since practically everything humans make eventually becomes waste, waste can only be reduced, never eliminated. When our society is obsessively focused on consuming more and more, waste must inevitably increase over time since it is directly related to consumption. Furthermore, improvements in efficiency are limited by the laws of physics and chemistry. Technology may often appear to pull rabbits out of hats, but this is deceptive. Again, in any society whose reason for being is unlimited growth of consumption, improvements in efficiency will be continually off-set by increases in consumption. Eventually, efficiency improvements for a given technology will no longer be possible or affordable, but consumption will be running along unabated.

One of the most intractable limits on our technology is the Second Law of Thermodynamics, which we are soon to meet with respect to oil consumption.[15]

The "oil crisis" of the early 1970s sparked fears that oil reserves might someday be totally depleted. Yet new reserves continue to be discovered and, based on these discoveries, we have enjoyed three decades of false assurances. While new oil continues to be discovered, we hear very little about how deep these new reserves lie in the Earth's crust, how far from markets they are located, or how difficult they will be to extract compared to reserves we have already tapped. In fact, humanity has already picked the "low hanging fruit," and it takes progressively more energy and resources to recover each additional barrel of new oil. Oil reserves will *never* run out. The reason for this is that before they do, we will stop extracting them because we will reach a point, sometime before the year 2025, when it will take more than a barrel of oil's worth of energy to extract a barrel of oil. This is the case because it takes energy to produce energy. At the point where it takes more than one unit of energy to produce a unit of energy, we might as well be pouring the oil back in the ground.

Thus, since reducing waste and improving efficiency (of the use of energy and resources) are certainly the first steps toward simpler living, they are not the final word and only go part way toward achieving their environmental conservation potential.

Another way we can practice simplicity for the sake of our environment is through *de-junking*. De-junking is the practice of removing clutter from our lives and eliminating (recycling, re-using, handing along, giving away) material possessions that we no longer use.

Another way we can practice simplicity for the sake of our environment is through de-junking. De-junking is the practice of removing clutter from our lives and eliminating (recycling, re-using, handing along, giving away) material possessions that we no longer use.

In North America in particular, many of our houses are actually warehouses for unused (and sometimes forgotten) possessions. We accumulate for the sake of accumulation to the point where we no longer really know what we own. We trip over this junk, insure it, maintain larger-than-needed houses to shelter it, pay for security services to keep it from being stolen, fret over its safety, curse its oppressive effects on our emotions and activities, search through it to find what we *really* need to get on with our lives, trip over it in the dark, and then, at last, relegate it to a landfill.

Junk represents a hidden inventory of potentially re-usable and recyclable resources. It also represents an on-going but often over-looked environmental deficit as we continue to live in larger houses than we actually need and continue to consume the resources and pay the price of maintaining them, fueling them, insuring them and, finally, demolishing them. When we hold on to junk, we are choosing to hold on to larger than necessary financial obligations, a larger than necessary share of compulsory consumption (once we have "things", there are all sorts of legal and social pressures at play coercing us to maintain them), and some share of resources that might be used to meet the real needs of someone else. De-junking moves these resources out of "storage" in our houses and back into circulation where they can be of some use and possibly reduce the need to harvest more resources from the ecosphere to supply future production.

I recommend a "contemplative" approach to de-junking. That is, going about removing clutter with attention to our emotions, memories, and intuitive connections with things as well as our intellectual opinions regarding how useful they may or may not be to us in the future. We can form strong emotional attachments to material things, and it's not helpful to be too cavalier about them. They need to be honored like any other relationship. When we feel it's time to clear out a drawer or cupboard, a room or a house, it is helpful to "sit" mindfully with the stuff housed there until we feel the full weight of its presence in ourselves. In mindfulness of the real emotional significance of our material possessions, we are in a better position to make sound decisions about what to keep and what to pass along.

De-junking often occurs in rounds over a period of months or years. Healthy de-junking leads to feelings of lightness, joyfulness, order, peace, calm, cleanliness, spaciousness, and freedom. Simply being free of things is not an end in itself. If we approach the process impulsively or thoughtlessly, we could easily dispose of things we need and only wind up replacing them later at further cost of resources to the Earth and money to ourselves. It's probably best to be conservative, go slowly, and make gradual but lasting changes.

The third way in which we can live simply for the sake of our environment relates much more directly to the central focus of voluntary simplicity, that is, the deliberate choice to *reduce consumption.*

Reducing consumption goes beyond maintaining consumption while reducing waste, or clearing away the backlog of clutter produced by our history of consumption. Voluntary simplicity involves continuing vigilance to maintain the lightness of being we achieved through waste reduction and de-junking, and further extending it if possible. It involves *refraining from re-acquiring* the baggage we just discarded. It involves cultivating a less "thing-oriented" way of life.

At first this movement toward simplicity may sound negative, as if we must live in a continual state of tension between wanting things and restraining ourselves from acquiring them. But if this is the case, we haven't really changed at all. Joyful simplicity is possible when we start wanting things other than "things." "Restraint" and "vigilance" then become exercises in protecting and sustaining something we have come to prize rather than a puritanical form of self-denial for its own sake. Sustaining and extending our practice of simplicity takes on feelings of joyfulness and accomplishment when it is clearly linked to enjoying and protecting non-material values.

> *Joyful simplicity is possible when we start wanting things other than "things." "Restraint" and "vigilance" then become exercises in protecting and sustaining something we have come to prize rather than a puritanical form of self-denial for its own sake.*

Once this fundamental change in the orientation of our identity and activity spins itself toward a new way of living, it has profound environmental benefits. The reason for this is what Alan Durning has termed the "environmental wake" left by everything we consume.[16] All the material things we are urged to buy come to us upon a more or less invisible "wake" of environmental impacts. Durning observes that what appears to be just a cup of coffee is actually coffee beans grown in Columbia shipped to New Orleans on freighters built in Japan fueled with oil coming from the Beaufort Sea, being roasted in New Orleans using gas that arrived in a pipeline from Oklahoma, only to be bagged in sacks made with fiber grown in Africa to be shipped on trucks built in Georgia and Michigan to consumers in California who use water piped from the Rocky Mountains, electricity generated on the Columbia River, a coffee maker made from a dozen different materials imported from Sweden, and a coffee cup made from glass that required silicates, chemicals, and natural gas to manufacture. What we actually *see* is only the cup of coffee. But when we come to be mindful of the environmental wake it represents, we appreciate the fact that the decision not to consume it in the first place saves not only the cup of coffee, but helps terminate the entire environmental wake required to produce it. The act of buying the coffee then comes to be repositioned in terms of a truer understanding of its meaning and consequences. Refraining from consuming the coffee, therefore, becomes not mainly an exercise in self-denial (though it is also that) but mainly an *affirmation* of something we prize more: ecological sustainability. Moreover, we are not even asking ourselves to go thirsty in this case, but merely to consider making a substitution, drinking something else that comes from closer to home with fewer steps of processing, like mint tea from the back yard.

Perhaps one of the most important contributions in several years to the practice of simplicity for the sake of the environment has appeared in a recent book published by the Union of Concerned Scientists titled *The Consumer's Guide to Effective Environmental Choices*.[17] While it is true that every material thing made or used by human beings drags along its own "environmental wake," some wakes are much larger than others. As we have often observed, voluntary simplicity is not necessarily about practicing across-the-board frugality, though for some it may indeed be that, and we respect those who take this path.

The Union of Concerned Scientists has done voluntary simplicity a great service by conducting quantitative research on exactly what forms of consumption have the greatest detrimental impacts on the ecosphere. They discovered that by reducing or changing the pattern of relatively few categories of consumption, we can drastically reduce environmental damage. Their contribution now gives us a short list of very important things we can do (and avoid doing) that will help save the Earth — a decided advance in "simplicity" over the hundreds and sometimes thousands of suggestions that characterized earlier action-oriented books which, despite their soundness, served as much to overwhelm as to inform.

Thus, to make a very large contribution to reducing most major forms of environmental harm, we are urged to (a) reduce and preferably eliminate the personal use of automobiles, recreational vehicles of all classes, and air travel; (b) reduce and preferably eliminate the consumption of meat; (c) reduce and preferably eliminate the consumption of foods grown by conventional agricultural methods and substitute for them, as much as practicable, local, organically grown foods; (d) reduce the overall size and increase the overall energy efficiency of our homes, especially the use of energy for heating, domestic hot water, major appliances, and lighting; (e) if possible, switch to an electricity supplier offering renewable energy. These changes should receive priority in any program of voluntary simplicity if we are practicing it wholly or partly for environmental reasons because these changes, challenging as they are, produce a very large environmental benefit compared to other consumption changes.

Moreover, the Union of Concerned Scientists prepared a list of activities that are especially environmentally damaging. Total environmental damage from these activities is not particularly high because not many people engage in them, and when they do, it is usually not for long periods. But when they are pursued, the environmental impact per dollar of consumption is extremely high. They include (a) the use of powerboats (marine engines) of all sizes and classes; (b) the household (yard and garden) use of pesticides and artificial fertilizers; (c) the use of gasoline-powered yard equipment, or any device with a two-stroke engine and no pollution controls; (d) the use of fireplaces and low-efficiency wood stoves; (e) recreational off-road driving; (f) the household use of hazardous solvents, paints, and cleaning chemicals; (g) the consumption of products made from endangered or threatened species.

The Union of Concerned Scientists provide detailed quantitative explanations to back up their recommendations, which fall beyond the scope of this book to summarize. The interested reader is encouraged to consult this resource directly.

For some practitioners of simple living, however, reducing consumption for the sake of the environment will involve refraining from most forms of consumption not directly connected with basic needs, rather than just making selective reductions or substitutions. This will be the practice of simplicity based on non-material values such that attaining our values leaves no room whatever in our lives for this or that acquisition. For example, some people seeking to promote ecological sustainability through their practice of simplicity see no place in their lives for something like a Sport Utility Vehicle — *at all* — *ever*. This is "hard core" voluntary simplicity at its most eloquent.

The decision to forgo consumption is the most direct, effective, immediate, and "market sensitive" step that an individual (or a group) can take toward ecological stewardship. It leaves species, resources, energy supplies, and natural cycles intact by never exploiting them in the first place. I cannot imagine any more elegant or direct method of preserving wilderness, silence, space, and species for future generations.

6

Simplicity and Spirituality

For then, we grow by subtraction. We study to un-learn.
We hold fast to letting go. We seek clean lines, short paths with few steps.
We dream deeply in simple words.[1]

"Spirituality" implies having regard for things that are invisible. It pertains to a realm of experience that may produce its effects and reflections in the world of visible events and things, but in itself is somehow "set apart" from them. This immediately places spiritual talk on a different plane from those human endeavours that concern only what can be observed and measured in a public, objective way. Of course, this also means that anything we say about our spiritual experience is metaphorical rather than precise, and to some degree personal, though not exclusively so.

Spirituality also involves a *search for meaning*, the desire to find and know the *truth about things and oneself*. The *meaning* of a thing (or a person's life) is that for the sake of which it exists and without which the thing (or person) lacks context, place, connectedness, embeddedness. So we might say that spirituality concerns that which *connects* us to some larger whole within which we have a unique "place" that "makes a difference", i.e., *has meaning*, and without which the pattern as a whole would be incomplete.

In a more personal sense, spirituality has strong connections to *love* and to *insight*. In both Christian and Islamic traditions, the *truth* we seek and the *meaning* of our lives are discovered in the dialogue of love between God and the human soul. It is the working of divine love in the soul that knits us into the larger whole that shows us the meaning of our existence. Love itself is invisible, of course, until it is "incarnated" in some way through our actions, thus "revealing" the invisible through something visible. But in the end, it is love that brings us *insight* into the nature of the world, of others, of ourselves, and of God.

In Buddhist spirituality, it is *insight* we seek through the practice of the dharma, which itself embodies the truth that insight reveals. When we experience this insight in a personal way, i.e., attain to some measure of "enlightenment," the ripening of this insight produces *love* (compassion). Our place in the great reality of the dharma has always existed, and it is through the insight of enlightenment that we come to know this in an irrefutable way and become conscious of the meaning of our existence.

Having regard for the invisible, searching for meaning and connection, necessarily entails attention to other ways of knowing about life than exclusive reference to our sensory experiences. Thus, spirituality accords value to *intuitive* knowledge as well as empirical knowledge.

Living spiritually involves organizing our manner of living according to a larger pattern, which we learn about and follow intuitively. It means having regard for both that which is visible and that which is invisible and is, therefore, a more complex way of living than having regard only for the physical universe.

There is a frog said to live in the Amazon that has a split lens in its eyes. The bottom half of each eye is adapted to seeing below the surface of the water, while the top half of each eye has a lens suited to vision in the air. The frog can thus sit half-submerged with the water surface precisely crossing the boundary between the two lenses of its eyes and can see beneath the water to guard against predators and above the water as it waits for insect prey. Similarly, having access to two realms of experience at the same time and fusing them together in consciousness is a descriptive, if crude, metaphor for spiritual living.

Practices that help us reconnect with our intuitive sources of knowing can be called spiritual practices. For many centuries, across many spiritual traditions, voluntary simplicity (by many different names: religious poverty, renunciation, non-attachment) has been an essential part of spiritual practice.

Thus, living spiritually acknowledges there is more to life than meets the eye. It means having regard for both an inner and an outer world, the subjective and objective world, the invisible and the visible worlds. These "worlds" are not really separate, but becoming conscious of the inner world requires paying attention to and respecting one's inner life.

For millennia, people have noticed that paying attention to their inner life is more difficult in the midst of the hubbub of commerce, power lust, manipulation, scheming, and control fantasies that in our age have accelerated to a frenzied pitch. By focusing entirely on image to the exclusion of substance, on appearance rather than reality, and on the transient and visible rather than on the lasting and the invisible, consumerism denigrates our inner life, authentic emotion, and intuitive knowledge — and we lose contact with life's spiritual meaning.

Practices that help us reconnect with our intuitive sources of knowing can be called *spiritual practices*. For many centuries, across many spiritual traditions, voluntary simplicity (going by many different names, such as religious poverty, renunciation, non-attachment) has been an essential part of spiritual practice. Experience has shown it is possible to develop and sustain a spiritual consciousness amidst a consumer society, but it can be extremely difficult for some people and immense effort may be required. The work required — the need for paying close attention to changes in feelings and mental imagery, to the symbolic as well as the literal dimensions of our experience, sometimes involving working with dreams or special physical disciplines like yoga or marital arts — can shrivel and die in the aggressive, noisy, and extroverted atmosphere of consumer culture.

Once some of these practices have been developed and our perspective on living has changed as a result, it is possible to continue spiritual practice amidst the uproar of modern life which, at times, can even become part of spiritual practice. But people who can maintain a vital, conscious connection with the spiritual dimension of their experience in the rush of consumer culture have often cultivated this ability over a considerable period and to a high level of proficiency.

To make a start, to continue to grow, and even to sustain access to intuitive knowledge and self-awareness, simplicity, solitude, and silence are supremely useful. For some people, the choice to live more simply is part of their decision to cultivate the spiritual dimension of their life.

Simplicity as a Form of Spiritual Practice

Many spiritual traditions have taught that the single-minded pursuit of the accumulation of material things, and even the pursuit of non-material things, in short, the pursuit of anything that tends to strengthen the ego, the false self, or whatever name we wish we give it — the pursuit of self-aggrandizement by any name — leads to a loss of connection with reality, to suffering, in a word, to trouble. It's not that material things are evil, quite the contrary, but that they are treacherous because they can become objects of craving and attachment. Our cravings and attachments to things that arenot really conducive to our spiritual growth can so occupy our attention that they soak up all the time and energy, which might otherwise be applied to cultivating knowledge of things that are more conducive to our growth.

There are many examples from a variety of spiritual literatures that commend the practice of simple living as also representing a spiritual practice:

> *Riches destroy the foolish, if they look not for the other shore;*
> *by his thirst for riches the foolish man destroys himself*
> *as if he were his own enemy.*[2]
> — Swamigal, *Dhammapada*

It is easier for a camel to go through a needle's eye,
than for a rich man to enter the kingdom of God.
— Matthew 19:24

Excess and deficiency are equally at fault.[3]
— Confucius, XI. 15

They are most happy and nearest the gods that need nothing.[4]
— Socrates

Fill your bowl to the brim
and it will spill.
Keep sharpening your knife
and it will blunt.
Chase after money and security
and your heart will never unclench.
Care about people's approval
and you will be their prisoner.
Do your work, then step back.
The only path to serenity.[5]
— Lao Tse, *Tao Te Ching*

First, the practice of simplicity can be part of modeling one's own life along the lines of the life of a revered spiritual forebearer or mentor. Christian monks of the orders of St. Francis, the Jesuits, the Dominicans, and vowed hermits promise to live simply (to take vows of poverty) to conform their lives to the example of the founders of their respective orders, and ultimately, to conform them to the example of Christ himself. Likewise, the followers of Buddha, Taoist monks, and Hindu yogis also practice more or less radical forms of simplicity to help free themselves from attachment to material things. This practice is based on the belief that part of a spiritual teacher's teaching is also carried in his or her way of life, and that those who share in this life will thereby absorb the truth of the teaching.

Practicing voluntary simplicity has also been seen as a way of disencumbering oneself for service to others. Concern for many possessions, complex business affairs, the demands of social commitments, etc. take time and energy. Yet many forms of spiritual practice stress the value of service to others, especially to those who cannot repay the service. Moreover, being fully open and responsive to the intuitive promptings of the spiritual life implies being relatively free to follow them. The practice of simplicity thus becomes essential.

Similarly, spiritual practice can itself have a "sign" value or a symbolic significance as well as a literal effect on the lives of others. How one lives communicates something about what one believes and values. According to St. Basil the Great, simplicity is a sign of one's belonging to God. Moreover, it communicates something about those with whom we stand in solidarity. Voluntary simplicity can be a powerful symbolic statement that we look beyond the material aspects of life for meaning. Also, voluntary simplicity can be a proclamation of solidarity with the poor — those for whom, in the Western spiritual tradition, God shows special care and who, in Eastern traditions, offer us special opportunities for practicing compassion.

An important way in which the practice of simplicity can be a spiritual practice is as a means of reducing demands that interfere with all the other practices we might pursue in order to heighten intuitive awareness, cultivate stillness, and grow in mindfulness. Developing the inner side of our lives requires getting in touch with what is going on in there and then actively cultivating a relationship with it. The traditional means of doing this include meditation, contemplation, service to others, various devotional practices, some of the martial arts, and a variety of fine arts. All of these require long periods of uninterrupted practice for their development, usually including silence, solitude, privacy, and freedom from distraction. In the endeavor to cultivate our character rather than expand the quantity of our possessions, simplifying life to its bare essentials has traditionally been a practical thing to do. Speaking of an intensive period of practice known as "spiritual retreat," David Cooper observes:

Developing the inner side of our lives requires getting in touch with what is going on in there and then actively cultivating a relationship with it.

> On retreat, one sits, walks, eats, sleeps, dresses, and takes care of personal hygiene. These are the basic physical needs. Keep it as simple as possible — clean, light, uncomplicated, spacious, empty — and use this pristine external form as a vehicle for and reflection of what we want for our inner being.[6]

Some spiritual teachers have taken this principle another step, indicating that not only does simplicity have an *instrumental* value in clearing the deck for practices that contribute directly to our spiritual growth, simplicity is also *intrinsically* effective in predisposing us for a more intimate relationship with Divine Being. In the Rule of St. Benedict, for example, the monk's love of poverty (simplicity) is grounded in love of the poor, and in them, the love of Christ.[7] The practice of simplicity is not seen as *leading* to the love of Christ, but rather, as *being equivalent to* the love of Christ — and this love grows through practice. This notion has strong resonances in Buddhist teaching, which says that by adopting the manner of life of the Buddha, by adopting his physical position in sitting meditation, by finding refuge in the sangha (the spiritual community), the devotee *already* manifests Buddha-nature (enlightenment), whether or not he or she has consciously realized it yet.[8]

The practice of simplicity is also valuable as an effective means of orienting oneself toward values that are grounded in spiritual truth rather than embracing the illusions of sense experience (Eastern) or concupiscence (misdirected and exaggerated desire) for things that have no inherent value or capacity to fulfill our deepest longings (Western). The practice of simplicity shifts the "center of gravity" of the personality away from attachment to what can be seen and possessed over to what is invisible but nonetheless real and imperishable:

> Lay not up for yourselves treasures upon the earth, where moth and rust consume, and where thieves break through and steal: but lay up for yourselves treasures in heaven, where neither moth nor rust doth consume, and where thieves do not break through nor steal: for where thy treasure is, there will thy heart be also. (Matthew, 6:19 - 21)

In the Dominican practice of simplicity, "evangelical poverty" is an economic rejection that is governed by a spiritual motive or insight. Following Christ means breaking away from the pomp (arrogance) of the world and its institutions. It may thus be understood as an action that bears a double aspect: a mystical adherence to Christianity on the one hand and the rejection of an established abusive economic system on the other. Adopting evangelical poverty forms both the symbol and the guarantee of the rejection of what the "worldly" economy has to offer.

Simplicity is never an end in itself. It is always a means in service of other ends.

We pick up some overtones of this theme even among those who practice simplicity for entirely non-spiritual reasons. Modern institutions might be characterized not only as spiritually "pompous," but also as embodying a certain political hubris and technological arrogance that, partially anyway, accounts for the extreme inequity with which their benefits are distributed in society and the violent invasiveness of their methods of economic production and social control. To practice simplicity is, then, so far as it lies within the power of an individual, a stepping back from this status quo in a silent but highly visible protest.

Having said all of this, however, we must enter a caveat that surrounds the practice of simplicity, especially as spiritual practice: *Simplicity is never an end in itself.* It is always a *means* in service of other ends. In the Western tradition, the practice of simplicity is properly subordinated to love and exercised in service of love — love for oneself and for others, to be sure, but most importantly, the love of God. Christian Scripture is striking in the mystical importance it attributes to poverty: (a) the poor person's confidence and source of security as he or she confronts life are not derived from the power of money or any other wealth held in reserve, they are based on trust and confidence in Divine love and providence; (b) the real object of possession for our deepest fulfillment is Divine Being. The poor in spirit are blessed, not because they possess nothing but because they possess only the kingdom of heaven. Mistaking the practice of simplicity for the divine relationship for which it prepares us would be to mistake practicing one's scales for the concert performance.

This is also the case in Eastern traditions, where those who seek liberation are continually warned not "to mistake the finger for the moon" — to believe that a particular practice is the same as the end for which it prepares us. Autism is a state of profound psychological "lack of attachment" to anything or anyone in the material world, but no one would mistake it for enlightenment. In the same way, practising simplicity is not, in and of itself, the end toward which it provides invaluable assistance.

Simplicity as a Fruit of Spiritual Practice

The "goal" of spiritual practice is to predispose us to fall in love with Divine Being and to realize that more and more of our needs are provided for through this love relationship. In the Western tradition, the development of this disposition, as well as its fruition in the birth of love within us, is from beginning to end the work of Divine Being itself, assisted by our willingness to co-operate with its action and to allow it to express itself in our lives. In the Eastern tradition, enlightenment is more of an individual achievement, but is nevertheless strongly supported and nurtured through one's roshi (teacher), one's sangha (spiritual community), the Dharma (truth), and countless generations of previously enlightened beings (Bodhisattvas) who continue to support and sustain the efforts of all beings to attain enlightenment and hence liberation from suffering.

Since my own spiritual tradition has Western roots, I will continue to speak from that tradition rather than presume too much upon my slender understanding of Eastern teachings.

What can happen for people who begin seriously to turn their attention toward cultivating the spiritual dimension of their lives is the ignition of a kind of "cycle" of simplification and spiritual growth that feed on each other. As spiritual practice becomes more important, we seek more time and privacy to pursue it. This involves practicing a certain measure of simplicity. As we grow spiritually, however, this experience is so profoundly joyful, peace-inducing, and warming that we are naturally drawn to more and more practice. But to find time and freedom from distraction to engage in more practice requires another round of simplification. This process may take years. Its basic trajectory is much like the toddler on the beach stripping off first this and then that in a squealing gallop toward the ocean of cosmic love. Eventually, we have no tolerance for "clothing" of any kind, and no desire to be anywhere but in that luminous ocean.

When this happens, a "shift" occurs in our personality where we come to understand that our essential nature is really "amphibian," that we belong as much to the divine realm as to the material one, that the two suffuse each other, and that there is really no longer any need for anxiety — about *anything*. Since the greatest engine of modern consumerism is fear, the diminishment of our fear has a profound effect on our future willingness to participate in the self-absorbed hyperactivity of modern life. Simplicity then becomes as much an *expression* of our spirituality as a practice that sustains it.

Of course, this process can also move in the reverse direction. There are occasions when we may find ourselves plunged into the ocean of Divine Being without having consciously set out to cultivate the dispositions that welcome it. Sometimes these "graced moments" happen spontaneously at the pleasure of Divine Being, entirely unconnected to anything happening in our daily lives. More commonly, they come when the circumstances of our suffering or state of "illusionment" bring our customary lives to a complete halt. This can happen through loss of a loved one or a career or through some important achievement; it can also descend on us through accident, illness, or a brush with death. In such cases, the "collapse" of life as we have always known it brings with it the *involuntary* "simplification" and silencing of our inner world — or enough of a silence so that we can begin to hear some ringing overtones to life we have previously ignored. We have no choice. Flat on our backs, we *must* listen. There isn't anything else to do.

In the best case, these sorts of experiences trigger the "shift" mentioned above that tilts our inner center of gravity in such a way that our outer life changes. We say we appreciate more. We say we can now focus on "what matters." We say we've done a lot of "separating the wheat from the chaff" when we were sick. We've "soul-searched." Having lost this person, we now appreciate how much we were taking for granted and will henceforth live more mindfully and with more gratitude. These kinds of inner changes often spin out into actions and affect how we shape our way of life; they are expressed in a greater preference for simplicity, honesty, directness, and authenticity in our relationships. In such cases, it is a round of spiritual growth that triggers an outer simplification of life. And, as in the first example, this simplification helps support and sustain a continuing relationship with the spiritual aspect of our being.

゚ℰ

The voluntary choice to simplify our lives thus has a long history in spiritual practice both in the East and the West. On the one hand, simplicity can be a practice that supports our spiritual growth and helps create the conditions in which we can deepen into Divine Being. On the other hand, it can be a fruit of this deepening, expressing and carrying forward changes that have happened in us either by sheer grace or by graced rescue from the calamities of trying to live while "sleep-walking." Wherever simplicity first begins, a preference for it often comes linked together with spiritual growth in a self-reinforcing cycle that grows stronger as it spins itself into realisation.

PART III

HOW TO PRACTICE
LIVING SIMPLY

7

Cultivating Mindfulness

In this section we begin exploring the *practice* of voluntary simplicity. Now that we better understand what it is and may have discovered convincing reasons for practicing simpler living, the question becomes: Just *how* do people go about it?

One of the most important things that distinguishes those who are enthusiastic about simple living is their taste for cultivating mindfulness. In 1996, I conducted an Internet survey of people subscribed to a major discussion list on voluntary simplicity. I asked them, among other things, what they thought the essential practices of simple living might be? The cultivation of mindfulness by one means or another was an essential part of many respondents' practice of simplicity.

Cultivating mindfulness means learning to pay full attention to whatever we are experiencing in the present moment. It means being fully awake and fully here for whatever is going on. We speak of "cultivating" mindfulness because it can be learned and deepened through practice. We may experience mindful moments by accident, as when we have a close brush with death or something surprises us into heightened awareness. It's also possible to take drugs to artificially induce a subjective sense of heightened attention. But these methods of being mindful are unstable and transient. The deliberate cultivation of mindfulness as a more or less continuous state of consciousness that can be maintained during daily activities is another thing altogether.

Learning to wake up and *stay* awake is the very basis for voluntary choice. It is the essential requirement for a life of freedom and self-determination. Otherwise, one drifts through the day in a coma-like state of habit, reflex, and impulsive reactions triggered by momentary appetites and advertising jingles. This is very good for consumerism because many purchases are made on impulse, even big purchases. Impulse is not particularly conducive, however, to aligning actions with values or to maintaining a meaningful attunement with one's intuition and inner feelings.

While mindfulness is a simple concept and the quality of consciousness it represents is clear and uncluttered, cultivating it requires lifelong practice. And yet, this is pleasant. Mindfulness practice is like dancing or playing the piano.

Beginners' steps and practice pieces are simple ones, yet from the very beginning the practitioner is dancing and making music. We take our place among *all* dancers and musicians and experience pleasure in what we can do. At the same time, however, there will always be room to develop and polish the practice of dancing or making music.

Cultivating mindful-ness means learning to pay full attention to whatever we are experiencing in the present moment.

Similarly, with the cultivation of mindfulness, the ability to stay awake, to pay attention in the present moment, on purpose, without pre-judging one's experience, will at first be sporadic and unreliable. In ways that escape easy description, cultivating mindfulness can become an essential part of life, something a practitioner misses daily practice is skipped. It adds a dimension to experience that cannot be gained in any other way. The world gains the dimension of depth. We still see the same people, trees, streets, houses, but everything has acquired another side, another aspect that adds a new quality to every experience.

Living simply helps establish and maintain the conditions (time, silence, solitude, freedom from unwanted distractions) that contribute to the cultivation of mindfulness and strengthens the motivation to continue. Interestingly, the cultivation of mindfulness enlarges a person's capacity to find pleasure in simple living and to practice it. Thus mindfulness and simplicity feed each other — it's a positive feedback loop.

The significance of mindfulness to voluntary simplicity is not just circular causation, however. There are two aspects at play here.

First, we all have moments when we are suddenly a bit more aware, more mindful, of some situation or habit that has developed in our lives. Sometimes this comes as a pleasant surprise, such as realizing that someone we liked for a long time has become someone we love. Sometimes we may be unpleasantly surprised, such as when we discover that we're being exploited by a trusted friend or misled by a respected community leader. In both cases we get a spontaneous taste of how simply *paying more attention* to our daily experience can help us live it with more responsibility, involvement, and clarity. Mindfulness can thus help us avoid or desist from causing harm to ourselves, others, or the planet. In fact, we cannot choose the lives we live unless we are first aware of some choices and also of ourselves as choosers.

Second, most of us have spontaneous moments of heightened awareness when very simple things bring us great pleasure or hold keen interest. This often happens when we're doing something new because it is in trying new things that we are most attentive and open to new learning. We come to our experience with a "beginner's mind." In a beginner's mind, things we will later take for granted are still full of interesting details, unexplored facets, hidden dangers, new discoveries. Often though, after our first explorations, we cease paying attention and move on to the next new thing. In fact, we can develop a deeply ingrained *habit* of only paying superficial attention to experience, especially when we add in the distracting effects of imagination, anticipation, and recollection running in the background of consciousness as well as the roaring confusion of advertising that characterizes the general ambience of a consumer culture.

But what if we could learn to *cultivate* mindfulness and *practice* it like dancing or singing, rather than just waiting for life to hand us our next surprise? What if mindfulness could grow, like appreciation for art or music? And what if we didn't have to resort to expedients like bungee jumping or "extreme sports" in order to force a temporary state of awareness?

Fortunately, there are ways of cultivating mindfulness that can form a regular part of daily activity. The role they play in voluntary simplicity is twofold:

First, mindfulness enhances awareness of the power of choice we can exercise in our lives. We become more aware of what we are doing, feeling, and thinking and of how we are acting. This is a tremendous help to acting in ways that serve life, promote goodness, protect us and those we love from harm, and promote in society the values we believe in. There is also a sense in which "mindfulness" implies *vigilance*. Once we learn to live more simply, sustaining our simplicity requires continual vigilance lest we succumb again to habit and impulsiveness and wind up acquiring additional stuff that somebody else profits from at the expense of complicating our lives.

Second, mindfulness brings quality and depth into whatever moment-to-moment experience brings us. We discover that we don't need *much* in order to live *deeply*. Consumerism tries to substitute for depth and quality a continuous stream of new, ever-changing but quite superficial experiences — for those who can pay for them, of course. The "bargain" it offers is exactly like the difference between a really stunning movie and real life. The movie is changing all the time, it's vivid and loaded with flashy special effects that can be riveting and spectacular. There is no doubt it can also be entertaining. But in the end, we are only watching a two-dimensional image on a flat screen, a shadow of what we are capable of experiencing. We may see the *illusion* of depth presented on the screen, but not its reality. The longer we stay in the theatre, the more restless we become, the more conscious we are that despite its attractions, the movie lacks something. Consumerism invests billions of dollars every year trying to make its "movies" as seamlessly realistic as possible so that we will never want to leave the theatre.

There is another dimension to life — a *depth* dimension — that is as different as strolling in a park is from seeing a park in a film. We can get up and walk out of the theatre. We can see real trees, a real sky, a real ocean. It is by cultivating mindfulness that we can do this. It is by learning how to enter into the depth of our experience that we escape the fate of bouncing off the surface of life never realizing that there is a dimension of our experience that allows us to plunge in.

Before we start cultivating mindfulness in a disciplined way, it can be helpful to form an inner image of our future, more mindful selves. Imagine yourself for a moment living in a more mindful and attentive way. See yourself moving more slowly through life, taking time to notice things, time to find your balance as you walk, time to notice how things look and smell around you. See yourself looking deeply into other people's eyes as you talk with them, studying their faces with attention and sensitivity. See yourself deeply enjoying the pleasure of love-making, a fresh salad, a starry evening sky, walking barefoot in wet grass. Imagine yourself gazing steadily inward, knowing and accepting yourself, your feelings, longings, spiritual intuitions, dreams. See yourself so clear, so centered and strong, that you can calmly remain with those in crisis, listening, loving, understanding, giving.

If this image of a future self appeals to you, let it grow in you, let it become clearer and clearer, let it become more and more an inner reality for you. As the image grows in clarity, you may also experience a growing desire to realize it in your life. It has the capacity to become an expression of one's "seed potential," carrying its own charge of energy and its own load of meaning. This inner image can strengthen your commitment to cultivate mindfulness. It can provide the energy to support your discipline of practice when you would rather do something else.

Once an inner image of this sort is born in us, we can nurture and protect it. The manic, debasing imagery of popular culture and the media can quickly erode our belief in the possibility that a mindful person can even exist, much less that we ourselves might learn to become such a being. When something good and admirable is born in our imagination, it's worth protecting. So part of the practice of cultivating mindfulness entails simplifying our lives and getting rid of those influences that may distract us from realizing this so-recently emerged potential within ourselves.

℅

Mindfulness practice is very ancient; many people have contributed to its development and advocated its practice. It is the exact opposite of "something new and exciting." When the cultivation of mindfulness is developed through formal sitting meditation, it can sometimes feel boring. But neither its antiquity nor its failure to deliver a steady stream of spine-tingling novelty at every turn in any way diminishes its value.

At its most basic, *we practice mindfulness whenever we pay close attention, on purpose, to one and only one thing at a time.* Many people find this challenging. Not the least among the challenges is overcoming the mistaken expectation that practicing mindfulness produces an altered state of consciousness that is either continually ecstatic or at least exciting. On the contrary, when developed through sitting meditation as described below, sitting practice can be low-key, punctuated by cycles of losing one's focus, only to return again to paying attention. It may be decidedly barren of spiritual "highs" or mystical insights. In fact, many spiritual teachers have referred to experiences of this sort as distractions from genuine practice, not the fruits of it.

> *Mindfulness practice is very ancient; many people have contributed to its development and advocated its practice. It is the exact opposite of "something new and exciting."*

So why would anyone continue practicing? The short answer is that if we can be patient, self-forgiving, persistent, and faithful to practice for a significant time, if we can find the help we need (if we hit a snag), and find support and affirmation for our efforts from another person (if we need that), then something wonderful begins to unfold in our lives that seems to be connected to the practice. I don't claim to understand *how* this happens. The change is very subtle at first — so subtle that we may not even notice anything happening until one day we're startled at how beautiful the world seems, how calm we feel inside, how we find energy or idealism for something we didn't know we had, how we feel connection with other people and species we never enjoyed before, and how our growing feelings of security leave little energy for desiring the things we used to want so much. The "messages" that advertisers want us to hear so badly, messages we may even have been interested in at one time, now seem like "noise" masking this deeper melody we've learned to hear. Sitting practice may continue to be boring and frustrating at times, but as we grow more certain about its effects on the texture of consciousness, we become more tenacious in practice.

The most time-honored method of cultivating mindfulness is the practice of formal sitting meditation. The advantage of sitting practice is that it is available to anyone regardless of age, income level, or background. It requires no special equipment, expensive travel, or specialized facilities. Yet there are some things that are helpful to sitting practice that may be difficult to find: silence, solitude, freedom from distraction, and preferably beautiful, or at least neutral, surroundings. Given these, the steps of sitting practice are very simple:

- **Find a place of solitude and silence where you can sit for at least thirty minutes without interruption.** It is helpful if you sit in the same place every day and if this place is furnished and decorated in a way that is conducive to sitting practice (i.e., simply).

- **Take a sitting position** on a firm but not hard chair, feet flat on the floor in front of you, spine erect but not stiff, chin level, hands cupped in your lap or palms on your thighs (palm up or down as feels most natural and appropriate), gaze straight forward, face, forehead, jaw and neck muscles as relaxed as possible in an alert, erect position. Sit on the floor if you wish, in lotus position if you can, but whatever position you finally adopt, it should present *minimum discomfort* and bodily stress, yet not be so relaxed as to induce sleep. Avoid over-stuffed chairs or recliners.

- **Close your eyes. Take three or four deep breaths and then let your breathing find its own depth, rhythm, and pace. Pay attention *only to your breathing* — to nothing else.** No thought, no memory, feeling, desire, expectation, goal, fear, worry, image, sensation, perception, or other event, inner or outer, should draw your attention away from your breath. Many things, pleasant and unpleasant, will arise inwardly, and there will also be external sensations, but all of these we simply let go and return to concentrating on the breath. Some people find it helpful at first to *count* their breaths as they breath, repeating sub-vocally "one" on the inhale and "one" again on the exhale, counting up to ten, then counting backwards again to one, then starting over. If this helps you, do it. If not, don't.

- **Practice sitting and breathing for 30 minutes twice a day, letting go of everything,** no matter how brilliant, insightful, or holy it may seem, or how dreadful, urgent, or vulgar. During sitting practice, we *only* sit and breathe. That is all. It's that simple.

By practicing this form of sitting meditation, we cultivate a capacity for non-judgmental, deliberate attention to here-and-now experience. We also cultivate the capacity to "let go," to *renounce* whatever is entering consciousness. Paradoxically, gaining inner freedom depends upon the ability to both focus energy in the experiences of the moment and to let go of them.

There are a number of things that help and hinder the development of mindfulness, whether it is deliberately cultivated through sitting practice or in other ways:

- Physical surroundings that induce rush, haste, clutter, noise, or general uproar or that are physically dangerous or unhealthy tend to distract attention, sometimes for good reason. Such surroundings are not conducive to learning mindfulness, although it is said that people accomplished in practice can practice anywhere under any circumstances. I find it difficult.

- Ingestion of mood-altering drugs or foods, even substances within the realm of social acceptability, such as alcohol, tobacco, and caffeine; over-eating, especially of fatty or protein-rich foods; and even the effects of many prescription drugs can hinder concentration and sitting practice.

- Our general state of soul, that is, whether our daily lives reflect our general intention to become more peaceable, loving, generous, and civilized people or not, influences our ability to cultivate mindfulness. As Shinzen Young, a Buddhist meditation teacher, is reported to have said: "...when you have been out stealing and killing all day long, it is hard to settle your mind for meditation at the end of the day."[1] It has also been the normal counsel in the Christian spiritual tradition that sacramental confession is a good (often necessary) preparation for a prolonged period of concentrated spiritual practice, such as a retreat.

- Patience, trust, and generosity are important aids to cultivating mindfulness.[2] Because practice takes considerable time to make any noticeable difference (at least months, and often years) and because we may become frustrated with how many times our attention may wander, we require great patience and gentleness with ourselves if we are to persist. Likewise, we must trust that the process leads somewhere worth going and be generous enough to give ourselves to it, at first on the hypothesis that by practicing we do good that touches others as well as us, until we come to know this as a subjective reality and see it come to pass as an objective fact.

- Clinging of any kind can hinder practice. We are especially prone to cling to pleasant experiences — brilliant insights, gentle thoughts — when they happen and to want to repeat them. Yet the heart of practice is letting go — letting go of everything, every thought, every feeling, every idea — not to be totally empty of thoughts, but to become emptied of *clinging* to them, especially of identifying with them or confusing the contents of thoughts or feelings with our most authentic self. Learning to let go of illusion and suffering requires letting go of everything.

- Letting go of the idea that cultivating mindfulness is a purely selfish thing to do happens somewhat later in practice. As mindfulness grows, so does compassion, and as compassion grows, it's easy to feel that further practice is self-indulgent. The famous Buddhist spiritual teacher Thich Nhat Hahn[3] points out that since everything is interdependent and connected, it is literally impossible to be alone, even though one may be in solitude. Any practice that advances one's own spiritual growth inevitably benefits the whole of humankind. There is a somewhat corresponding notion in Christian spirituality associated with the "communion of saints" wherein doing the "work of God" — *opus dei* — benefits the entire "people of God," that is, everyone, since we all form one divine body.

For many people who have chosen to live simply, the cultivation of mindfulness — whether through the practice of formal sitting meditation or some other means, such as a martial art, sport, fine art, dance, gardening, music, contemplative walking — forms an essential and often daily part of the person's life. Several people have commented that once they understood what it meant, the only alternative to cultivating mindfulness appeared to be returning to a *mindless* way of life, something they no longer found appealing.

8

Knowing When Enough Is Enough

He who knows he has enough is rich.[1]
— Lao-Tse, *Tao Te Ching*

In our first explorations of the meaning of voluntary simplicity, we pointed out that simplicity is not the same thing as destitution, or self-imposed deprivation. The practice of simplicity is all about *sufficiency* or there being *enough* — what the ancients called "the Middle Way" or the "Golden Mean." It has to do with finding a graceful balance in life where we have enough material possessions to provide for our basic needs, plus some comforts and luxuries that may not be required for basic survival but are appropriate to a dignified and self-actualizing life. As we might expect, there is considerable latitude here in deciding exactly how much is enough, and how much of what sorts of things. This will naturally vary with the individual, to some degree with the culture, certainly with geography, and with our state and stage in life.

Supposing that we may have made at least one "de-junking" pass through our living quarters, we're faced with the practical question of *how not to slide slowly (or rapidly) back into the mire of accumulation?* This requires cultivating discernment in how much is enough as well as cultivating the mindfulness necessary to balance on that graceful point without allowing ourselves to be pulled or pushed off. There are two things that will be of some help in achieving this: First, cultivating mindfulness of our governing values and all those things we most love in our lives. This means developing a regular practice of remembering who we are, why we are here, where we came from, and where we are going. Awareness of our personal answers to these questions, however tentative or hypothetical they may be at this time, is a powerful way of staying connected to our own sources of inner wisdom and meaning. This awareness is what helps us stay connected with what we love rather than letting ourselves become distracted by what others are trying to get us to want. (This practice of cultivating mindfulness was described in the previous chapter.)

Another thing that can be of some help in learning to discern how much is enough is developing an understanding of the dynamics of desire, that is, of why we seem to crave more and more without limit.

One story we tell ourselves about the nature and purpose of human existence is that of *consumerism*. Consumerism positions the meaning and value of life in the endless stimulation, satisfaction, and re-stimulation of desire for the consumption of material things. As well, consumerism deliberately confounds the satisfaction of non-material (psychological, social, emotional, spiritual) human needs with the production and consumption of material goods and services for profit. Since the "profit motive" is itself a *learned* desire, there are no built-in physical limits to its satisfaction. Only other social or psychological factors can restrain it or direct its expression.

In our society, an unlimited desire for profit welds the enormous flexibility of human learning to a growth-oriented economic and technical system that feeds upon a physically limited planet. The effects of this system on the Earth are being magnified by a galloping population growth, rapidly developing technology, and the "good-life-through-growth-in-consumption" ideology shared by business, governments, and most ordinary citizens. This combination is inherently unsustainable. We know this. Yet we actively export the ideology of consumerism to the rest of the world. Consumerism isn't what we *profess*, of course, but it is what we *do*, and what we do speaks far louder than what we say.

The culture of consumerism grows out of the rather sloppy "philosophy" (if it can be called that) of hedonistic materialism. Modern economics simply states that human beings are, by nature, greedy, self-interested, and pleasure-hungry without limit. Paradoxically, in our pursuit of the satisfaction of our greed and appetites for pleasure we are also supposed to be "rational". Consumerism really doesn't offer any explanation for this state of affairs, being content rather to accept it as being "just the way people are," and proceeding from this premise to devise ways of making as much money as possible from it. In the process, it preaches the very theory of human nature it assumes and, to the extent that we uncritically accept these sermons, consumerism's theory of human nature becomes a self-fulfilling prophesy. If television advertising tells us we are power-hungry, pleasure-seeking, violent, self-interested, vulgar, and unspiritual beings by nature, then perhaps we are; and if we are, then all the stuff they are offering to satisfy these desires seems quite logically to fit in with what we're told we need.

Has this description of human nature *ever* characterized the majority of human beings? It certainly *does* characterize an aggressive, powerful, and prominent minority who exercise an inordinate influence over our collective destiny. After some reflection, we can usually cite dozens of examples of other people who behave generously without thought of personal advantage, who extend themselves and sometimes die for the sake of others, who enjoy pleasure but certainly aren't ruled by it, and who do not spend every waking moment of their existence planning ways of extending their personal advantage or expanding their hoard of possessions. Most people of my acquaintance more closely resemble this latter group than the former. I mention the "economic theory" of human desire because it is so ubiquitous in the media and seems to be the fundamental assumption of most economic and political thinking in our society. Moreover, this scheme of human nature has become depersonalized and institutionalized in the form of corporations — a most ominous development.

Another theory about why we often feel drawn to acquire more than enough is proposed by the cognitive psychologist Timothy Miller in his book *How To Want What You Have*.[2] Miller argues that all species evolved the basic genetic program to acquire as much of the pre-requisites to successful mating and survival as possible (land, food, power, mates, status, etc.) for the simple reason that any creature that might have evolved with an "enough switch" for these things would have been at a reproductive disadvantage compared to those who had no enough-switch. Our more or less insatiable appetite for accumulation, therefore, may be biologically rooted, quite natural, and, until fairly recently, have been adapted for assuring the survival of the species. In modern times, however, insatiable desire has come together with powerful technologies and large populations, both of which are threatening ecological ruin if we continue with business as usual.

Miller also observes, cogently, I think, that while this innate biological programming to acquire, accumulate, and protect had a certain usefulness in assuring biological survival, *it is inherently incapable of delivering happiness or contentment.* It is not necessary for an animal to be happy or contented in order to reproduce and be an evolutionary success. Most of us know from our own personal experience that in terms of some emergent aspects of our human nature (our spirituality, our complex psychology, our social relationships) simply reproducing is not much of a reason to survive. We are more than fish swimming upstream, more than insects just trying to find a place to lay eggs.

Going further, Miller suggests (in the good company of orthodox Buddhist thinking) that when we mistakenly believe that the satisfaction of our biologically rooted desires will lead to contentment and happiness, the way is open for all varieties of competition, struggle, conflict, loss, sorrow — in a word, suffering. Paradoxically, the way to peace and happiness is *not* found through the satisfaction of desires for the simple reason that desires cannot be satisfied in a lasting way. Instead, the satiation of desire simply leads sooner or later to another round of desire, or else a fear of loss. Consumerism is actually a social system designed to strengthen desire and heighten fear of loss because these motivate people to consume much more effectively than contentment and peace, even though contentment and peace (satisfaction) are often what consumerism *promises* will follow from the consumption of products.

Desire likely has a biological origin in human nature and is no more a matter for guilt or self-blame than our need to eat or drink. It may be natural to want stuff; it may even be natural to want more and more stuff. The truth is, however, getting more and more stuff doesn't leave us better off. Yet, the competitiveness that is so stressed in consumer societies implies that it is possible for one person to enjoy a significant advantage of comfort over his or her neighbors, with peace and security to boot. Moreover, consumer societies believe they can maintain advantages of comfort and security at the expense of neighboring societies. These ideas are mistaken because they rest on the illusion that there can be such things as separate individuals and societies when, in fact, everything and everyone is systemically linked.

In its simple-minded way, consumerism just accepts this situation and seeks a way to use it systematically to enrich the minority (who are just as much its victims as anyone else!) at the expense of the freedom and contentment of the majority who are exploited. Miller offers more hope, pointing out that humans are not just bags of chemicals blindly driven about by biological instincts, but that we also have a mental and emotional capacity to counterbalance our innate desires with *understanding* and *insight* regarding their truth and consequences. Miller believes that we can counterbalance the effects of our innate propensity to want more and more by cultivating habits of thinking and ways of paying attention to our experience that are better matched with what we know is the nature of our existence. This involves establishing the mental practice of *gratitude* (the habit of perceiving and appreciating the positive aspects of our here-and-now experience), *attention* (the habit of non-prejudicially paying attention to our here-and-now experience), and *compassion* (the habit of thinking of other people as being just as ensnared in the pain of insatiable desire and chronic fear and subject to the same sufferings as are we ourselves).

The most encouraging aspect of what Miller has to say is that an "enough switch" may not come as part of our inborn biological equipment, but that we *can* install one. We can learn contentment. We can learn "how to want what we have." We are not necessarily condemned to inevitable personal burn-out, social conflict and inequity, and ecological ruin for lack of choices. We can cultivate an awareness of how much is enough and live accordingly, though not without some effort to maintain mindfulness, and not without *practice*.

There is yet another perspective on desire that has a very ancient pedigree and deserves mention here, and that concerns the spiritual aspect of desire with its repercussions for our individual well-being and the health of our relationships and our environment.

The Buddhist perspective on desire is very similar to Miller's description in that desire itself is the enemy of liberation from suffering. If desire can be stilled through insight (enlightenment), then suffering of every kind will be extinguished. Pain, both emotional and physical, cannot be extinguished because it arises from our nature as biological and psychological beings. But the *suffering* that arises from the fear of anticipating pain, the struggle to escape pain, the memory of past pain, decisions that can lead to pain, desires and fears that renew and sustain pain — all these things *can* be extinguished through the right practice of mindfulness and right understanding.

The Judeo-Christian heritage takes a somewhat different perspective, namely that desire is a normal and healthy aspect of human nature implanted in it by the Creator, but that the desiring part of human beings mistakenly desires things that *cannot* satisfy it. Our human nature has received a primordial spiritual wound. The normal object of all desire, as the Creator originally intended, is loving communion with Divine Being, in which all other desires find their meaning and appropriate fulfillment. But the effects of the primordial wound have been to confuse and misdirect the energy of human desire, to confuse our understanding of who provides the proper object of our desire, and to weaken our will even to know who that proper object is. Desire is "insatiable" because it represents the unquenchable thirst we have for communion with the Divine, which is not fully satisfied with anything less than the Divine. We were designed this way: to desire the communion of love above everything else. The fact that daily life presents us with virtually no experiences of the stilling of desire (contentment) is not a condemnation of desire itself, but a mere *effect* that follows from our seeking the equivalent of communion with the Divine from objects that cannot provide it. This is why much suffering occurs in life, and at the feet of the blind misdirection of desire can be laid all of the environmental, personal, and social harms that make up so large a proportion of the human situation. This same tradition asserts that the "primordial wound" that so distorts everything in our lives arose in some mysterious way because of *our choice* — not, to be sure, a *personal* choice, but a choice that nonetheless affects us collectively *and* personally.

We suffer then from a malady that is so mysterious and so distant from us in time, so deeply rooted in our nature, so far beyond our individual power to undo, and so pervasive and subtle in its effects that, left to our own devices, we stumble from one calamity to the next and finally to destruction. But according to the Christian tradition, there is good news as well: through the deepest of all mysteries, Divine Being was incarnated to human form, and through the working of this incarnation "Jesus of Nazareth", the primordial wound was healed. This healing is offered through *relationship*, which is ongoing and almost totally one-sided — our relationship with Divine Being. Our role in this healing is to recognize our need for it, desire it, and accept it. Yet even the ability to play out our role is brought about by Divine Being. All other healing in ourselves, our relationships, and our relation to the living world is effected through the action of Divine Being working in us through our acceptance of this activity.

Considering these different perspectives on our desire for more and more, the consumerist, economic perspective doesn't offer very much except irrational subjection to insatiable craving. This is not a particularly happy prospect for humanity, especially when this treadmill vision of existence is set up as the "engine" that drives all human progress. What progress can it be if we just drive deeper and deeper into insatiable desire?

The perspectives of cognitive psychology and of Buddhism offer us decidedly more optimistic possibilities, though neither understates the challenges. Insatiable desire for more and more is natural and also inherently incapable of leading to human happiness. By cultivating new habits of thinking and more insight into the nature of our motivations, life situation, and behavior, we can gain liberation from desire and the suffering it entails. For Buddhists, this can be achieved through assiduous practice of meditative disciplines that change the quality of consciousness itself. For cognitive psychology, it entails learning new habits of thinking, new patterns of "self-talk," concerning the world, ourselves, our lives, our relationships, etc. We are the active agents of this un-learning/re-learning process.

From the Christian perspective, desire isn't the problem, but rather a spiritual wound that misdirects desire, a wound that requires healing and that can be healed by disposing ourselves to receive the healing action of Divine Being that is continually on offer. In this tradition, we *receive* the "peace that passes understanding" rather than *achieve* it.

Without debating which of these views may ultimately be correct (if they even need to be *exclusively* correct to be helpful), observe that the roots of desire are very deep in human nature — whether because they were implanted in us through the mystery of the creation of our nature, or because they emerged in us through the natural evolution of our nature. Observe as well that *we have a choice*.

Clearly the description of human nature that serves consumerism is not the only way of making sense of our daily experience of desire. Ironically, a cultural system like consumerism, which so trumpets its desire to offer us choice, offers us no choice regarding its view of us. That doesn't mean that there is no choice, or that its view is the correct one. So the first point at which we can exercise the "voluntariness" of our choice is the decision of whether or not to accept what consumerism says to us about our identity: that we are helpless before our insatiable desires and have no option but to spend our lives trying vainly to satisfy them when, even by consumerism's own definition, they are insatiable, that is, incapable of satisfaction. We have a choice to not accept this alternative.

We might also choose to keep looking for other descriptions of human nature that better fit with our experience. Have we experiences that show how changing our thinking or our state of conscious awareness can bring contentment? Have we experiences that show we are capable of receiving a deep spiritual healing that in turn can "bring us home" to a place of stillness, love, and peace? If so, there may be more to us than our earning power or our credit rating. It may be that we contain possibilities that can take us far beyond the treadmill of insatiable desire — or if we must walk this treadmill, then we can at least walk it lightly, with conscious mindfulness that it does not lead to contentment or happiness, that we walk it only as much as necessary to provide for our basic needs, and that we direct our best energies elsewhere, toward those activities and relationships that *do* promise something better.

ℬↄ

All of these considerations have so far focused our attention more or less within our own skins on what it may be about *us* that explains our desire to consume more and more, more than we actually need, or even more than what is good for us. However, there is another aspect of developing mindfulness that is highly relevant here.

During the 20th century we developed an entire *culture* — and an industrial and economic system to serve it — with the principal purpose to abolish any idea of "enough," to orient every waking moment of human existence toward consumption for its own sake and promoting insatiable desire as the defining characteristic of human nature. In every historical period there have always been individuals whose identities were so fragile that they felt compelled to conspicuously display their wealth, make waste to a vulgar degree, accumulate far in excess of personal need, and accede to the self-indulgent pursuit of novelty for its own sake. But at no previous time in history has such an odd philosophy of life been adopted as a

During the 20th century we developed an entire culture — and an industrial and economic system to serve it — with the principal purpose to abolish any idea of "enough" ...

social norm, systematized in economic policy, served by the most powerful technology ever developed, and elevated to the center of the political arena.

We live in a *consumer culture*. We simmer in its broth day and night. When there is very little, if anything, in our social milieu, in the media, in economic and technical development, or in political discourse that in any way suggests that moderation might be a comprehensible, even desirable way of life, it is hard for individuals to keep any sort of grip on how much is enough. Therefore, getting an inkling of what "enough" might mean almost inevitably implies getting some *distance* (intellectually and emotionally) from life as most of us live it. This is not easy.

No evangelizing faith, no conquering army, no plague of nature has ever been more pervasive than consumerism and its propagation system — advertising. The entire planet is now bathed in microwave, television, and radio signals 24 hours a day. The medium of television itself has the power to alter brain functioning and, after gradually lulling the viewer into an uncritical state of diffuse semi-awareness, it implants semi-conscious images and messages that have been psychologically designed to "trigger" consumption in the presence of the appropriate stimulus.[3] It has been estimated that by the age of 20, the average American has been exposed to nearly one million advertising messages, that he or she will spend a total of one year of his or her life watching television advertising. Two-thirds of newspaper space and 40 percent of our mail is unsolicited advertising.[4] The advent of telemarketing and internet marketing as well as the gradual commercialization of public spaces allows for even more intrusive advertising in our daily lives. These developments and many others establish the "background reality" (and often the "foreground" as well) in which we live and raise our children. It's not much of a stretch to imagine that if advertisers could conceive a way to broadcast directly into our brains, they would certainly do so.

Fortunately, all electronic media still come equipped with "off" switches and allow the user a choice of channels. Stopping the influx of marketing propaganda is relatively easy. It is much more difficult (and often impossible) to *select* the entertainment and information portions of the media stream from the glut of advertising, "infomercials", and "entertainment" programs that are really thinly disguised advertisements. Separating the wheat from the chaff thus requires considerable time and no small amount of technical ability.

Even more daunting will be reversing the flood of commercial advertising that is rapidly covering every visible surface of every structure built by humanity. Should we want to do anything as innocent as walk in a park, attend a baseball game, go to a concert or art gallery, or even go to school, there is no escaping advertising that we more or less passively "consume" simply by looking at things around us.

In such a social environment, coming to a personal awareness of how much is enough to provide for our well-being requires mindfulness to be sure, but also a measure of "self-defense." Those who succeed in identifying a gracefully sufficient way of life for themselves often say they maintain it at the cost of feeling that they stand amid a social current constantly rushing in the direction of renewed consumption, a current that always inclines to pull them along with it. This brings to the practice of simplicity, in our current social reality, something of the quality of a struggle. Helpful in this contest is giving ourselves extended periods of retreat to solitude to reconnect, again and again if necessary, with our personal sources of value in life, to regain a sense of proportion and sufficiency, and to deepen gratitude for what we have. Also helpful is the practice of exercising a fairly ruthless selectivity in our choice of entertainment, our use of media, and our willingness to endure the come-ons of all sorts of marketing people.

ൠ

How much is enough? That depends very much on how we see ourselves and on how exactly we find the "satisfaction" we seek in life. If we are little more than a credit rating linked to biologically rooted insatiable desire, there will *never* be enough. But if the stillness and freedom we desire are found along other avenues than the consumption of material things, it may be that very little is enough. The celebrated British economist E.F. Schumacher expressed it this way:

> For the modern economist this is very difficult to understand. He is used to measuring the "standard of living" by the amount of annual consumption, assuming all the time that a man who consumes more is "better off" than a man who consumes less. A Buddhist economist would consider this approach excessively irrational: since consumption is merely a means to human well-being, the aim should be to obtain the maximum of well-being with the minimum of consumption.[5]

An ability to grow more mindful of how and what we consume and of the degree to which each instance of consumption adds or detracts from our quality of life seems to be the key to knowing how much is enough, that is, to know what is the necessary minimum of consumption that delivers the maximum of well-being.

One way of getting a practical handle on this was proposed by Joe Dominguez and Vicki Robin in their important book *Your Money Or Your Life*.[6] In it the authors present what they call the "Fulfillment Curve," which has the same shape as a "bell curve" and also the curve that illustrates "diminishing returns" in economics. On the vertical axis we have increasing Fulfillment, on the horizontal axis Consumption, or money spent. As we increase consumption, first for basic survival, then for some comforts, then for some luxuries, we also increase fulfillment. But there is a point at which this relationship starts to "flatten out" and paradoxically (from the point of view of consumerism) heads in a negative direction. We reach a point where spending more and more for additional luxuries adds less and less to our sense of fulfillment in life and will actually begin to detract from it as we endure greater stress to earn more money to support higher consumption, sacrifice time with family and community, and suffer the environmental damage and health effects that are incurred to support high levels of consumption. The point at which the curve reaches its peak of maximum well-being on the minimum of consumption is the point of "enough."

Dominguez and Robin suggest that we can actually chart this point of "enough" by keeping careful track of all monthly expenditures and then reviewing them on a regular basis to assign a "fulfillment score" to each expenditure. In this way, we can identify and eliminate major expenses that deliver little reward. Gradually, we optimize our "joy-to-stuff" ratio and identify for ourselves the point where we have enough stuff to give us maximum joy with minimum expenditure and waste.

This is a very useful tool, as far as it goes. It helps us identify "enough" fairly effectively when it's the current consumption of things that can be purchased with money that most complicates our lives. For many of us, this is where we will begin bringing mindfulness to our daily lives in practicing voluntary simplicity. But documenting current expenses and rating their fulfillment value doesn't address the "stuff" we already have in storage which may or may not be contributing to our well-being, nor does it address a number of non-material issues. For example, how many social engagements per week are enough? How many committee memberships? How many meetings? How many communications gadgets that beep, chirp, or ring at us do we need? How many lessons, classes, "enrichments," or "options" do we need? The concept of "enough" applies equally as well to these aspects of our lives as to the choice to live simply in relation to them.

ॐ

We have often pointed out that the practice of simple living is a highly individualized affair. While simple living embraces a general tendency towards "sufficiency" rather than accumulating more, what we discard, what we refrain from re-acquiring, and what we continue to own are personal decisions. This general principle has implications for how much is "enough."

For example, one person may find that the passionate center of his or her life seeks to unfold through some artistic endeavor that requires many supplies, materials, and a suitable working space. To supply these things, the person refrains from owning many clothes, driving a car, or living in a large house. The art studio itself may be a very cluttered place and the "consumption" of art supplies may continue apace even as the artist practices voluntary simplicity in most other parts of his or her life.

Neither is it easy to identify how much is enough simply by tracking monthly expenditures. For example, a musician may be living very simply in every way and yet need to purchase a tuxedo for performances, spend tens of thousands of dollars on a piano or violin, and engage in considerable travel. A good violin or cello is a physically small object that incurs negligible environmental impact to produce, yet may cost thousands of dollars.

These examples illustrate the mistake of thinking of voluntary simplicity as something people would practice for its own sake by adopting a sort of mindless, across-the-board reduction in consumption. It is realizing the deeper values that simplicity serves that makes the practice of simplicity rewarding. Not many people would embrace simplicity just to own fewer things. Rather, it is usually practiced because it makes possible the pursuit of one's art or music, the rearing of one's family, spiritual growth, access to freedom, or contributions to a worthwhile cause.

One of the greatest challenges of voluntary simplicity is in creating a rich and meaningful way of life not only by finding a personal definition of how much we think is enough, but by fitting that harmoniously into how much the Earth can provide in a healthy and sustainable way.

Discerning how much is enough also involves placing our personal consumption of things in the context of environmental sustainability, social justice, and inter-generational equity. In this realm, we move beyond considerations of what may be expedient or comfortable in terms of our individual lives and consider ourselves to be part of a much larger whole.

In the section on Simplicity and the Environment (Chapter 5), we pointed out that even current rates of consumption could not be sustained if everyone on Earth participated in the consumer economy to an equal degree. Deciding how much is enough for us, then, must also involve some awareness that for most North Americans our "enough" must be found somewhere *below* about 30 percent of our current consumption of resources and energy. For some North Americans, living on their "fair Earth share" — the amount of resources available equally to every person on Earth — might involve a 90 to 95 percent reduction in their consumption, while for others, it may actually represent an *increase*. One of the greatest challenges of voluntary simplicity is in creating a rich and meaningful way of life not only by finding a personal definition of how much we think is enough, but by fitting that harmoniously into how much the Earth can provide in a healthy and sustainable way.

The other aspect to consider is that of justice. Mahatma Gandhi made it a personal principle to own nothing that was not equally available to the poorest person on Earth. He considered any consumption of luxuries to be tantamount to theft from the needy as long as there was anyone who could not meet his or her basic needs in life or who did not enjoy equal access to the luxury in question. We might consider this position to be so harsh that few could hope to practice it, but it addresses a perennial issue that is growing in urgency.

Just as the Earth displays biophysical limits to its productivity and regenerative capacities that must be taken into account as we develop mindfulness of how much is enough, there are also social and economic equity limits on how much my "enough" can exceed your "enough" without creating intolerable social tensions. What use is it to own a luxury home that must be surrounded by guards, dogs, and electric fences? How much can one enjoy a new limousine or Bentley when it must be made bullet-proof and outfitted with seats for guards and gun ports? What can possibly be gained by a gated, idyllic existence when just beyond the fence one cannot walk in safety or let one's children play? Who, after all, is the prisoner in this situation?

A great deal of psychological research reveals that one way people determine how satisfied they are with their lives is through social comparison. If we see ourselves doing as well as or better than our neighbors, we tend to feel happy and optimistic about our lot in life. But in the current environmental and social situation, we should probably be trying to teach ourselves the exact opposite, that if we see ourselves exceeding the lot of our neighbors by too large a degree, this is a danger signal both for the wellness of our communities and for the environment. This is not to say that all distinctions in society need to be leveled or that everyone must own exactly the same material possessions. Instead it points out that special hazards attend living out the dreams of the consumer culture where so much of our identity, our sense of self-worth, and our sense of success in life is directly tied to the possession and consumption of material things.

Finally, consumerism strongly encourages people to live as if they have neither ancestors nor descendents. Both seem to be relevant only insofar as they can contribute to marketing goods and services. Thus, historical buildings or artifacts have value if they will attract tourists or form the centerpiece of a theme park. Children are important if, in the words of one Disney marketing executive, they can be "branded early" to identify product logos and establish purchasing habits for one's products. Consumerism's insatiable hunger for novelty is prone to sweep away all history, and its insatiable greed for growth and its naïve belief in technical progress make it prone to discount the interests of future generations except if they can be numbered as future consumers.

The late 20th century may have been the first time in history when large numbers of people had no sense of personal identity rooted in the past, nor any sense of responsibility to future generations. Yet not only are we socially connected through relationships of economic and emotional interdependence and ecologically connected through evolution and biological interdependence, we are also historically connected to our ancestors and our descendents. Awareness of these connections can serve to immeasurably deepen and enrich an individual's identity. We are not unique entities who just "pop" into existence in this lifetime to "pop" out of it again when we die. We exist because of countless acts of love and self-giving that reach back into the dimmest mists of time (possibly even to times when "love" and "self-giving" were not consciously human acts). And we are the channels, biologically and culturally, through which whatever remains of human history will pass into the future. We cannot step out of this stream even if we want to. Our only decisions concern how we want to participate in it. In this context, the decision about how much is enough has profound implications.

The late 20th century may have been the first time in history when large numbers of people had no sense of personal identity rooted in the past, nor any sense of responsibility to future generations.

The world we inhabit is something we will be passing along to future generations, whether or not we can precisely calculate the economic significance of this gesture by "discounting" the value of natural resources or placing a "premium" on our hopes for technical breakthroughs. What we leave behind — both our wisdom and our trash — will have its effects on future generations. It is only a hopelessly self-centered and spiritually impoverished people who could ignore this responsibility or even seriously ask, "What have future generations ever done for me?"

ॐ

To summarize, voluntary simplicity is a way of life based on "enough," on the middle way of sufficiency in all things. It appears that we are not innately "wired" to be satisfied with sufficiency. Whether our tendency to want more and more without limit is the result of natural evolution or a spiritual malady, it is a fact of life. Happily, however, we *are* capable of understanding the nature of incessant desire, its destructive effects on our lives, relationships, and the environment, and we are capable of developing other ways of thinking and living based on a truer understanding of what will really bring us peace and contentment.

In the current North American social reality, putting these insights into practice requires that we continually swim against the prevailing current of advertising, social custom, and what passes for "common sense" in our day. Developing mindfulness about the nature and dynamics of innate desires, culti-vating "defenses" against commercialism intruding into our lives, and staying conscious of how much money, time, and energy we spend and the value we receive in exchange for them, are all helpful ways of identifying how much is enough and then letting that awareness guide our life choices.

9

Simplicity, Time, and Money

How many times have we heard from those on their deathbeds
that their greatest regret in life was not having spent more time at the office?

— Senior US Department Secretary announcing
the reason for his early retirement

We take up the exploration of the relationship of voluntary simplicity to time and money as a single discussion because in modern society, time and money are very much confused and very often linked.

People who adopt simpler living often cite time as one of their most important reasons for doing so. More time for oneself, for one's family, for making contributions to the community, for pursuing some important life work, for true leisure, which consists of creative work unconnected with making money — these are all key reasons people simplify their lives.[1] It is helpful to our practice of simplicity, therefore, to get a perspective on time and money because, perhaps surprisingly, living simply won't create more time nor can living simply be strictly equated with saving money or frugality. But, living simply can confer an enormous financial freedom as well as greater freedom to use the time we do have on the things that matter most to us.

Time is the ultimate democrat. We all have the same amount of it — 24 hours per day — whether we are rich or poor. No matter how much money we have, we cannot increase the number of hours in a day. Yet we are often confused by the notion that if we were rich, our wealth would somehow increase our available time. This confusion is propagated vigorously by commercial interests, which profit from it, by telling us that they can invest our money for us toward a day when we should have so much of it that we can "buy" our freedom from unpleasant tasks. And to some degree, there is a kernel of truth in this.

Many people feel they are in a "time crunch."[2] Time management seminars are popular among both the stressed-out business class and ordinary folk. We are often on the lookout for time-saving conveniences and are vulnerable to marketing pitches that promise that this or that gadget will either reduce the time we spend on a particular task or increase our productivity. But the truth is that no one can manage time. Time passes at the same rate regardless of what we do. The only thing we can directly manage are our *activities*, that is to say what we actually do with the 24 hours we have each day. Time management is therefore really *life* management. The stress we experience is not the result of having too few hours per day, but rather of feeling that we must respond to too many unwanted and uncontrollable demands and that the way we are spending our 24 hours is not returning the kind of satisfaction, sense of meaning, or feeling of accomplishment we desire.

> *People who adopt simpler living often cite time as one of their most important reasons for doing so. More time for oneself, for one's family, for making contributions to the community, for pursuing some important life work, for true leisure...*

Finding more time for the things we value most comes down partly to shifting our attention and activity in the direction of doing those things. Like all the other aspects of simple living we have addressed so far, it requires *mindfulness* both of what we value and of how we are currently spending time — in other words, mindfulness of daily activities.

The values of consumerism have gotten mixed up in how we think of time. Recall that for the consumer the value of life is measured quantitatively. More is better. It follows then that a consumeristic approach to managing time consists of trying to cram as many activities, as much productivity, as much money-making as possible into every hour of the day and night. Here we meet the speed-reading programs, the courses on developing a photographic memory, the computerized "productivity tools" that schedule every micro-second of our existence, the cell phone, the pager, the telecommunications revolution that promises more and more "access" faster and faster. In this land we also meet the unending work day, the supper meeting, the weekend strategy conference. We meet the parents who work overtime in order to provide "options" for their children, and we meet the children with daily schedules as jammed as their parents' because a child who has more "experiences" is thought to be better off than a child with fewer experiences — as if the 24 hours in every day did not hold the same quantity of conscious experience for everyone! In such a world there can never be enough time, enough experiences, enough options. Accepting this view of our existence condemns us to a treadmill of activity that runs faster and faster without much sense of where it is going.

The practice of voluntary simplicity includes a shift in focus from this "consumer" perspective on time, where quantity and speed are the key considerations, to a perspective that stresses *selectivity* and *quality*. The number of things we achieve in a day becomes secondary to *how well* we achieve them and how directly linked they are to our most central values. Simplicity subordinates increasing the number and variety of life experiences to the depth of awareness and appreciation we bring to the experiences we have. We deliberately choose meaningful activities that bring us richness in life, and we attend to them with care, attention, consciousness, and appreciation. Just as dumping junk out of our closets contributes to a sense of physical spaciousness in our lives, the practice of simplicity in our use of time implies cutting away "schedule clutter." When we do this, the things that money can buy are sometimes helpful, but nowhere near as helpful as we might at first expect. As Jon Kabat-Zinn observed in his book on cultivating mindfulness, voluntary simplicity "involves intentionally doing only one thing at a time and making sure I'm here for it."[3]

As with learning how much is "enough," there is never enough of anything if we think that contentment and peace can be found only by trying to satisfy the incessant cravings arising from inborn or acquired desires. If the philosophy of life is that "he who dies with the most toys wins," if the goal in life is to accumulate larger and larger résumés, to pack more and more options and experiences into our children's lives, then no amount of money spent on any number of time-saving gadgets or organizers will ever be enough. Each time we achieve an increment in time saving, our incessant desire for more will be right there prodding us on toward the next step in increasing speed. As Mahatma Gandhi is reported to have said: "There's got to be more to life than increasing its speed."

We can seldom live a joyful simplicity in relation to how we use time until we believe there is more to be gained by slowing down and exercising a mindful selectivity in our activities than by speeding up and trying to jam as much as possible into every moment. How might we move in this direction?

I suggest there are three steps to practice:

First, we renew consciousness of what it is in our lives that we most value, we reconnect with those things that are most meaningful, we remember who we are.

Second, it's difficult to live with voluntariness and deliberation if we are living *unconsciously*. To become conscious of how we are *actually* using our time requires the simple expedient of keeping close and honest track of what we are doing. If we practice this even a little, it is sometimes startling to notice how much of the day is consumed in more or less "automatic" routines such as commuting to work, household tasks, or mechanical work — routines that have long ago become almost reflexive. Thus we sleepwalk through a large part of the day, entertaining ourselves with fantasies, or consuming the fantasies created for us by the great dream machine of advertising and what passes for "entertainment." Say we stop for even a moment and try to remember our activities from the previous day, the television we watched, our conversations, our route to work — if we can't recall these events, we were probably not "present" for them. Living life like this day after day, year after year, can result in an enormous, though often unconscious, sense of loss. Is it any wonder then that so many people reaching midlife, having already spent the best of their youth, are afflicted by diffuse depressions and vague anxieties and feel as if something is missing or as if life has slipped by and something precious has been lost?

So it is salutary to take whatever steps are necessary to become aware of how we spend time and what activities fill our day. Simply being conscious of this is not enough. Consciousness provides the springboard to life affirmation and to life change.

The third step of practice concerns how we can group our various life activities. I suggest using an old time management prop that consists of a diagram like a window frame with four panes in it. Across the top we define two categories of activities that are either Important or Unimportant and along the side two categories of activity that are either Urgent or Non-urgent. We can then drop every one of our daily activities into one or another of these four boxes.

Some activities are both urgent and important, such as dealing with physical emergencies like fire alarms or bodily needs that cannot be deferred.

Other activities might have a high level of urgency but turn out to be unimportant, especially many of the things that are matters of urgency to other people (like telemarketers or co-workers) but which have no importance for us.

Yet other activities, like cleaning out old files or alphabetizing our recipe cards, are neither very urgent nor very important. The world keeps revolving, regardless of whether or not we get to them.

The fourth group of activities, however, is very important but not urgent. This is the group of things that we keep planning to get to some day and that matter to us a great deal but that can be put off in the short run. Examples might include taking our children fishing or spending that long, leisurely night with our partner, a bottle of wine, and a vial of massage oil.

When we take up the practice of keeping track of what we actually do all day, a common pattern is to see much, if not all, of our time going to urgent but unimportant interruptions and non-urgent and unimportant mechanical routines punctuated by the occasional urgent and genuinely important emergency. Unfortunately, little or no time may be going to the things we value most: really important things that have, however a low level of urgency. These activities, the ones we know bring us the most reward in life, keep getting displaced from our lives by activities that we allow to have a higher level of urgency.

Hence the third step in practicing simplicity in the use of time is to *give urgency to the things that are most important*. In a practical sense, we do this by getting rid of "to-do" lists — the list of things we have to do just to respond to outside demands and keep our heads above water — and substitute a *plan* for how we will spend the next 24 hours. The plan is based on giving the most important things priority and finding ways to fit in the less important things when we can find time for them. When we adopt this practice, it becomes clearer what are meaningful activities and what constitutes "schedule clutter." It is schedule clutter that we can then take steps to eliminate.

Perhaps one of the most annoying customs of the consumer culture is its tendency to elevate trivia to the status of "emergencies." One sign of this is the growing prevalence of alarms installed on every imaginable gadget. The telephone is one big alarm system, warbling its incessant demand to be answered immediately *in case* the person calling has something of consequence to say. Busy people with important things to do often insert either a human or mechanical answering service to cut off this source of incessant interruptions at the pass. But there are cell phones that chirp away in our pockets, beepers that go off at the most awkward moments, voice mail in case we "lose" that important message, key alarms in our cars, smoke alarms, "bag full" alarms on vacuum cleaners, back-up warning alarms on our rear bumpers, computer software that is replete with incoming mail alarms, chat notices, virus alerts, meeting notices, error prompts of every kind, yard-watering alarms, various gas alarms, meat timer alarms, washer load imbalance alarms, dryer overheat alarms — the list is endless. And in all of this, will we even hear fire alarms, police sirens, or civil defense alerts? *Must life be so alarming?*

Developing mindfulness of what are our highest values, then becoming aware of how we are actually spending our time, and then consciously planning the day to provide time for what we value and clearing away the schedule clutter are effective steps toward living more simply in relation to time. Time is the most precious possession we have because it measures the span and contains the experiences that constitute our lives. To allow it to disappear in meaningless urgencies and trivia, hyperactive consumerism, and mindless rushing about is cause for great regret.

There is yet another important dimension to the experience of time that has less to do with consciously planning activities and more with cultivating a contemplative, receptive attitude toward life. It recognizes the "uses of nothing" or the value of "emptiness" and the availability to spontaneous, unplanned happenings as key aspects of living a more soulful life.

The psychologist Ira Progoff offered a useful perspective of time when he distinguished between *chronological time* and *qualitative time*.[4] Chronological time is "clock time" as we understand it. Our discussion of time up to this point has concerned this clock time and stategies to use less of it on things that don't matter and consciously to re-allocate more of it to things that do matter. Chronological time is what people try to "save" by spending lots of money on things that go fast because they mistakenly think that reducing the expenditure of clock time per unit of production will increase life's value. Generally, however, the experience of value in life is associated with qualitative time, not with clock time.

To understand qualitative time we need to turn inward and explore the nature of conscious subjectivity — the ways we experience life from the inside. One characteristic of this inner world of consciousness is that it doesn't "flow" by at a uniform rate the way clock time does. Instead, it is "stretchy," depending on the depth and focus of our attention, our emotional state, and the meaning of the experiences we're engaged in at the moment. We have only to recall an afternoon doing something we enjoyed and how time seemed to "fly" or, conversely, the time we may have spent in traffic jams or in the dentist's chair, to appreciate how elastic time can be in the inner landscape of the soul. So we have this subjective capacity to "telescope" time so that years can feel inwardly compressed to the blink of an eye when nothing of significance really happened to the soul, but an afternoon of love or a moment of deep insight can "expand" to fill the soul with a sense of beauty and meaning.

We live in two worlds at once: the world of chronological time running on the "outside" and the world of qualitative time running on the "inside." It is the experiences being conveyed to us on the ocean of qualitative time that tend to carry value for the soul. This sense of value is available to us when we can take sufficient chronological time to notice it, live out its meanings, honor its value. But it is the demands of chronological time in a consumer society that keep pulling attention away from the inner, subjective world of qualitative time. It may be that we've awakened to a particularly tender and opportune moment for making love with our partner, yet we can't enjoy this moment because a mechanical clock says we have to be at work in 30 minutes. Or it may be that it is especially important to attend to a dying relative or to a needy child whose needs just aren't occurring "on schedule" or at a time that is chronologically convenient for everyone concerned. Nevertheless, it is acts of love, communication, and caring shared with real people that constitute what we have elsewhere called the person's "Lifeworld" — the very source of meaning for the soul. It will be the degree to which we have, or have not, been available for these sorts of experiences that most determines how rich our life experience feels.

What we are referring to here is a sort of "dialogue" that is carried on between our subjective awareness of feeling and meaning on the one hand and the events and relationships in the "outer" world of our daily experience on the other. Chronological time measures and regulates the activities of machines and people who serve them. Qualitative time measures the growth and movements of the soul. Since the soul lives and moves in its own world, mostly outside the tiny spotlight of conscious awareness, it is almost impossible to "schedule its spontaneity." Soul responds to what it wants to, when it wants to. Our inner world really doesn't care much about what a clock says. Thus, the critical issue for inner growth only partly concerns the question of whether or not we are scheduling enough time for activities that have a high value. It also concerns the question of whether there is enough "empty time" so that we are available for and can respond to *surprises* that are meaningful to our souls.

Part of the meaning of practicing simpler living is, I believe, deciding to leave enough flexibility, enough "empty time" in the daily round to bring to all our activities a certain quality of unhurried attention.

Part of the meaning of practicing simpler living is, I believe, deciding to leave enough flexibility, enough "empty time" in the daily round to bring to *all* our activities a certain quality of unhurried attention. It also means, at least most of the time, cultivating a life that is not so packed and so rushed that we must hurry away from a moment that speaks to the soul in order to attend to something else that is rigidly scheduled to meet some goal set by the ego. I think it is nonsense to think that "quality time" can be scheduled. The experiences that bring quality into life happen when they happen — like falling in love, birthing babies, dying, moments of spiritual connection, or happening upon something beautiful. Consumerism believes in such things as mate-selection services as handy ways of scheduling life's less predictable passages, but these could never be ways of honoring or nurturing the soul.

ॐ

Time and money are closely connected in the popular imagination. We often hear that "time is money" and that saving time and saving money are interchangeable. Both propositions are false. But let's further explore the relation between money and simple living in general before we take up the question of how money and time might be related.

Many people who live simply also live frugally. But more than anything else, living simply is about *living with conscious focus on our highest values,* not about living cheaply for its own sake. It is possible to have a great deal of money and still live simply, and the most refined wealth expresses itself this way, namely by applying itself to acts of philanthropy and generosity toward others while maintaining a modest simplicity at home. It is possible to live simply while at the same time spending considerable money on the few possessions, carefully chosen, that we see as essential to our well-being and our livelihood. But for the wealthy practitioner of simple living, financial means never find display in affluent living, never become a source of envy to neighbors, never are mistaken for sources of security in life or its ultimate meaning or goal. They are means of achieving a higher social or cultural good, funds held in trust to be managed not just for one-self and one's family, but for the larger good they can bring into the world.

A more useful way of viewing money in relation to simple living is to bring mindfulness to our use of it like everything else. Many people who live simply also live frugally. They do so because the chief purposes of their lives have noth-ing to do with the accumulation of money, so they spend as little time on it as possible. There are many practitioners of simplicity who have no plan, no inten-tion, and no desire ever to become financially independent because they have found or fashioned something more precious instead: a way of earning their livelihood that expresses their highest values in life for which they are also just-ly and fairly compensated. Why would someone with this sort of work to do ever want to "retire?"

In addition to those who perform wholesome and honorable work for which they receive wages, there are also those who are entirely unconcerned with money and have found a means of livelihood without it. In this company we find the prophets, the mendicant beggars, the holy men and women possessed of a passion for the spirit, poets and wandering minstrels, the troubadours of "Lady Poverty," and every mountain hermit feasting on nettle broth and lentils. While such figures may seem distant from modern urbanized ideas of the good life, many have walked this road in the past, and the door is always open to any who would enter, even today.

The example of people who have managed, or who are managing to live largely without money holds an interesting lesson — and also a hope — for the rest of us. Most of us find the idea of living without money totally unimaginable. This is, however, more a reflection of the "monetarization" of consciousness and our dependence on the market than it is any inescapable fact of life. What is absolutely necessary to human life can be found or produced given a bit of land and the appropriate skills. No financial transactions are required. But modern life has moved so far away from subsistence living that we can scarcely even form a picture of it or have any inkling that it might hold its own rewards.

This mental "box" that so confines us has serious implications for the envi-ronment, for society and, of course, for individuals. If we are thoroughly enough convinced that money is the *only* way to get food, shelter, clothing, and love, then unemployment is a catastrophe. We feel compelled to earn and hoard or steal money regardless of what sort of activity is involved in getting it. A "retirement plan" is an investment scheme designed to increase our hoard of money. Moreover, we are totally dependent upon (and therefore totally vulnerable to) those who control our access to money (employers and banks) and those who make it possible for us to exchange money for the real things we need (corporations and markets).

Those who have learned to live without money, no matter how demanding their way of life, defy the rule. They illustrate that a "retirement plan" may consist of a hundred acres of trees being grown and sustainably harvested, supplying both an income in perpetuity for its owner, an ecological service to the planet, and a recreational and aesthetic asset for the entire community. Those who grow or gather their own food illustrate that industrial agriculture, chemical pesticides, food processing, and large-scale retailing are not essential to eating. Those who learn to play a tin whistle demonstrate that we don't need Hollywood.

> *Thus, while it is obviously true that we have constructed an enormous economic and monetary machine that enmeshes nearly everyone, it is a cage of our own making, not a law of nature. Consumerism simply accepts the cage. Voluntary simplicity tries to find a way out.*

Thus, while it is obviously true that we have constructed an enormous economic and monetary machine that enmeshes nearly everyone, it is a cage of our own making, not a law of nature. Consumerism simply accepts the cage. Voluntary simplicity tries to find a way out.

֍

Let's now return to the question of how time and money might be linked. As mentioned above, we often hear that "time is money." This is false. Time is time and measures the flow of our life activity. Time only becomes money when we choose to trade our life activity for someone else's money by doing what they ask us to for a given period of time. This reality is highlighted by Joe Dominguez and Vicki Robin in their book *Your Money Or Your Life*.[5] It is essential to become more mindful of the meaning of money in our lives, especially if we wish to practice simplicity. *Money is something we trade our life-time for.*

Thinking of money as something we trade our life-time for — not as something in itself but as the symbol of a trade we have made — helps us stay tuned to the question of exactly what we may be giving up in exchange for money. When we have earned some money, what have we traded for it? Dominguez and

Robin offer some helpful tools for getting a grip on these questions, including tracking all monthly expenses, expressing these expenses not only as dollar values but also as the number of hours of life-time required to procure them, and then consciously deciding whether this expenditure, this trade, brings comparable value into our lives. If so, be thankful. If not, try doing something different with that time and/or money.

There are also a number of insights that, even though they may not be able to liberate us entirely from the impact of money on our lives, will nevertheless help us keep it in its place.

The old saw that "it takes money to make money" is more than just advice to those who might hope to reap interest without investing capital. When we search for paid employment from other people or corporations, the salary or wages offered for the job are often the chief attraction. Less appealing and often less visible is the very real cost in time and money that *we* pay simply to be employed. The impact of taxes and mandatory deductions for "benefits" are only the most visible losses from the black ink side of our personal ledger. Almost every job requires special clothing, commuting time, "decompression time" after work, and a variety of subtle and not-so-subtle obligations connected with participation in the workplace, such as charity donations, fundraisers, sports pools, sporting activities, or other social events that may not be exactly what we had in mind in taking the job. All of these cost money. We may incur additional expenses for lunches, coffee breaks, etc. Many employers now expect workers to work unpaid overtime, attend unpaid professional training programs, provide their own child care and emergency child care arrangements, pay for parking and security for their vehicles, subscribe to professional publications, and support collective bargaining units. In some lines of work, special tools are a major investment.

At the end of the day, the only true way to know whether or not we are farther ahead by taking or leaving a job is to calculate the total number of hours, paid and unpaid, both on the job and on our way to and from it, including all the overtime and stress leaves, and to divide this number into the actual pay remaining after *all* the costs of employment have been deducted — costs we would not incur except for being employed. This calculation returns our actual rate of pay and can be dishearteningly small when everything is considered. The lesson is that *any* involvement with money costs money as well, and while some involvement is probably unavoidable in modern life, the world of money itself represents a sticky morass of entanglement that can wind up taking the best of our time and energy if we fail to be mindful.

Current trends in the development of "financial services" are making this morass even stickier. With the advent of "credit cards" (really *debt* cards), direct payment cards, and electronic commerce, every transaction includes a service charge. As "cashless" forms of financial transaction become the dominant means of conducting business, the fees levied at every stage of the process become increasingly inescapable and costly. It costs money simply to have it, and certainly to transfer it, add to it, change its form, or spend it.

Another aspect of the relationship between money and simple living has to do with the inherent tendency of consumerism to insert market transactions between us and every one of our life needs. In consumer culture, everything is for sale, even things that don't need to be bought and sold, even things that *should not* be bought and sold. There is a great psychological momentum set up that inclines us to turn to buying and selling as the means of meeting all our needs, even needs that really can't be met in this way. The long-term effect of this process is to monetarize every aspect of life and to disempower people from doing what we can for ourselves. In some respects, this trend has taken on truly frightening proportions.

Because modern life for most people is so urbanized and so "monetarized," we take it for granted that living as an adult in the "real world" implies working for someone else to earn money and, with this money, purchasing all the necessities of life. This has not always been so. One of the key values espoused by many who embrace simpler living is the idea of self-reliance and direct involvement in providing for one's basic needs in life. We will explore this in more detail in Chapter 10: Simplicity, Work, and Livelihood.

In his book *How Much Is Enough?*[2], Alan Durning points out that the modern house is designed to be a consumption center rather than a production center. As recently as the mid-20th century, houses were still designed with pantries, workshops, sewing rooms, large kitchens, storage cupboards, laundry rooms, and root cellars. Modern houses have none of these features except for "galley" kitchens large enough only to re-heat pre-cooked and pre-packaged foods. This change in architecture reflects a larger social shift in the role of the home in society from its earlier, more self-reliant function as a center of productivity for the family to its current function of being merely a sleeping, eating, and entertainment center between work shifts. Even though the advent of the "home office" in some ways begins to reincarnate the home as a productive place, we still work in the office to make the money we then trade for food rather than simply growing and processing the food ourselves. Ironically, some of these same home office denizens scramble to free up a few hours each week to work in their backyard gardens or spend exorbitant sums hiring others to look after them!

Many people who practice simplicity begin from the principle of never purchasing anything that is within their ability to provide for themselves by a more direct means, through direct personal involvement, when this activity would clearly add to the quality of their lives. For example, rather than working for money to buy organic vegetables that are grown far away and shipped a great distance to a local market, those who enjoy gardening might grow their own vegetables. The same principle can be applied to repairing our own appliances, maintaining and renovating our homes, providing our own entertainment, education, health care, and child care, and engaging in artistic pursuits. In these activities and many more, the "middle steps" of earning and spending money can be removed through direct personal action. A side-effect of this action is that we often meet our neighbors, re-acquaint ourselves with our children, and develop skills of real value that increase our self-esteem and contribute to self-reliance.

The tendency of consumerism to monetarize everything becomes especially dangerous when economic thinking distorts reality to a hazardous or tragic degree. The most pervasive example of this is the widespread belief that money provides security. This may be true, but only to a very limited extent. The real security human beings can enjoy in this life is defined by personal health, rich community and family relationships, and intact and healthy ecosystems. Money cannot provide any of these, but the hunger to get money threatens every one of them. We are continually urged to believe that money *can* provide substitutes for these life needs. We invest in retirement savings plans and watch their growth with anxious alertness all the while unaware of and unconcerned about the growth of highways on the outskirts of town, the growth of poverty in our communities, the growth of a tumor in our own bodies. Money certainly has its uses and, in a totally monetarized culture like ours, it has very important uses. But there are forms of security it cannot provide. Practicing simplicity includes developing mindfulness of what real security is, where it comes from, how most directly to provide it, and exactly what role money can play in this, if any.

10

Simplicity, Work and Livelihood

"Normal" is getting dressed in clothes that you buy for work,
driving through traffic in a car that you are still paying for,
in order to get to the job that you need so you can pay for
the clothes, car, and the house that you leave empty
all day in order to afford to live in it.[1]

Sometimes, simple living is portrayed as a life of irresponsible laziness. This is often also true of "retirement." Both those who refuse to participate in the general scramble and those who have profited mightily from it may find themselves idle, but the rich have society's respect because they are still consuming, still "contributing" to the economy, whereas the social drop-out has neither real estate nor investment assets and, on that account, is almost "invisible" in a consumer society.

There may indeed be some folk who practice simplicity as economic indigence and a few others who have attained financial independence and, having thus become people of means, are at liberty to combine periods of activity and inactivity as they feel inclined. But the middle way of simple living for most of us will be found somewhere between the extremes of poverty (even if freely chosen) and affluence (however that was achieved).

Many of those who practice simplicity need a means of livelihood, work that produces a living (carefully distinguishing this from making piles of money) but avoids compromising simplicity. The greatest creative challenge is found neither in dropping out nor in piling up investments, but rather in fashioning an unpretentious, honest, life-giving pattern of livelihood that allows time for productive work that nurtures the unfolding of one's seed potential and that also allows enough time and energy for appreciating and savouring the values that are found in good work. Moreover, this must be fashioned in the rushing stream of a consumer society headed in a very different direction and propelled by very different dynamics. Thus a means of livelihood is required, but it must be a *skillful means.*

The standard approach to earning one's living in our consumer society is well defined. Soon after birth, children are "branded" by advertisers and taught to want what a consumer economy produces. As soon as they can walk, children are introduced to an accumulation mentality when they are sent to pre-schools and day-care centres to begin acquiring "skills." These are the behavioural tokens needed to succeed later on in the general competition for grades, recognition, privilege, access to opportunity, employment, sales, getting raises, and for professional status, mates, and power. One of their most challenging tasks will be developing the capacity for simultaneous co-operation and competition so they can detect the subtle interpersonal and situational signals that require that they conform, comply, and self-censor on the one hand, but be instantly ready to compete, contend, and be aggressive on the other.

This journey begins in earnest when a child enters school and is encouraged from every side to "do well," which means learning things, of course, but it also means learning all about how to manipulate systems and other people for desired outcomes, how to shape other people's perceptions, how to establish and maintain an image, how to "spin" situations to personal advantage, and, most of all, how to conform one's consumption choices to those of one's peer group in order to maintain social acceptance.

These days, the academic and emotional side of education has almost nothing to do with introducing young people to how to create a rich life for themselves whether or not they have money, or even preparing them for active participation as citizens in a democratic society. Rather, it is a sort of oracular exercise wherein students, parents, counsellors, and teachers all try to augur the future shape of a chaotically changing economy, anticipate what "skills" will be required by multinational corporations, and then instill those skills in students. Meanwhile, the students are in heated competition for access to the best teachers and the most prestigious sponsors and patrons. Never mind that most jobs in the fastest emerging sectors of the economy either didn't exist five years ago or can scarcely be named even today!

Despite their best efforts to maintain educational standards, both schools and teachers are under heavy pressure from corporations, and sometimes governments, to teach young people to be savvy consumers, to balance chequebooks, to make wise selections of pre-processed foods (about the production of which they may have very limited knowledge), to establish long-range retirement investment plans, to compare the rates of usury associated with different "credit" cards, and above all to write effective résumés. Learning critical thinking skills can get marginalized by learning shopping skills. Learning how to provide directly for some of one's basic needs can be displaced by assurances from corporations that all these needs can be satisfied in the marketplace. Since almost anything one might imagine (and many things one would rather not imagine!) are already "in the pipe" of the consumer economy, "education" must be about making prudent (usually defined as least expensive, most comforting, safest) selections from the array of products and services on offer. There are many dedicated education professionals struggling mightily against these pressures and helping students achieve admirable learning goals. There are also some institutions striving for higher goals than preparing young people for the marketplace. Nevertheless, I think the social and political momentum of the last few decades has been oriented toward education for a life of production and consumption and not education for citizenship in a democracy.

During the last few decades, public schools have come under immense pressure from governments with their reduced budgets as well as under social pressures and corporate influence to deliver "no frills," "back-to-basics" education. This has sometimes meant that from their earliest days in the school system, students acquire industrially uniform "skill sets" that are later assembled into "competitive" résumés to be presented, hat in hand, to corporations, the ultimate arbiters of access to the rewards of a consumer society (which are meanwhile being intensively imprinted in both the child's conscious and unconscious mind as the principal reason for existence). Advancing through the various levels of formal education does little to this general pattern except intensify it.

Emerging upon graduation, and strongly "motivated" both by hunger for consumer goods and staggering education debts, students begin to compete for jobs. Once employed, they continue to compete for "success" and "advancement". Both these are pursued through a dizzy whirl of lay-offs, repeated re-engineering of one's career and "skill sets," and occupational self-reinvention until, with luck, we find ourselves expelled from the yonder end of this meat-grinder with a sizeable pile of material possessions, a handsome pension fund or golden parachute, and an otherwise vague role in society, apart from our inalienable value as consumers.

This admittedly hyperbolic description of a "normal" career path in a consumer society I still think generally expresses the rule. By and large, modern life pits people against each other in competition for access to its supposed rewards. It insists that people shape themselves, their aspirations, their behaviours, and even their feelings to the patterns it requires to advance its economic interests. Of course all societies "socialize" their newborn members to the customs and traditions of the group, and ours can be no different. But our society is signal in the very narrow range of livelihood pathways it commends to the attention of its young people. One can either be an entrepreneur or work for one. One either conforms to the functional slots within corporations or is relegated to the margins of society and the economy.

Moreover, the economy itself has become so technical, so dependent upon an extreme specialization of tasks, that it employs mostly workers who do one or a very few things that have little utility outside the specialized needs of one or a very few employers. For example, Canada recently transferred its tax collection functions from a government department (formerly Revenue Canada) to an arms-length agency called Canada Customs and Revenue Agency. In the process, hundreds of employees were displaced from their positions who had spent their entire careers processing only a few lines or specific sections of income tax returns. Their skills were so focused and so specialized that they were virtually unmarketable as generic accounting skills that might be useful to other businesses or employers.

In this way, many highly skilled employees are also the most specialized, and the most specialized become increasingly vulnerable to unemployment because their employment options are limited. Upon losing their jobs, they need to be retrained because their "skill sets" aren't transferable to new jobs.

Given this rather peculiar way of organizing our affairs, is it any wonder that so many middle-aged parents have a story to tell about a young adult child who continues to lurk in the basement, continues to sleep all day, pierces every orifice in mute, masochistic protest, and appears generally devoid of "career goals?" Can it be that hard to understand why so few young people feel so little attraction to, and so much hostility toward, a mainstream culture that asks so much from them and yet offers so little soul, so little real poetry, so little to believe in?

❧

The important question for anyone seeking a skillful means to a richer way of life is this: Are there any alternatives to what now dominates the social and economic landscape? Our explorations of voluntary simplicity so far should provide some points of departure in the search for alternatives.

First, the practice of simple living in general implies reducing or eliminating debts, reducing the consumption of material things, making more mindful choices about future consumption, and generally reducing the overall material scale of our life. This alone represents a movement toward the margins of the consumer mainstream — a place where the continuing demand for income and the incessant need to compete with others for scarce opportunities and goods becomes less pressing. A life of modest scale only requires modest effort to maintain.

One consequence of reducing the complexity and costliness of our way of life is that we open up many new employment opportunities because the need for income is decreased. This means that lower paid but perhaps less stressful or more rewarding forms of employment become practical possibilities.

Second, we have been careful to emphasize the fact that the practice of simplicity often includes a heightened awareness of and an increased willingness to honor the inner, intuitive, spiritual, artistic "depth" dimension of our existence. So in addition to reducing the overall urgency of meeting our material and physical needs by reducing their number and scale, any new pattern of livelihood we might fashion will also honor our desire for what Buddhists often refer to as "right livelihood" — a way of life that does no harm, that honors spiritual and psychic realities, that contains depth and quality.

In Chapter 2, we referred to the work of Ira Progoff[2] and his metaphor of a unique "seed potential" that contains all the possibilities and processes necessary for the development of a fully actualized human personality. Again drawing on this metaphor, we can say that it is the unfolding of the seed potential within each person that forms the inner, psychic "landscape" of the life of that individual. This inner aspect of our being has its own agenda, its own goals, and its own developmental needs. It also has its own potential and gifts to bring into the world.

Complementing the seed potential within is the "outer" world of physical and social realities that present their own possibilities and limitations. "Development" of the self occurs in the "dialogue" relationship that grows between the seed potential striving to realize itself in the person's life and what it finds available in the world with which to tinker itself toward visibility and reality. In a manner of speaking, something within us that is at first invisible plays with what it finds in the outer world and thus discovers its own identity and possibilities.

This sort of process is exemplified by the work of some artists and musicians when they respond to "inspiration" — the prompting of the seed potential to find outward expression — by playing with an artistic medium or with sounds until they create forms or patterns that express their inspiration. Sometimes it is through the very process of playing with a material that artists become more conscious of the inspiration itself and what it is asking of them. As artists interact with the medium, the characteristics of the paints, clay, or sculpting material can also "feedback" to change the artists' concept of what is being created. Thus, inspiration and medium *interact* in the process of the seed potential striving for objective expression. The nature of this interaction closely resembles a dialogue or conversation in which we have something of our own to say, the expression of which, however, is shaped and influenced by the person with whom we speak and the limitations and possibilities inherent in the words we use.

Knitted between the lines of this dialogue is another skein of requirements that arise from the realities of physical existence. Whatever may be the poetry of our lives that is playing itself toward visibility in the shared world of social and physical existence, there is also the need to eat, to stay warm, to find safety, to leave offspring. To say that these needs are "basic" is not to say that they are more important than a person's actualization needs, but only to note that they belong to a more physically and biologically rooted aspect of our existence. Life, lived as a whole person, involves finding ways to honor both of these realities at the same time. Obviously, this is not easy. It is discouragingly easy to veer one way or another and become either a starving idealist or a "hard-headed realist" someone who is economically and materially successful but whose soul is a wasteland.

In cases where a person has an ear tuned to both worlds and is inclined to give each its due, however, there exists the possibility of creating an alternative both to the mainstream wasteland and the idealistic misfit. Since we are all familiar with the ways in which the outer world makes its demands known, we will turn our attention instead to how the seed potential speaks to life.

What distinguishes a work from a job is that a work contains its own charge of passion. It is intrinsically worth doing. If it is ignored, we feel a sense of self-betrayal, of inner loss, of sadness of soul for not pursuing it and bringing it to life to the best of our ability.

The notion of a "seed potential" is just a way of referring to the observed tendency of life to be inherently in motion. Life contains its own intrinsic dynamism. It is going *somewhere*, not just anywhere. In the life of a developing human being, "whatever" simply won't do. In a manner of speaking, the seed potential presses for realization through what Progoff refers to as specific *works*. Sometimes works are born as vague intuitive longings, semi-conscious fantasies, or images in night dreams. But sometimes they can burst into conscious awareness with the force of "revelations." They are tasks or visions or projects that engage our passionate attention, our loving care, our deepest commitment, and the most unstinting application of our energies.

"Works" of this sort can take any form: works of art or music, books, life projects like raising children, making a home, growing a garden. What distinguishes a *work* from a *job* is that a work contains its own charge of passion. It is intrinsically worth doing. If it is ignored, we feel a sense of self-betrayal, of inner loss, of sadness of soul for not pursuing it and bringing it to life to the best of our ability. If we fail to acknowledge these inner passions, we live without soul, speak without conviction, give without love, work without delight. Our works express what the life force within us is striving to manifest in the world. Our works are both the way we develop as individuals and also, at their best, our contributions to the greater flow of life of which we are a part.

By contrast, a *job* is a task defined by someone else that we agree to perform in exchange for money that we in turn spend to provide for our physical needs. Some jobs can be very rewarding monetarily. Some jobs can even have some of the characteristics of works and engage not only the compliance of our physical bodies and brains, but also offer significant opportunities for us to grow as persons. But in many cases, jobs consist simply of assigned tasks performed by workers in exchange for money. The workers make little or no contribution to defining the job and, compared to those who are hiring them, reap relatively little reward for performing it. The consumer economy offers jobs. It can never offer works because a work, by definition, is something that spontaneously springs from within a growing person. The consumer economy *violates* people when it demands that they abandon their works and conform their lives wholly to what is needed for jobs.

In creating skillful means, however, we should not aim to land a high paying job but *to provide the necessities of life through pursuing our works*, or at least to provide for these needs in ways that distract us as little as possible from our works. This is an entirely different project. This would be work with some poetry in it.

It is revealing to reflect on how often we hear about the importance of jobs, creating jobs, job training, job readiness, job success, etc., and how seldom today we hear the more traditional term "vocation." Not long ago young people were encouraged to discover their vocation. The word "vocation" is derived from the Latin root "vocatio" which means to "call." The "caller" in this case was not a corporation, but *God*. The "callee" was not an anonymous individual with a certain "skill set" who could be exchanged for any other individual having the same skill set, but a specific human person, known and loved by God and called to develop divinely endowed talents through a specific form of *work* rendered as a gift of service either to God or to the community. In exchange for cooperating with the divine inner voice, a person had a moral claim on fair compensation for work well and honestly done, since "the worker is entitled to a wage."

The perspective on life carried in the very short word "vocation" is one with room for the divine, the inner world of spiritual intimacy between every person and the supernatural source of all life. It assumes that people will look inward for their direction in life and honor what they find there. It admits that there are practical issues to be addressed in the getting of one's livelihood, but at the same time the very idea of "vocation" testifies to a mingling of practical and divine activities in all work, no matter how humble.

This sort of understanding vastly ennobles work because the seed potential, representing in a sense the inner aspect of the divine "voice" speaking deeply in the human soul, is present in every worker and every work. Work thus becomes a pathway for spiritual growth as well as a means of livelihood — something that was clearly recognized in the form of fraternal organizations that had both a spiritual quality and clear links to an occupation, such as in Freemasonry or the Canadian custom in the 1920s and '30s to call labor union assembly halls "temples." A similar sensibility is expressed in eastern traditions such as *karma yoga*, the path of spiritual realization through work. In many aboriginal societies, young people were considered to be children until they undertook a "vision quest," a prolonged period of special ceremonies, secret teachings, physical trials, meditation, and fasting, culminating in a solitary ordeal that did not end until the initiates met a spirit guide who revealed to them their divinely ordained role in the tribe and became their life-long companion in pursuing it. Only then did "children" become "adults" — people who knew who they were and who had a recognized and respected role in the community. Contrast this with the endless circling in low orbit without landing instructions that characterizes adolescence in our consumer culture.

A skillful means of livelihood would honor the claims of both this inner, subjective, personal, and sacred dimension of human life as well as its outer, practical, and objective exigencies. Clearly we must eat, but not bread alone.

These insights can be brought to bear on the practical tasks of daily living at two levels: (a) steps that can be taken by individuals to fashion more life-giving approaches to livelihood, and (b) steps that can be taken by groups of people to collectively do so.

We have already seen how practicing voluntary simplicity can substantially reduce our need for money and consequently the pressure to obtain and keep paid employment. The value of simple living as an individual means of "reducing demand" for income remains valid and effective throughout life.

But unless we are prepared to accept a subsistence livelihood (which itself implies access to certain resources such as land, water, seeds, wild foods, etc.), there will continue to be some need for money to purchase things we cannot or choose not to make ourselves. To meet this need, consumerism offers indenturing oneself to an employer, with very few exceptions on a full-time basis. Or one can become an "entrepreneur," which could mean creating gainful work for oneself, but could also mean serving an unsustainable urge to amass a personal fortune. What are the alternatives to being a cog in a corporate machine or a solitary worker?

Discovering and creating alternatives begins with re-conceptualizing work, as we started to do above. It also includes re-thinking the getting of money, being ever mindful of how much is enough and of how desirable it is to allow room in one's life for activities that both meet life's physical needs and also support its deeper energies of inspiration, creativity, and self-realization. In many cases, this will entail a pattern of livelihood that is more flexible, more involving, more self-reliant, and more under one's personal control than most "jobs" offered by traditional corporate employment. Moreover, since its object would be to meet our need to provide for money for physical needs and to advance the works of our souls, amassing money itself would not be the principal objective.

In his highly useful book *How To Survive Without a Salary*[3], Charles Long suggests that self-employment in a variety of forms (temporary, casual, part-time, contract, seasonal, etc.) and involving a variety of activities (entrepreneurial self-employment, wage labor for others, investments, home production of some necessities) can provide a highly stimulating mix of activities, many "choice points" to take advantage of new opportunities, the chance to cut loose from abusive employment situations, and opportunities to learn new skills. This approach to earning one's livelihood is not as "simple" as working for one employer or doing just one thing. Like other "opportunistic" species, the "voluntary simpleton" would always be open to opportunities, always on the lookout to make small sums doing appealing things, always mindful of how to reduce expenses or deploy assets in particularly effective ways. It may be necessary to work very hard for short periods as well as budget for "gaps" in income. On the other hand, one is never totally committed to any one enterprise or activity. It is often much easier to earn small sums on short term contracts than to land high paid permanent jobs. Like a well diversified "stock portfolio," some activities will make money while others may not. But iif one doesn't fall victim to the entrepreneurial temptation to "go for broke on the big one," both gains *and* losses are modest, opportunity for learning is maximized, and, over the long haul, earning a modest living becomes, in a sense, a casual affair.

In this endeavor it is important to be mindful of the *costs* associated with being employed by someone else (as discussed earlier) and also of the point at which the cost of producing something or offering a service to others purely for the sake of making money begins to reach its point of "sufficiency" beyond which continuing the enterprise requires that we adopt a different way of life.

For example, a person of my acquaintance makes part of his living by keeping bees on a rural acreage from which he derives a few thousand dollars of income every year. His beekeeping operation involves only a few hives, a small, mechanically simple extractor, and small "warehousing" needs. The work is seasonal and requires little time. He sells his honey locally to his neighbors. Compared to many "companies," his return on capital investment in percentage terms is astronomical even though the actual amount of money is small. If he were suddenly to decide to go into the honey business "big time," he would face much higher costs and risks, much tougher competition, and the need to ship his honey to distant markets because local buyers could no longer consume what he produced. This would shift the entire enterprise into a different league and place very different demands on his time, energy and financial resources. Reflecting on these possibilities, he has recognized that the success of his honey operation (defined not in terms of how much money it makes, but of *how well it fits into the rest of his life*) rests entirely on knowing *where to stop*. Are we undertaking a certain activity to make a living or to make a *killing?* Herein lies the difference between enterprises that serve *life* by observing the appropriate limits of both the ecological carrying capacity and financial realism on the one hand and the "sky's-the-limit" expansionistic aspirations of consumer capitalism on the other.

Of course one can be just as opportunistic in the spending of money as in the getting of it, and to some extent this is implied in the practice of thrift as an essential part of voluntary simplicity. Charles Long points out that another important skill of living without a salary is to keep our eyes open for bargains as well as income opportunities. Auction sales, garage sales, consignment stores, estate liquidations, and all sorts of transactions that serve to eliminate "middlemen" from the sale help to conserve hard-earned money. Exercising this sort of opportunism is the exact opposite of the impulse buying that characterizes mainstream consumerism. One who uses skillful means is always mindful of exactly what and how much is needed and uses this mindfulness to take advantage of opportunities when they present themselves. This is very different from living in woolly-minded confusion about the difference between a want and a legitimate need and knowing when "spending in order to save" is working to one's own advantage and when it is not.

We have already mentioned that for some people, practicing simple living involves directly producing part of what they need for themselves, such as growing some food in an allotment or backyard garden or learning to do routine household maintenance. A logical extension of this is the general principle of *substitution*. After identifying a need or a desire, we should estimate how much money is required to purchase whatever is necessary to satisfy it. There may be other approaches that involve little or no money at all.

In many communities there is a growing interest in barter and trade networks that allow participants to swap goods and services directly with other network members. The only monetary aspect of these transactions is the collection of sales or income taxes. In this case, a community agreement has been substituted for money.

Another approach involves a further exercise of mindfulness, namely looking closely into the exact nature of the need or desire we experience and then discerning how best to satisfy it. For instance, if we want to read a certain book, it may not be necessary to purchase it, especially if it's something we're sure we won't be referring to again. Most communities have public libraries that also have added recorded music and videotape collections and offer free public access to the internet. Some communities have tool-lending and toy-lending services that function just like libraries. In general, if we need or want something only for a short period, a single use, or a specific project, it may not be necessary to *own* the item when it can be borrowed or rented at much less cost. It advances the practice of simplicity to substitute owning something with borrowing it, or trading something you no longer need for something you need now, rather than just purchasing and then discarding it.

Another individual approach to cultivating skillful means involves a shift in how we see ourselves. We have already illustrated that consumerism strongly promotes the idea that people are bundles of (natural or artificial) "needs" and that we are essentially dependent upon markets for the satisfaction of those needs. But the practice of simplicity through using skillful means invites us to see ourselves as *productive* human beings. From this perspective, what we should aim to "grow" is not our hoard of material possessions or investments, but our *productive capacities*, that is, the abilities, attitudes, and aptitudes required for self-reliance and constructive citizenship. In the chaotically changing vicissitudes of an increasingly environmentally, economically, and socially compromised future, it may be of more use to know how to maintain personal wellness, grow nutritious food, and repair basic household machines than to rely exclusively on a fat investment portfolio.

In the chaotically changing vicissitudes of an increasingly environmentally, economically, and socially compromised future, it may be of more use to know how to maintain personal wellness, grow nutritious food, and repair basic household machines than to rely exclusively on a fat investment portfolio.

$\mathcal{P}_{\mathfrak{D}}$

Of course the need for a means of livelihood is not exclusively an individual one. There are many exciting possibilities for collective activities that can also help sustain the individual quest for skillful means. The arch-conservative agenda that so dominates public discourse in North America insists that the only effective approach to meeting human needs is a corporate-controlled global economy. All assets should be "privately" owned, even if the "persons" who privately own them are disembodied legal fictions accountable to no one but their shareholders. According to this agenda, the distribution of costs and benefits in society should be entrusted to markets; such blind operation of economic principles will secure every imaginable social and environmental good.

Despite the fact that practically all media are controlled by these same corporate interests and politicians seem totally incapable of questioning economic orthodoxy, much less daring to offer any alternatives to it, alternatives are being shaped where every new thing has always been shaped: underground, at the margins, in harsh circumstances where innovation becomes a necessary means of survival. The results of this work now represent an impressive array of technical and social innovations which, taken together, offer not just a menu of one-issue "fixes" for particular problems but rather a coherent alternative agenda for the future cultural development of human societies. The only missing ingredient is a sufficiently effective mechanism to link all of these innovations (and their proponents) into a single, well-articulated agenda. But the appearance of this agenda can only be a matter of time.

There are clearly alternatives to corporations for organizing groups of people for productive activities that more equitably share the benefits of those activities, namely co-operatives.

Co-operatives have represented an alternative to profit-oriented corporations since the early part of the 20th century. In North America, co-operatives have grown up to counterbalance some of the worst abuses of corporate capitalism in manufacturing, housing, agriculture, and financial services. In Europe, many co-operatives were outgrowths of the Marxist-Leninist social critique of the 19th century.

The usual process of forming a corporation involves filing articles of incorporation to create a legal "person," the corporation. Money (capital) for financing corporate acquisitions and operations is provided by shareholders who purchase "shares" in the corporation in the expectation that they will also share in the profits derived from corporate operations (dividends on share capital). The managers of the corporation usually hire other people to perform the actual work necessary to produce profits. Thus the owners of the corporation are its shareholders while its workers are employees who trade their labor and expertise for wages or salaries. This establishes a situation in which the interests of shareholders and employees can (and often do) differ.

By contrast, co-operatives are legal corporations whose employees are the shareholders or are "members" of the co-operative in such fashion as to benefit directly from its operations. Thus, the "owners" and the "employees" are often the same people. Like traditional corporations, co-operatives enjoy limitations on financial liability equal to their corporate assets without recourse to the personal assets of members. Members can be paid wages or salaries by the co-operative that employs them, and they usually also enjoy various sorts of dividends, end-of-year bonuses, rebates, discounts, or share returns that distribute profits to co-operative members rather than to often distant shareholders whose only involvement with the enterprise has been the investment of their money. Most importantly, co-operative members have a direct say in the strategic planning decisions that determine the future of the co-operative and follow a one-person-one-vote regime in decision-making, rather than the one-share-one-vote scheme prevalent in traditional corporations. Obviously, under the latter arrangement, people with sufficient capital to purchase a majority of a corporation's shares determine how the corporation will be managed. In co-operatives, decision-making is more equitably distributed among members.

There are, of course, many variations in the organization of co-operatives. Since the 1920s in North America, thousands of co-ops have been created to market agricultural commodities on behalf of farmers, to run a variety of manufacturing and retailing enterprises, and, through credit unions and caisse populaires, to provide financial services. There are also many examples of housing co-operatives (where residents own an apartment complex or some other housing development and rent it back to themselves rather than pay rent to a non-resident landlord) and consumer co-ops (where people organize quantity purchasing to avail themselves of savings through bulk buying of goods and services).

The relevance of co-operatives to social sustainability has never been greater; there is no better example than the Mondragon Co-operative movement in the Basque region of Spain. In 1988, the Mondragon "system" was reported to embrace 21,000 workers organized in 166 co-operatives producing goods and services valued in 1987 at $1.6 billion, with $310 million in exports. Among Mondragon's many enterprises were light manufacturing, insurance, retailing, education and training, and advanced technology and research. Like any business enterprise, the Mondragon co-operatives are concerned with producing goods and services efficiently and profitably. But as various enterprises developed and expanded, they approached their own internal reorganization through *retention* and *retraining* of the existing workforce, rather than through "down-sizing." In addition to investing in new technology to increase productivity, Mondragon managers also invested heavily in the professional and technical upgrading of members. These operational principles have helped the co-operatives maintain jobs and contribute to the social stability of their communities and regions. The Mondragon co-operatives also limited the scale of their operations in order to retain certain valued features, such as a democratic organization, participatory approaches to decision-making, self-management, and community solidarity. Maintaining fixed ratios between the wages of production workers, managers, and technical staff also helped to maintain equity in the workplace and community.

The general concept of co-operatives can be applied at almost any scale of organization, from those exemplified by Mondragon to groups of a few individuals who might want to establish a small consumer co-operative, a child care service, a housing co-op, or some sort of co-op enterprise for their own employment. Many of the co-housing experiments now under way are co-operatively based enterprises. While there is nothing inherently environmentally sustainable about co-operative business ventures, they are intrinsically more socially equitable and can be configured toward greater environmental sustainability as readily as any other social institution.

A concept closely related to that of a co-operative involves people banding together for the specific purpose of meeting a particular life need through collective action. One exciting example of this has been the formation of "co-housing", developments[5], housing collectives, and "Eco-Villages."[6].

The North American "dream" has traditionally included a fully detached, single family suburban house with manicured lawn, backyard pool, and a minivan parked in front of a three-car garage housing at least one more car and probably a boat, snowmobile, or mobile camper. It is no accident that this dream continues to be strongly promoted through advertising imagery that presents it as the most desirable, most "normal" way to live. It is also the most consumptive pattern of settlement ever developed by human beings except for the multiple country estates of the very rich. There is no better way to spur consumption than to convince people that distance be kept between neighbors and that each one own as personal property all sorts of machines and physical amenities of life that could much more efficiently be owned in common and shared. It is more profitable to corporations, for example, if everyone owns his or her own automatic washer and lets it stand idle 99 percent of the time than if ten families shared one machine and let it stand idle only 50 percent of the time!

Co-housing arrangements attempt to address some of these concerns. Co-housing developments consist of residential quarters designed for a group of people with varying degrees of shared amenities and services. What is shared and what is private property varies with the group, but it is common that co-housing schemes include private sleeping, living, and sometimes light kitchen facilities, with shared larger kitchens, dining facilities, recreation areas, and laundry facilities. Facilities consist of clusters of attached single-family dwellings or else larger multiple-family buildings with more units. Sometimes they incorporate garden spaces, meeting rooms, and workshops, as well as services such as daycare, small retail outlets, and car pools or shared transportation. They may also include shared water and energy services, recycling and composting operations, and a variety of educational, recreational, social, or cultural programs. The co-housing concept allows for members to determine how much they wish to do in common and how much in private.

Whereas traditional condominiums are built by developers, sold to residents for profit, and maintained for a monthly occupancy fee, co-housing facilities are often developed by co-operatives or collectives whose members are the residents. Accommodation is leased from the co-operative. This protects residents from real estate speculation and makes dwellings available to families and individuals at much less cost than traditional single-family houses.

When co-housing facilities are built from scratch, they offer many opportunities for sustainability, including an energy conserving design, an optimal use of passive solar energy, an efficient use of space in general as well as workspaces, integrated green spaces, and a pedestrian environment. To the degree that members develop (or possess) the social skills and attitudes necessary to successful interdependence, the lives of individuals can become materially much simpler and financially more secure. This is the case because much of what once had to be purchased, maintained, and repaired as one's own property can now be shared, conferring an extra measure of personal freedom from possessions that are only infrequently needed.

Eco-Villages are intentional communities (communities established "on purpose" rather than higgledy-piggledy over time) that may include or spring from co-housing agreements but are deliberately organized around the pursuit of ecological sustainability. They often, from the very beginning, aim to integrate into community design such features as off-grid renewable energy supplies, local organic production of some foods, pedestrian transportation, waste recycling, and provisions for local, community-based enterprises. To the degree that some eco-villages include many co-operatively organized businesses and attract individuals with a strong preference for voluntary simplicity, they might be counted as early harbingers of the alternative integrated development agenda suggested above.

Co-operative businesses, co-housing developments, and eco-villages all represent potential skillful means for those seeking to extend their practice of voluntary simplicity while trying to meet their livelihood needs in ways that are more in harmony with their values but all of these options may represent fairly substantial changes in lifestyle.

Gentler, yet equally promising innovations include Local Exchange Trading Systems[7], Community Shared Agriculture, and Community Land Trusts.[8]

ॐ

Economies are sustained through the production and consumption of goods and services. The medium that lubricates the gears of these transactions is money. Of course goods and services can be traded directly through barter transactions, but the practicality of these arrangements depends on the parties trading articles or services of approximately equal value over very short periods of time. It is awkward, for example, to barter turnips against the building materials needed for a house, or music lessons in exchange for a piece of land. Money, handy invention that it is, allows the grower of turnips to sell, and hence convert to money, many small amounts of turnips, to save some of this money over periods of time she could never have saved turnips, and to then exchange the money for building materials of much larger aggregate value than any single lot of turnips.

In the current social and economic reality, money is printed by governments who scrupulously control the total supply of currency and use other economic instruments, such as interest rate policies, to control the value of the national currency. They can also regulate the use of credit and the terms on which credit can be extended, thereby controlling access to credit as well as money. This system creates the quite bizarre and socially destructive possibility that if money is unequally distributed throughout society, some people may have more of it than they need and others less. That is, money can become scarce and people can compete with each other to get it. Indeed, people with valuable skills and legitimate needs may not be able to purchase what they need or sell what they have simply because they lack money to enable the exchange.

In 1983, Michael Linton, a computer programmer in Courtenay, B.C., invented *Local Exchange Trading Systems (LETS)* to address this situation. With LETS, people who lack money simply print their own. LETS networks are often specific to a region or local community, although the only "system requirement" is that they be limited to a specific network of subscribed members. Under some systems, a local currency is printed and issued to members of the network that can be traded to other members of the network for goods and services. In other systems, transactions are logged as "credits" on a computer that keeps track of the positive and negative balances of all subscribers and their transactions with each other. Subscribers can "spend" credits they haven't accumulated yet without being charged for "credit." Other subscribers can offer goods and services and accumulate credits that they agree to eventually spend within the network.

The long-term picture of a well-functioning system will show about half the subscribers in a transaction "deficit" position and half in a surplus position at any one time. Since subscribers sign agreements to balance purchasing transactions with earning transactions over the long run, the system facilitates the movement of goods and services within the community without letting money "leak out" to distant profit-takers.

Some LETS networks allow transactions that involve combinations of the local currency and the national currency. The unit value of a credit or local currency note is "pegged" to the value of a national currency (in the UK LETSystem, one credit value is equal to one pound sterling) or to the average hourly wage in the community or region (as with "Ithaca Hours," which are valued at about $10.00US, the average hourly rate of pay in Ithaca, New York). The value of transactions is estimated in the national currency as well so that taxation regulations can be observed and sales taxes remitted when they would normally be levied on such transactions. The effect of LETS arrangements is to establish semi-autonomous local economies that are largely free from the depredations of chartered banks, national governments, and international currency speculators. LETS place a medium of exchange in the hands of local people so that the benefits of local commercial transactions, often diverted out of local communities, can be recaptured to meet local needs.

... these systems provide a basis for re-igniting local economies and breaking the grip of corporations and financial institutions on local development. They are inherently compatible with bio-regional and eco-village scale communities and relatively impervious to the many economically, socially, and environmentally distorting influences of large scale, monetarized economies and transnational corporations.

There are dozens of LETS networks emerging and operating in Canada, the United States, Australia, and the UK. Increasingly sophisticated computer software is being developed to manage such systems, and many of the legal and taxation details have been amicably worked out. Since LETS networks are essentially bookkeeping systems for the promises that members make to each other to trade goods and services, the system reflects patterns of commitment among its members. Such a system is eminently *local* and *human*. It is insulated from outside speculation and protected from the economic forces that customarily cause nationally issued currencies to be drawn away toward enterprises that promise the highest rates of return, usually found in large cities. Thus local communities, whether urban or rural, gain a measure of protection from interests that would extract wealth from communities without reinvesting it.

The relevance of LETS to simplicity and skillful means of livelihood is that these systems provide a basis for re-igniting local economies and breaking the grip of corporations and financial institutions on local development. They are inherently compatible with bioregional and eco-village scale communities and relatively impervious to the many economically, socially, and environmentally distorting influences of large scale, monetarized economies and transnational corporations. Since one of the requirements for participation is full disclosure of all members' transactions and commitment balances, the whole trading system is "transparent" to all participants, which is far more than can be said for traditional approaches to business.

ℰ

For many people, the corporate influence on community life, along with personal health issues, environmental issues, and economic development issues, comes to a focus in the agro-food system — that set of social, economic, technical, and productive arrangements through which our food is produced. In her now classic book, *Diet For A Small Planet*[9], Frances Moore Lappe draws parallels between the production of food, personal health and nutrition, the environmental impact of different sorts of food production systems, and the role that large agro-food corporations play in configuring both our diets and the economics of food production. Not surprisingly, we have created a society of mostly urban dwellers who consume food but don't know much about where it comes from or how it is produced; agricultural producers who grow the food but seldom meet the people who consume it and realize very little profit from their labor; and, in between, an immense, environmentally destructive and largely parasitic system of food processors, distributors, transportation interests, pesticide and fertilizer manufacturers, slaughterhouses and packing plants, advertisers, retailers, and commodity market speculators who claw in huge profits from their various operations. Lappe and others have seen in this an inherently unsustainable system that leaves farmers undercompensated for their land and labor, rural communities depopulated because of the shift away from family farms toward corporate industrial agriculture, malnourished urban dwellers being sold "empty calories" in novelty packages, landscapes environmentally compromised as land is "mined" for maximum profit and poisoned by agri-chemicals, and genetic diversity dangerously diminished as transnational corporations try to lock up the world's germ plasm by patenting cultivars of many of the most important human foods. And in the middle of it all are banks and stock market speculators who make very sizable returns on the lending and marketing commissions necessary to make all these wheels turn.

Community Shared Agriculture (CSA) aims to cut through many of the destructive and unsustainable features of our existing food system. Under CSA schemes, consumers (usually urban dwellers) enter directly into contracts with farmers whereby they purchase "shares" redeemable in food in advance of its production. How much food they receive depends on how well the farmer's crop does during the growing season. Thus the risk of production is shared between both the farmer and the consumer. Some CSA farms offer organic produce, but under all schemes, food buyers get their products fresh, in season, and unprocessed or treated beyond the farm gate. Producers can offer food at prices well below those of retail outlets because all the "middlemen" have been eliminated, while at the same time realizing a higher and more equitable rate of return for their own work. Many CSA arrangements include opportunities for purchasers to help with crop production, thereby increasing their own awareness of how food is produced, the risks involved, and the intimate links between our food supply and the ecological health of the bioregion. CSA helps individual "family farms" obtain some part of their operating capital up front at seeding time, interest-free, and without having to borrow it from banks. This helps stabilize the farm family financially, and as a result, rural communities are stabilized as well. CSA shortens the transportation lines between field and table, saving transportation fuels and the resources, chemicals, and packaging that would otherwise have gone into processing and retailing the food.

The first CSA farm was opened to customers in Canada in 1992 near Winnipeg, Manitoba. Within one year, 30 more CSA operations opened in various regions across the country. As the CSA movement gains momentum, it promises to tighten the links between the producers and the consumers of food. It may also help sustain family farms.

Our right in North America to the ownership of private property, specifically land, is one of our strongest and most cherished traditions. It confers many benefits to landowners and provides a legally secure basis for forms of livelihood, such as agriculture, that require a land base for production activities. But the protections and prerogatives that extend to the private ownership of land also enable serious abuses of both the land itself and others in society. One individual may purchase some marginal land and undertake a reforestation program, immensely increasing the ecological sustainability and social value of the property. Another individual might take another plot of land and totally deforest it, pollute it with toxic chemicals, or allow wind and water to erode its topsoils. In the current legal reality, as long as these activities don't affect anyone else beyond the property lines, the landowner can use the property more or less any way he or she wishes. Since corporations are legal persons, they can also own land. And of course, any landowner can speculate with land, hoping to sell it at a higher price than was originally paid for it.

The notion that land can be a personal possession, or that it can be used for one's personal benefit rather than the benefit of one's group as a whole, is a comparatively recent and isolated cultural development. Historically, the notion that one can own land would have seemed as outlandish as making the claim today that one might own the air or the stars.

Nevertheless, given that we have this peculiar notion about land ownership, it follows that those who have money or access to credit are in a better position to purchase land and use it as they wish than people who have little money or no access to credit. It also follows that since the owner of land can set any price he or she wishes to resell the land, land can become a speculative commodity and price can be used to exclude whole groups of people from access to certain areas of land. Moreover, the various levels of profit that can be derived from different uses of the same parcel of land can dramatically influence how it is used, and not always in ways that enhance its overall social and environmental sustainability. In the current economic reality, for example, it is more profitable to "develop" an area of land into a golf course than to retain it as agricultural land, and less profitable still to preserve it as wetland or marsh or forest even though these are *ecologically* immeasurably more productive than a golf course.

Land trusts are now being developed to address these and many other potential abuses and inequities arising from the private ownership of land. Proponents of land trusts are not against private personal property, but rather are trying to establish a network of institutions that secure land against the extension of the concept of private property to all land. This is motivated by social, environmental, and, in some cases, historical or cultural interests rather than by the desire for profit.

Land trusts are not-for-profit corporations formed by individuals or groups, with articles of incorporation establishing the company to exercise trusteeship over land according to certain guiding principles. Land trusts can be established for any purpose, but one of their principal effects is that lands that become trust properties are permanently removed from the market and are no longer available for sale or speculation. This immediately insulates the land against fluctuations in market prices and conforms the uses of the land to those specified in the articles of incorporation. Land trusts are being rapidly established in dozens of areas across North America. There is no requirement that they be of any particular size. Land trusts acquire property either by direct donation of land or by cash donations from supporters of the trust who then use the money to purchase land.

Conservation land trusts have been established in rural and wilderness areas to protect these lands as biodiversity reserves, wildlife sanctuaries, or recreational areas. Trusts have also been established to preserve specific areas containing sites of archeological or historic interest.

Community land trusts have been created in urban areas to purchase properties in inner cities so that building sites or rental accommodation can be leased back to community residents at affordable prices and free from the threat that future speculators will sell the properties out from under the current residents. The leases are often long term (99 years) and inheritable.

Establishing land trusts in no way prevents land from being used for residential or commercial purposes if such uses are mandated in the trust's charter. Properties for residential uses are *leased* to individuals at rates established by the trust and usually aimed at achieving some measure of environmental or social sustainability, rather than profiting the shareholders of a corporation. Improvements to the property belong to the leaseholders.

A major catalyst of the land trust movement in North America has been the Maryland-based E.F. Schumacher Society. Established in 1980 to promote a decentralist vision of locally based, human scale, and more environmentally sustainable economic development, and inspired by its namesake, the British economist Fritz Schumacher, the Society actively promotes the formation of land trusts and produces excellent training material and information packages to help local groups establish such trusts. There are also many home pages on the Internet for specific land trusts around the world that describe their charters, goals, and activities.

ॐ

The options described above are just a sample of the many innovative schemes now appearing, as well as of arrangements that are time-tested and known to be workable, that present real alternatives to a "nine-to-five-to-sixty-five" way of life. Clearly, individuals can take up the personal practice of simple living as an ecologically sustainable, socially equitable way of life. It is also possible, indeed necessary, for us to work together to fashion collective alternatives to the culture of consumerism.

11

Simplicity and Economy

One question (or a group of questions really) that often comes forth in dinner conversation about voluntary simplicity is how its adoption would affect "our" economy? As significant as the question itself is the tone in which it is posed, as if people are saying, "Well, let's get serious here and talk about this in terms of the *real* world of hard cash and jobs and earning potential." Just as prevalent is the prejudice that before voluntary simplicity can be taken seriously on *any* score, it must make its case in terms of economics. Economics seems to be the dominant religion of North America in the sense that it sets the background of "absolute" categories against which we judge the realism, practicality, even sanity of one's arguments for or against any other value or human project, actual or proposed.

Not being an economist, I confess a distinct disability in framing arguments that would be compelling to professionals in this field. Being a human being, however, I claim my right to comment on issues that affect my life, and given that economics dominates today's thinking, it is a key issue for better or worse. It will be in this limited and qualified sense, therefore, that I offer some reflections.

It's Not "Our" Economy

It is always somewhat puzzling to hear individuals who are clearly victimized by the current economic system refer to the economy with a possessive pronoun. The current economic system of North America clearly does not belong to those it exploits, though the system labors mightily to create that impression. Hearing people fret about what would happen to "our" economy if voluntary simplicity were widely adopted sounds as misplaced as a person suffering from addiction worrying about what might happen to his pusher if the supply of street drugs were ever to dry up.

"Our" economy is controlled primarily by corporations that are growing larger and fewer by the day. The wealth created by the economy is becoming progressively more concentrated in fewer and larger private fortunes, a trend that has been underway for many decades. While there are more millionaires than ever before, the amount of wealth they control relative to their numbers is enormous, and the percentage of millionaires within the total world population is vanishingly small. Moreover, how can we suppose that the number of millionaires in a society is in any way a good measure of the overall social well-being?

The current economic system of North America clearly does not belong to those it exploits, though the system labors mightily to create that impression.

Governments, for their part, are more and more often engaged by corporations to "manage" populations, legal processes, appeal procedures, and regulatory regimes to the advantage of the corporations. Governments are increasingly serving as "buffers" that shield "corporate citizens" from interaction with and accountability to real citizens. Moreover, those elected to govern are so mesmerized by the superstitions of economics that they have largely come to accept that the best thing they can do for humanity is to dismantle themselves and leave the world "open for business." The effect of our cultural dedication to economic growth as the measure of all human progress has been both to increase the total monetary wealth in society and at the same time to concentrate that wealth in fewer and fewer hands. Our dedication to economic growth has achieved this wealth transfer while "externalizing" its environmental and social costs. Voluntary simplicity merely proposes an alternative to this inequitable and violence-prone system.

How the adoption of voluntary simplicity might affect the economy can be asked in a number of ways. For example, might simple living result in job losses?

On the face of it, such a question is logical. If people consumed less, then consumer demand would drop, production would drop, and job losses would ensue. We would presumably see both an economic recession and increased unemployment.

At one level, however, some of the lowered demand for labor devoted to the production of goods and services would be compensated precisely by those practicing simpler living and choosing to work fewer hours. Total GDP might decline, but there might be very little net change in the demand for labor as compared to the available supply of workers. Thus, employment might remain high.

At another level, the assumption that any departure from the status quo is undesirable because it may result in job losses or recession is, well, more than a little peculiar. Many jobs now consist of work that is directly or indirectly destroying the ecosphere, the very foundation of future prosperity. To insist that such jobs stay in place is exactly like arguing that no cure should be sought for cancer because oncologists might lose their jobs or that no steps should be taken to treat drug addiction because a local drug trafficker may go on the dole.

It is totally nonsensical to insist that a person currently employed in sawing off his own arms and legs continue doing so because the alternative would be unemployment. Yet such an argument is often made in the "Oz" of modern economic thinking.

Another way of posing the question might be to ask if the widespread adoption of voluntary simplicity poses a threat to the overall economic development or to business as usual.

Voluntary simplicity represents a significant cultural change. Businesses that are intelligently attuned to meeting people's changing needs would simply use their already highly developed skills for tracking and responding to such changes to develop new business opportunities. There is nothing particularly scary or mysterious about this.

It is widely acknowledged in many quarters that existing business and accounting practices are unsustainable, if not unrealistic, because they do not adequately factor in the environmental and social costs of producing many goods and services. The sort of cultural transformation that voluntary simplicity represents can thus be seen as the same sort of transformation needed to secure the future of business. To meet the needs of an expanding population (market) within the ecological limits imposed by the Earth, business will have to both increase its production efficiency (an essentially technical task) and participate in a general social transformation that "dematerializes" our understanding of the good life (an essentially cultural challenge). Failing this, business will go down with the consumers and ecosystems it has chosen to exploit rather than conserve.

Should a "culture of simplicity" ever emerge, business could never be conducted as it has been in the past. Simplicity is about reducing the quantity of one's personal consumption in order to gain more quality in life. Any commercial venture producing *anything* in quantity (speed, noise, obsolescence, size, waste) would be under enormous pressure to change or perish. But of course, there will always be markets for those goods and services necessary to a decent human life: food, shelter, clothing, transportation, etc.

> *Simplicity is about reducing the quantity of one's personal consumption in order to gain more quality in life.*

Voluntary simplicity implies an overall reduction in the scale of business activity as we have known it: less energy and resource throughput, less waste, less advertising, less commercialization of everything, less physical space on the planet allocated to commerce. This doesn't necessarily mean a lower GDP in cash terms, however, or less financial wealth. It does mean a radical change in how that wealth is created and what defines it. Wealth will be derived from more intangible sources and relate to more intangible services and goods, e.g., knowledge, technique, and things that qualitatively improve human life.

Simple Living Will Not Cause Economic Collapse

The idea that the economy would collapse if people lived more simply is alarmist and, well, simplistic. Humans can't stop consuming altogether since we clearly need things to live, but the pattern of our consumption might shift from material things to non-material services, experiences, learning, etc. Beyond the personal scale, simpler living is at least partly about the *de-materialization* of the economy, not the abolition of it. De-materialization involves generating wealth by adding ingenuity, tasteful design, and efficiency improvements to products rather than generating profit simply by increasing the quantity of sales.

For example, the nature and types of goods and services available in a culture of simplicity would change dramatically with more durable, repairable, and aesthetically pleasing products being developed and many more people employed in maintaining, repairing, rebuilding, and recycling these products than we see today. Profits would still be made, but the "fair Earth share" of each person's consumption would be more in line with, and eventually below, the carrying capacity for one's bioregion. People would still buy and sell things, but the good life would no longer be defined by the *amount* consumed and wasted but rather by the quality and depth of fit between the goods and services consumed and the purchaser's most authentic needs.

In such circumstances, we might foresee the following goods and services:

- Services that enhance the quality of life relationships, provide solitude, support personal development, and bring people into contact with nature in an environmentally sustainable fashion.

- Products and services that help people experience themselves as *creators* of value, not as *consumers* of it, e.g., good paints and canvas, not paint-by-number sets; good musical instruments, not more stereo equipment; good tools and materials, not "no-fail-half-assembled-just-insert-batteries kits".

- Goods that are of higher quality, more durable, more user-serviceable; tools that extend creative and self-reliance activities, not highly automated machines that take over the tasks of living.

- Goods that combine beauty and function. There is no room in a simple life for products that are ugly or dysfunctional.

- Goods and services that display attention to environmental stewardship in every detail of the design, construction, use, and recycling of products.

Practitioners of voluntary simplicity will make their purchasing decisions based on the lifecycle cost of the product, not on the lowest price.

- Products and services that help people take responsibility for and maintain their own health, e.g., natural self-care products, health maintenance services, high quality outdoor clothing, sports equipment that enhances contact with nature and others (such as canoes versus power boats or hiking boots versus ATVs).

- Products and services that help people be more deeply and permanently rooted in community. They will be likely to patronize businesses with a similar commitment to permanence, place, and neighborliness.

- Businesses that strengthen and support communities, for example by including education components in their services or by providing community-oriented meeting places and services that make the development of community easier.

Any service or good is likely to appeal to practitioners of voluntary simplicity if it helps make their lives simpler. This means any good or service that promises to confer an increase in the quality of life at reduced input of material, energy, time, or labor.

Simplicity Does Not Abolish All Opportunities to Become Rich

A corollary of our discussion above is the notion that a de-materialized economy may offer just as many opportunities for those who wish to become rich because material goods that are better made, better designed, longer lasting, and repairable would probably cost more than disposable alternatives. An economy that produces these kinds of goods compensates job losses in manufacturing with job creation in repair, recycling, and maintenance occupations. Just as many dollars may circulate in the economy, but less would be tied to the consumption and waste of resources and energy, and they would be more equitably distributed. Moreover, it would seem less likely that repair and maintenance occupations could ever become as highly automated as the production of new goods from fresh raw materials. This would virtually assure higher levels of employment.

Getting the Question Right

Critics challenge advocates of voluntary simplicity to justify the effects they suppose simplicity would have on the economy. But is this the right question? Might it not be more appropriate to turn this around and ask how apologists for the economy can justify its effects on communities and the ecosphere? After all, the economy, we are forcefully told, represents the *real* world and has an established track record. Simplicity offers both people and ecosystems a chance at sustainability. Consumerism assures our extinction within two or three generations. What benefits does consumerism confer that justify extinction?

Critics challenge advocates of voluntary simplicity to justify effects they suppose simplicity would have on the economy. But is this the right question? Might it not be more appropriate to turn this around and ask how apologists for the economy can justify its effects on communities and the ecosphere?

Currently, business seeks to increase production and consumption of all goods and services because these are the source of ever-increasing profits, the *raison d'être* of business. The problem is that this is not sustainable. As Paul Hawken has described in detail, should business achieve its ultimate goal, given the current reality, it would paradoxically seal its own demise[1]; a regrettable eventuality for us all.

It is also important to distinguish different scales of "business." We use the same term whether we are referring to street vendors selling hot-dogs or to transnational corporations. But with the difference in scale represented by these extremes comes a great qualitative difference in their respective impacts on society and the environment. Voluntary simplicity is certainly consistent with individual and family-owned enterprises and small corporations that produce goods and services.

Of a different order altogether are gigantic corporations, some of whose budgets exceed those of national governments and whose decisions can have a massive sway on the outcomes of elections, the future of communities, and the survival of whole ecosystems. While such organizations *can* muster huge amounts of capital for projects that *sometimes* return the benefits of "economies of scale," as often as not they also create social and environmental "externalities of scale" in the process. ("Economies of scale" refers to the reduction in the per-unit cost of production when very large amounts of a product can be produced, as with the use of automation. "Externalities of scale" is a phrase I've coined to express the environmental and social impacts of production characterized by economies of scale.)

In addition, very large corporations have the resources not only to mass produce goods and services for the market but also to mass produce *markets* for their goods and services, irrespective of the relevance of their products to authentic human needs. As Wendell Berry has observed, when inescapable human fallibility is wedded to very powerful technology operating at very large scales, the results are ultimately disastrous[2]: witness Saveso, Bhopal, Chernobyl, Love Canal, and the *Exxon Valdez*.

To support more sustainable patterns of livelihood, business must re-engineer itself at a number of levels simultaneously:

First, business must rethink its mission in society, coming to see itself as *part* of society, not as its controlling element. Society and commerce are not coterminous. Business exists to serve society, not vice versa. We can see a few encouraging developments in this direction with the recent growth in interest in "business ethics" and some very notable examples of businesses (Nortel and VanCity Savings Credit Union in Canada, and Electrolux and IKEA of Sweden) that are successfully organizing their operations more according to social and environmental benefits while maintaining profitability and competitiveness.

By far the majority of private sector voices influencing the direction of governance and social development in North America has pursued a vigorous program of neutralizing the power of governments to protect the public good. They have shifted the focus of public discourse to the needs and priorities of business rather than the key requirements for social and environmental sustainability. They have also spawned a series of international agreements (FTA, NAFTA, GATT, and MAI) designed to institutionalize regulations and treaties favorable to business activities, with little regard for their effects on communities and ecosystems.

Second, as Paul Hawken has also argued, business needs to see people as potential *customers*, not as "consumers" to whom one markets "product." Commercial transactions are first of all *human* interactions and only secondly commodity exchanges. It should be the values humans hold that characterize the exchange, rather than the characteristics of exchange transactions coming to govern humans.

Again with only a few notable exceptions, the mindset of business, and particularly of accounting, has come to dominate discussion and planning in education, health care, the arts, and even religion in North America. In general, while this may be intended to bring prudence and efficiency to the operation of organizations and institutions not customarily thought of as "businesses," at another level it represents a profound and sad incursion of mercantile values into every aspect of life. Just as industrialized farming and forestry now seek to eradicate from landscapes all species of plants and animals except those they use in order to maximize profits, the dominance of business lingo in public discourse tends to eradicate every social value except those directly connected with consumerism and corporate profit.

Third, business must redesign its products, services, and processes to satisfy the system conditions that are non-negotiable requirements for living on a limited planet. Moreover, business might consider its activities in terms of the ends they are designed to achieve. The pressing nature of the environmental emergency that is manifesting itself everywhere around us clearly requires that we ask whether a good or service is being produced to more efficiently and economically meet an authentic human need or whether it is being manufactured simply in the expectation that a market can be created for it that will turn a profit? In the present reality, corporate charters are routinely granted (in perpetuity) simply for the purpose of making a profit. Neither society nor the ecosphere can continue the luxury of this practice.

Fourth, business must expand its concept of its ethical obligations within society and stop deliberately confusing non-material human needs with the promise of satisfying them through addictive consumerism. Advertising is specifically designed to suggest that social acceptance can be gained by consuming the right beer, that personal identity can be discovered by owning a particular car, that confidence can be found by using the right feminine hygiene product, or that family ties can be strengthened by drinking a particular orange juice. It is *profitable*, although *unethical*, to perpetrate this sort of confusion because its ultimate consequence is death — the death of individuals and the death of nature. Adopting a more responsible ethical position may reduce the quantity and types of goods and services that can ethically be marketed, but the alternative is in no one's long-term interest.

Finally, business should actively participate in the "de-materialization" of the economy. It is conceivable that new frontiers of innovation, new products and services might come to exist in a more de-materialized economic system (as well as on the pathway to it) that will help sustain corporate profits as well as pave the way to more sustainable patterns of livelihood. Such enterprises could also make major contributions to voluntary simplicity by helping shift attention from the quantitative aspects of material objects to the qualitative characteristics of experience.

A Culture of Simplicity Won't Appear Overnight

One of the favorite tactics of those who wish to discredit simple living as an alternative to the status quo is to imply that the transition to a culture of simplicity would (could) happen overnight — as if on signal, everyone would (could) instantly "down tools," walk away from their jobs, and go fishing! Such imagery is reminiscent of a general strike and easily conjures up fears of general economic collapse and social chaos. Yet there are very few historical examples of anything in human life being taken to its "logical extreme" in a few days or months, except in the woolly-minded speculations of sophists.

In practice and in fact, the stories of people who have already simplified their lives describe a process that takes many years and must overcome many personal and social hurdles. It is a practice that grows slowly in a life, comes about organically, by trial and error, and through the progressive accumulation of new tastes and habits. It is something people must think through, feel their way into, and repeatedly evaluate, re-invent, adapt to, and adjust. It is completely different from dropping everything and running off to the woods.

What would also slow the diffusion of simple living into the cultural mainstream, even if people became very determined to practice "hard core" simplicity, is the fact that many people are deeply mired in debt, do not have jobs or households conducive to simplicity, and may be part way along in raising families, which implies a very different approach to practicing simplicity than is available to single people and those who either never had children or whose children are grown-up. Debts would have to be paid off and scores of other decisions made about all sorts of life habits, living quarters, and daily routines. All of this takes time if the changes we seek are to be healthy, stable, appropriate, and meaningful.

Accordingly, as individuals and families launched into the practice of simplicity, the economy would likely also make a very gradual shift to "track" these changes in values and livelihoods. If the diffusion of simple living through society occurred at the very modest rate of only three percent per year, it would take an entire generation before the practice became universal. Moreover, it would take a generation to re-engineer education so that we were training ourselves not to be consumers, but to be self-reliant, co-operative citizens of democratic societies seeking a high quality of life for everyone.

Economics Is Not the Measure of All Things

Another way of looking at the question of how the practice of simplicity might affect economics concerns the possibility that raising the question at all actually constitutes a subtle way of re-asserting the primacy of economic terms and concepts as the most important measure of all values. We have already alluded to this tendency.

The American psychologist and philosopher William James[3] proposed that people are passionate by nature and that we passionately *want* to believe certain things.[3] One consequence of this intense desire to believe is that where human action is involved, the intensity of our belief and our willingness to act on our beliefs can cause what we wish to believe to come about. In the present case, the person who passionately believes that "money makes the world go around" behaves in such a way as to make this true, creating a self-fulfilling prophesy about how human beings behave and then mistaking that behavior for evidence of some natural "law" that compels human behavior.

Psychologically, such people perceive themselves to be compelled by their own choices. Economics has effected such a mindset in North American society.

An unfortunate corollary of this "will to believe," as James called it, is that anything that we don't want, we tend to disbelieve. This effectively closes the door on the possibility of considering alternatives.

When people insist that simple living must make its case in terms of economics or they will not seriously entertain any further exploration of the subject, they often state this with passion, and with passion comes the insistence that simplicity take up the language, ideas, and rationales of economics. None of this has anything at all to do with what might be good, or human, or even *true*. It is mostly the assertion of an intellectual prejudice, or a *preference* at least, namely that economic thinking be the measure and language that configures every other discussion. Under such circumstances, an open-minded exploration of what simplicity might hold for people in *any* part of their life becomes impossible.

$\mathcal{P}$

In his book *Ishmael*[4], Daniel Quinn suggests that all cultures could be classified as either "leavers" or "takers." Members of "taker" cultures believe that the world belongs to them and that it's okay to it as they see fit, even if that entails the death of other species or even other people. After all, they are all "prey," and we think of ourselves as predators.

> Modern economics is a taker ideology. Voluntary simplicity is something else again, something very much attuned to a more humble scale and to letting go. Which of these perspectives on human life we adopt with passion is a vote for the kind of future we will have.

"Leavers" have a different perspective on things. They are a lot more relaxed, believing that they belong to the world, and frequently to God. From this relationship of belonging, co-operation and compassion are possible, as is sharing what is available to meet the needs of all. The world controls itself. Our job is to notice how it moves and to join the dance, but to dance consciously and with appreciation on behalf of everything else that is dancing unconsciously. Our essential skills are not prediction, control, and exploitation, but rather letting go, letting be, and appreciation. Leaver societies position human beings in a humbler role, accepting more readily our tendencies to fallibility and therefore our need to work at smaller scales and with more care for each other. Fallible human beings look out for each other. Predators don't.

Modern economics is a taker ideology. Voluntary simplicity is something else again, something very much attuned to a more humble scale and to letting go. Which of these perspectives on human life we adopt with passion is a vote for the kind of future we will have.

12

Simplicity and Equity

When someone steals a man's clothes we call him a thief.
Should we not give the same name to one who could clothe the naked and does not?
The bread in your cupboard belongs to the hungry man; the coat hanging unused in
your closet belongs to the man who needs it; the shoes rotting in your closet belong to
the man who has no shoes; the money which you hoard up belongs to the poor.

— Basil the Great, Bishop of Caesaraea, A.D. 365

Simplicity as Non-Violence

A key reason that some people take up the practice of voluntary simplicity is that they believe it will in some way contribute to a more equitable and peaceable world. That the world is a distinctly inequitable and unpeaceful place scarcely needs demonstration and I won't bother re-stating the obvious here. The question of interest is whether the choice to voluntarily simplify one's life can be in any way a means of redressing inequity and violence?

Using "inequity and violence" as a single phrase is a deliberate effort to emphasize their correlation, and possibly even their mutual causation. To determine which comes first, the chicken or the egg, is impossible. But the observation that both inequity and violence arise as aspects of a single system is inescapable. Establishing their priority adds little to the picture.

The culture of consumerism, driven as it is by competition, social comparison, the continual stimulation of discontent, and differential rewards virtually manufactures inequity. As economic and social inequity grows, the process is similar to an electrical charge gathering in a thundercloud. The stronger the polarization between Earth and cloud, the likelier it becomes that lightning will flash, destroying whatever it touches.

While reasoning from analogy is always hazardous, it doesn't take great powers of observation or introspection to notice that as some people in society gain access to more and more wealth and social privilege and others have less and less, tension develops. Among the "have-nots" this is the tension of envy, of real (or perceived) injustice, of frustration, of the tension between what one's income allows and continually repeated advertising messages about things one should aspire to own but cannot afford. There also can grow up a sense of fear, insecurity, and helplessness as everywhere decisions are taken by the wealthy concerning how society as a whole will operate, what projects will be given priority, even what sorts of cultural and spiritual activities will predominate, while those of lesser means feel they can only suffer the results of these decisions and accept what is decided rather than become active architects and create their own communities. In such situations, where one is continually feeling "done to" by others, it would be natural to find growing suspicion as to the motives of society's more fortunate members, cynicism and apathy with respect to participation in civil society, and fear about what the future may bring.

Fear is perhaps the most equitably distributed product of the consumer society. For all their wealth and privilege, the "haves" experience their own side of the fear, suspicion, and helplessness equation. The greater the difference between one's own pile of possessions and that of one's neighbors, the more aware we become (consciously or unconsciously) of the potential for violence and loss inherent in the social polarization. Despite their arrogance and apparent security, the affluent too are trapped by the inequity others think they enjoy. We have only to ask if confident and secure people need to surround themselves with security devices, live in gated communities, join "exclusive" clubs, or be concerned with "risk management?" How often does the genteel velvet glove of privilege conceal just beneath the surface all the violence of law, of police, of armies, of guards and dogs and fences and bullet-proof glass? And who really is the prisoner: the one in front of or the one behind all this?

In our society, the mere assertion of the notion of private property also asserts the rule of violence, and the more property we claim, the more enmeshed we become in violence. The very notion that I may own something "privately" implies that I claim a right to its exclusive use and enjoyment and that I can decide who else may or may not use or enjoy the thing I own. Behind this idea stands a social convention, a widespread agreement that when something is privately owned, control over the exclusiveness of deciding how to use it is ultimately enforced by the power of the state through law, and finally, through the instruments of violence that are "legitimate" powers of the state, that is, the police and the military.

When a culture, such as that of consumerism, evolves that posits the acquisition and ownership of material things as the ultimate values of human life, the members of that kind of a society continually dance on a powder keg. Indeed, it is a miracle that we don't see more violence than we do. The manufacture of material goods entails inflicting violence on nature, which is magnified in direct proportion to our craving for larger and larger quantities of such goods. Competition for access to the goods also entails violence (though much of it is emotional and psychological rather than physical), and the ceaseless efforts of the consumer system itself to hyper-stimulate the desire for its products is another form of manipulative, often aggressive intrusion. That this sometimes reaches absurd extremes is evident in the comment of one Disney Corporation executive who announced to a marketing conference, "Antisocial behavior in pursuit of a product is a good thing."[1]

What is seldom widely appreciated is that inequity, violence, environmental destruction, and social unrest can interact in a positive feedback system that may drag the poor and affluent alike toward destruction. In 1994, Robert Kaplan published a much discussed article titled "The Coming Anarchy."[2] In it, he relates some examples of African countries where poverty forced the over-exploitation of ecosystems and contributed to the deterioration of the infrastructure and to political corruption. These conditions came to feed on each other in a way that was not only damaging to the immediate prospects of the societies engulfed in the difficulties, but also promised to compromise their future ability ever to fashion anything else. "Recovery" for these societies now depends entirely on outside assistance.

One of the most chilling implications of Kaplan's observations, however, is the possibility that consumerism might bring the entire planet to a similar fate. In such circumstances, trying to identify what is the first cause of the difficulty — corrupt political institutions, damaged environments, rampant poverty, or collapsing social institutions — is as useless as arguing about which comes first, the chicken or the egg. In this insttance, however, there would be no "outside" assistance available.

The choice to live more simply in a material sense is thus in part a decision to step back from this whole system — to step back from the violence done to nature in manufacturing unnecessary products, the violence done to one's neighbors (or the threat of it) implied by exclusive ownership, the violence left for future generations in toxic wastes, the remains of military campaigns, and the legacy of remembered suffering. The choice to live more simply is also the choice to step back from the whole cultural myth that anything of lasting value can be secured for human beings through the pursuit of limitless consumption.

Simplicity as Living on One's Fair Earth Share

Voluntary simplicity can also contain a "double movement": *both* a "stepping back" from consumptive materialism and the violence it entails *and* a stepping forward to take up the work of Earth-healing and creating justice and peace.

As we have already mentioned in the section on the ecological reasons for practicing simplicity (Chapter 5), the individual decision to desist from unnecessary consumption effectively leaves resources "in the ground." These resources are then potentially available to those who currently don't consume enough to satisfy even their basic needs as well as to future generations. Moreover, the decision to step back from consumerism directly avoids the creation of those toxic wastes that are inescapable by-products of many manufacturing processes. For those of us living in affluent, developed countries, such a decision may contribute to a reduction in what might be termed "environmental inequity", which of course has its economic aspects but consists essentially in the appropriation of resources and the ecological carrying capacity from beyond the borders of our own countries.

Rees and Wackernagel have clearly demonstrated that the consumerist lifestyle requires vast areas of "appropriated carrying capacity" outside the actual geopolitical boundaries of developed countries themselves.[3] For example, the lifestyle of consumerism in the Canadian city of Vancouver is sustained only because the population in the city proper draws upon a land area equivalent to 178 times its political area to supply food, fiber, building materials, and energy and to absorb its wastes.[4] The United States of America appropriates a carrying capacity about 1.8 times larger than its own land area to support the lifestyles of its citizens, while other industrialized countries, such as the Netherlands and Belgium, appropriate up to 19 and 14 times their own land area respectively.[5]

> *Affluence is attainable by a minority of Earth's people only because the remainder of the planet's resources, people, and oceans are exploited beyond the limits that would apply if everyone had a "fair share."*

These observations relate directly to issues of both domestic and international social justice and equity. Any society (or individual) living beyond its means must live at someone else's expense. Affluence is attainable by a minority of Earth's people only because the remainder of the planet's resources, people, and oceans are exploited beyond the limits that would apply if everyone had a "fair share." This situation sets the stage for a great deal of domestic and international violence, contention, and unrest. Those addicted to affluence are inclined to maintain (and, if necessary, enforce by use of arms) the social and economic arrangements that supply their addictions. Those who see their own share of resources dwindling before the ever-expanding appetites of the affluent are driven toward conflict by their sheer need to survive and their legitimate desire for some measure of comfort and security for themselves and their children.

Accepted doctrine claims that these inequities will be redressed through economic growth. The affluent need not share their wealth since the lot of the poor can be improved by increasing the overall size of the economic pie. This view is plausible, however, only if the "economic pie" grows faster than the population *and* if the growth of that pie is more equitably shared in the future than it has been in the past. Today, the argument is absurd. Today, the correlation between affluence in some parts of the world and the death of cultures, countries, and ecosystems in other parts of the world is stark.

The benefits of economic growth over the last three decades have disproportionately flowed to an ever-dwindling number of fantastically wealthy individuals and corporations rather than diffusing more equitably throughout the world. The Worldwatch Institute has estimated that between 1960 and 1990, the share of global income going to the richest 20 percent of Earth's people increased from 70.2 percent to 82.8 percent, while the share of income going to the poorest 20 percent dropped from 2.3 percent to 1.3 percent. During the same period, the ratio of the average income in affluent countries to the average income in poor countries shifted from 30:1 in 1960 to 64:1 in 1990. As well, there are growing income discrepancies even *within* the affluent societies themselves. Finally, the rate of growth in the world economy is itself grinding to halt: overall growth in global economic output peaked in the 1960-70 decade at 5.2 percent and has declined steadily to an estimated 0.9 percent in the 1990s, with *per capita* economic growth actually *declining* in the 1990s by -0.8 percent.[6] Thus, the social and environmental unsustainability of consumerism is becoming glaringly evident; its promise to redress social and economic inequity is clearly a hollow promise.

The choice to live more simply, to live within our means, is the choice to live more sustainably. This reduces not only the financial stress on individuals but also the energy and resource demands placed on the environment. Hence pressures to over-exploit resources and to appropriate the development agendas of other cultures and countries are reduced. To the degree that material needs are simplified, they can be met more sustainably through the resources available in our own bioregions. This can reduce the need to protect our means of livelihood through violence, militarism, and war. It is unlikely, for example, that the Persian Gulf War would have been fought if the United States, Europe, and Japan were all fully functioning solar economies.

Voluntary simplicity has the additional feature that it tends to position *sharing* rather than *growth* as the centerpiece of justice. Belief in growth allows us essentially to avoid self-examination and personal change in coming to terms with human needs. If I believe that the *economy* will grow and thereby resolve the problems of poverty, competition, militarism, and social injustice, then *I* do not have to grow in order to resolve them, which would be a much more challenging task than leaving it to "the economy." In this manner, a belief in economics and affluence can rob people of the opportunity to develop as human beings. It short-circuits all sorts of opportunities for moral deepening, developing social interdependence and solidarity, and learning how to realize aspirations for a just and equitable society through personal action.

Moving from the Personal to the Collective

So far, we have been exploring voluntary simplicity as essentially a *personal* practice of living. It is often observed, however, that the causes of poverty, militarism, and other forms of social injustice are *collective* and *systemic*. For some reason, we then infer that individual lifestyle choices will make no difference in reversing large-scale systemic problems. But to say that something is systemic is merely to say that it is widely shared or commonly practiced. To identify a problem as having a systemic aspect or wide prevalence in no manner invalidates individual responses to it. In fact, they are required.

The practice of voluntary simplicity implies the adoption of personal life choices that are inherently congruent with justice and equity, regardless of whether or not these are effectively addressed by collective institutions. The practice of simple living by individuals sets up a dissonance within societies systemically inclined toward inequity. Practicing simple living must eventually have its effects, and will certainly contribute more towards establishing justice than a society whose individual members actively collude with inequitable institutions.

In addition, those who embrace simpler living can also choose to apply their dividends of saved time, energy, and money toward the establishment of more just and equitable institutions. Indeed, surveys of the essential values and practices that characterize voluntary simplicity indicate strong commitments by many of its practitioners toward involvement as volunteers in social, environmental, and cultural activities. This is an instance of both stepping away from an old system of inequity and violence at the same time as stepping forward in favor of an alternative.

Voluntary simplicity has been termed "non-violent insurrection." In many ways, this description is apt. Simple living steps away from the "normal" methods of bringing about change in mainstream society, which are essentially violent. The system that enmeshes us is elegantly designed to deal with violent opposition. It sees the potential for violence everywhere, prepares for it always, lives in fear of it continually, and believes it to be inescapable. Much more difficult for it to deal with is even one individual who quietly shrugs and says, "I don't believe in you anymore."

Simplicity as an Act of Solidarity

A number of researchers who focus on the determinates of human happiness have noted that we often gauge our own level of well-being by comparing ourselves to others. Social comparison forms the basis for how we estimate the "progress" we are making in achieving the "good life." It has been our propensity to compare ourselves with others that some thinkers believe explains how we might quadruple consumption — as we have in North America since 1960 — without quadrupling happiness. While overall consumption (with its attendant effects on the environment) is increasing, we don't see ourselves getting ahead of our neighbors and so we're no happier, statistically speaking, than we were in 1960. This sort of finding must also give the lie to the argument that economic growth can be compared to "a tide that lifts all boats" and therefore has the potential to increase the general well-being. In fact, growth is a tide that seems to lift some boats while sinking others. But even if it did lift them all equally, what we think makes life better is seeing our own boat go higher than our neighbor's.

Some recent research on the relationship between poverty and health revealed the somewhat startling finding that the two are only very loosely connected.[7] While it is generally true that the rich fare better in terms of incidence of illness and life span than do the poor, the richer members of societies with low GDPs fare better than the poorer members of societies with higher GDPs. In some cases, the poorer members of richer countries are actually financially richer than the richer members of poorer countries, yet they suffer the same shortened life spans and increased rates of illness as their poorer counterparts in the less developed world. What seems to be at work in these data is not any very clear connection between the absolute number of dollars one earns and personal health (given a certain minimum), but the process of social comparison that contributes stress to the lives of those who perceive themselves to be less advantaged than everyone else they see around them.

It is in this context that we can see the practice of voluntary simplicity as an act of social solidarity that is driven by compassion. When people choose to live simply, they choose to stand shoulder-to-shoulder with those in society who may feel dispirited by their prospects as they compare themselves with others. By living simply, the practitioner ceases to be an object of stressful comparison for his or her neighbor.

More important is what the celebrants of simplicity can bring to the materially less advantaged members of society. It may be that a great measure of the emotional pain of poverty (involuntary simplicity) arises from the belief that the only life worth having is a life of affluence and consumerism. Advertising organizations spend billions trying to convince everyone that this is the case, wealthy and poor alike. But those who have embraced simple living voluntarily have usually done so for good reasons, reasons that hold sufficient value to compensate for the supposed "sacrifices" of stepping back from the general scramble for fashion and luxury. People who are in touch with such values have a great deal to offer to those who are not in touch with them and, in choosing a life in solidarity with those who have no choice, may, paradoxically, open new choices for those who thought they had none.

... choosing to live simply in solidarity with those who think they have no choice testifies to a hidden truth that gradually becomes more apparent as we grow in mindfulness: We are all connected.

Finally, choosing to live simply in solidarity with those who think they have no choice testifies to a hidden truth that gradually becomes more apparent as we grow in mindfulness: *We are all connected.* The efforts we make to appear better or more accomplished or more affluent than our neighbors are attempts to fashion "images" rather than to participate in the reality of our connectedness and relationship with all things. In the fear that grows out of the illusion of our personal separateness, we build artificial personas instead of intimacy, knowledge, and connection. Those choosing to live in simplicity and solidarity with others set aside these wasteful expenditures of money and energy to express in the outer pattern of their lives the inner connection they already experience with humanity as a whole, and with the greater life of the world. In this sense, the practice of simplicity becomes a visible sign of the honor we give to non-material values, an evidence of connection, a proof of love, another step along the path of walking the talk of justice and equity.

PART IV

HOW VOLUNTARY SIMPLICITY
BENEFITS US ALL

13

Writing a New Story for Our Culture: Simplicity and Belonging to the Earth

Simple living is not an end in itself. We may save money (but not always) and increase our freedom and security (again not always), and our life may reflect the special beauty of simplicity (but only if we cultivate the tastes appropriate to it). But more than anything else, simplicity is a means of clearing a "space" within which something new can be born. It is this "something new" that simplicity is for.

The "space" we clear can be physical as we reduce the clutter in our lives. It can also be social as we may trade some financial gains for more time to enjoy family, friends, and community. The "space" we open may be emotional insofar as we reduce stress, worry, fear, competitiveness, and so on. We may also gain relaxation, peace, and co-operative relations with others. The "space" can also be spiritual since the old gods of consumerism are deposed in favour of a new spiritual awareness.

There is another aspect of this "something new" that has to do with what *human beings* are for. It is the purposes of our lives that must expand to fill the space provided by simplicity if both simplicity and our lives are to be meaningful.

At its most basic, the gift of life is a gift of time, energy, and freedom. But nothing about simply being alive answers the next question: How shall we use our time, energy, and freedom to express the meaning of our life in the world? Put differently: What shall our being alive amount to?

We always answer this question in some way, even if we just repeat what we learned growing up.

In his thought-provoking book *Ishmael*, Daniel Quinn says that every society and every individual life is a story about the questions What is the world for? What am I for?

The basic story of consumer culture says that *the Earth was created for the use and pleasure of human beings and* that *the purpose of human life is to conquer and subdue the Earth for human purposes, including the delusion that we can live without connection to the sacred powers.* The result of living out this story is what we see around us: a damaged environment, social inequity and violence, psychological and emotional pain, and spiritual emptiness. If we find this story unfulfilling, two things are required: first, that we stop acting out the old story, and second, that we start acting out a new story. In general, people don't give up their old story until they have a new one.

Voluntary simplicity is a blank book in which we can write a new story ... Instead of telling a story about how the Earth belongs to us, we could tell a story about how we belong to the Earth.

Voluntary simplicity is a blank book in which we can write a new story. Daniel Quinn also suggests an exciting opening strategy: Instead of telling a story about how the Earth belongs to us, we could tell a story about how we belong to the Earth.

We are conscious, spiritual, reflective beings capable of living with simplicity and elegance in caring for the Earth we belong to. It would be a cause of regret if we just consumed the planet and left in its place the refuse of a very brief and selfish party. It would also be a cause of regret if we passed our days living in the fear of death, the denial of our interdependence with other species, and the futile delusion that we can somehow control and dominate the living communities that sustain us.

If human beings belong to the Earth and living things depend on each other, then we all belong to each other. Now a new story, which is also an ancient story, can begin. It will be a story about belonging and will express itself through acts of belonging and of relationship. This is the meaning of love, and love is life in consciousness of Divine Being. Might we come to realize that the idea of the human domination of the Earth is part of an old story that a growing consciousness of our life in Divine Being can change? Might we think that by becoming more conscious of Divine Being manifesting itself through us we aspire not to transcend our life on Earth but to live in a sacred and compassionate way within it, as part of it?

Simple living presents us with the challenge not to veer back into nostalgia, myth, primitivism, false asceticism, or any of the other "-isms" that have been part of our history. We cannot return to being hunter-gatherers. But we can tell ourselves different stories about the meaning of our being here on Earth. We can see simplicity as *part* of that new society that will appear based on the new story. *We belong to the Earth, and the Earth belongs to Divine Being.* We were made to tend a garden we belong in.

The emotional linchpin of the old/new story is our fear of death. Our society took a rather dramatic turn exactly when we humans tried to take control over our own lives and deaths in defiance of Divine Being. Our basic choice in life is either to try to hold our lives in our own hands or to entrust them to the hands of Divine Being. From this choice, everything else follows, for good or ill. Our lives are, *in fact*, in the hands of Divine Being — always have been and always will be. It is when we imagine that we can take them back that we harm ourselves, each other, and the Earth. The issue then is not really whether we will live or die, but whether we will live and die in the hands of Divine Being or alone in our own hands and the hands of our technology.

The fear of death may also account for some people's uneasiness with voluntary simplicity. Letting go of material possessions foreshadows the greater letting-go that is death. Maybe it is even a kind of training for it! Maybe we accumulate possessions to bolster the illusion that we are safe from death.

If I look into the "space" created by simplicity, I see people living differently. I see us applying ourselves creatively to belonging to the world and to each other. I see people using science to understand and appreciate the world we belong to, not to manipulate it for personal gain or to avoid death, but simply to understand and appreciate it and to know how to live in it with greater and greater harmony. I see us using technology to enhance our belonging to the Earth and to each other, not to increase profit and luxury for a few. I see people working hard to grow spiritually, to appreciate beauty, and to cultivate compassion, peace, tolerance, and social harmony. I imagine us travelling to the stars not as conquerors looking for new planets to subdue, but rather as people looking for other worlds and other beings to appreciate and understand.

Developing consciousness of our "belonging" to the Earth and to Divine Being calls for the practice both of *simplicity* (which provides the "space" for new awareness) and of *mindfulness* (which is the method for developing new awareness). We cannot understand that we belong to the Earth unless we somehow experience our belonging. We cannot experience our belonging unless we become aware of it. We cannot become aware of it unless we clear away whatever might distract us from developing new awareness and re-direct our attention to those experiences that testify to our belonging in creation.

Developing mindfulness requires no exceptional aptitude. If we could measure awareness, we would probably find out that we all have about the same "amount" of it. The issue isn't to "expand" awareness so that we "have" *more* of it, but to *redirect* our attention so that we notice different aspects of our experience and our place in the world. Both the artist and the art lover have the same kind of eyes. Yet artists direct their attention in such a way that their works of art draw *our* attention to things we never noticed before. The gift of artistic talent makes it seem that such people "see the invisible" when in fact we might see the very same thing if only we directed our attention appropriately.

So what is voluntary simplicity for? It is for developing mindfulness. And mindfulness helps us discover that we belong to the Earth and, together with the Earth, in the hands of Divine Being. Knowing this makes all the difference. It will help us tell a new story with our lives.

Endnotes

Chapter 1

1 Daniel Quinn, *Ishmael* (New York: Bantam Books, 1992).

2 Anthony Spina, "Research shows new aspects of voluntary simplicity," *www.sln.net*, 1999.

3 Duane Elgin, *Voluntary Simplicity* (New York: William Morrow, 1993), p. 3.

4 Richard Gregg, "Voluntary Simplicity," *Visva-Bharati Quarterly*, August 1936.

5 The "delphi method" was invented in the 1970s by social researchers to provide a vehicle for large numbers of people knowledgeable about a certain subject, but having different opinions on it, to arrive at a consensus. A delphi process begins with a standard set of questions to which all participants respond. The responses are collated in various ways and then fed back to participants. The participants read the summaries of all the responses and then answer the same or similar questions again. Through successive rounds of this process, a consensus of views tends to emerge, not necessarily reflecting complete agreement on all points but clearly identifying "core" areas of agreement on the subject at hand.

In 1997, I invited participants in an Internet discussion group on voluntary simplicity to take part in such a delphi process. It was opened with three questions: (1) What do you think are the *essential values* of voluntary simplicity? (2) What do you think are the *essential practices* comprising voluntary simplicity? (3) What do you think are the *key benefits* of voluntary simplicity? Among those participating in the process, a significant degree of consensus was reached after six delphi "rounds." While the results of this process certainly do not purport to be representative of the North American population as a whole (the process was not conducted with the rigor required for truly reliable social research), they were nonetheless interesting.

6 Paul Hawken, *The Ecology of Commerce: A Declaration of Sustainability* (New York: HarperCollins, 1993), p. 37.

7 Richard Rohr, *Simplicity: The Art of Living* (New York: Crossroad Publishing Company, 1991), p. 59.

8 David Shi, *The Simple Life: Plain Living and High Thinking in American Culture* (New York: Oxford University Press, 1985).

9   Henry David Thoreau, *Walden and Other Writings* (New York: Bantam, 1989).

10 Tracey McBride, *Frugal Luxuries: Simple Pleasures to Enhance Your Life and Comfort Your Soul* (New York: Bantam, 1997).

11 E.F. Schumacher, *Small Is Beautiful: A Study of Economics as if People Mattered* (London: Vintage, 1993).

12 Ernest Callenbach, *Living Cheaply With Style* (Berkeley: Ronin Publications, 1992). See also Amy Dacyczyn, *The Tightwad Gazette: Promising Thrift As a Viable Alternative Lifestyle* (New York: Villard Books, 1993).

13 Joe Dominguez and Vicki Robin, *Your Money Or Your Life: Transforming Your Relationship With Money and Achieving Financial Independence* (New York: Penguin, 1992).

14 Elgin, p. 113.

15 The Harwood Group, *Yearning For Balance: Views of Americans on Consumption, Materialism, and the Environment.* (Takoma Park: Merck Family Fund, 1995), p. 12.

16 Anthony C. Spina, 1999. "Research shows new aspects of voluntary simplicity," *www.slnet.com.* 1999.

17 Fritjof Capra, *The Turning Point: Science, Society and the Rising Culture* (New York: Bantam Books, 1982). See also James Glieck, *Chaos: Making A New Science* (New York: Penguin, 1987) and Margaret J. Wheatley, *Leadership and the New Science: Learning About Organization from an Orderly Universe* (San Francisco: Berrett-Koehler Publishers, 1994).

18 Alanna Mitchell, Karen Unland, and Chad Skelton, "Canadians pay for busy lives" *Globe and Mail,* July 19, 1997. p. 7.

19 Cecile Andrews, *Circle of Simplicity: Returning to the Good Life* (New York: HarperCollins, 1997).

20 Sarah Ban Breathnach, *Simple Abundance: A Daybook of Comfort and Joy* (New York: Warner Books, 1995).

21 Mark A. Burch, *Simplicity: Notes, Stories and Exercises for Developing Unimaginable Wealth* (Gabriola Island: New Society Publishers, 1995).

22 Mennonite Central Committee, *Trek: Venture Into a World of Enough* (Winnipeg: Mennonite Central Committee, 1997).

23 Michael Schut, *Simplicity as Compassion: Voluntary Simplicity From a Christian Perspective* (Seattle: Earth Ministry, 1996).

Chapter 2

1   The Harwood Group, *Yearning for Balance: Views of Americans on Consumption, Materialism, and the Environment* (Takoma Park: Merck Family Fund, 1995).

2 Margaret J. Wheatley, and Myron Kellner-Rogers, *A Simpler Way* (San Francisco: Berrett-Koehler Publishers, 1996).

3 Arthur Koestler, *The Ghost in the Machine* (London: Arkana Books, 1967).

4 Gregory Bateson, *Steps to an Ecology of Mind* (New York: Ballantine Books, 1972). See also his *Mind and Nature: A Necessary Unity* (New York: Bantam, 1979).

5 Fritjof Capra, *The Turning Point* (New York: Bantam, 1992).

6 Ira Progoff, *Depth Psychology and Modern Man* (New York: Dialogue House, 1969).

7 Jan Christian Smuts, *Holism and Evolution* (New York: MacMillan, 1926).

8 Edmund Sinnott, *Mind, Matter and Man* (New York: Harper and Row, 1957).

9 C.G. Jung, (private communication).

10 Wheatley and Kellner-Rogers, p. 100.

11 Lin Yutang, trans., "Book of Mencius," in *The Wisdom of Confucius* (New York: Random House, 1966), p. 283-4.

Chapter 3

1 Lin Yutang, trans., *The Wisdom of Lao-Tse* (New York: Modern Library, 1976), p. 87.

2 E. F. Schumacher, *Small is Beautiful: A Study of Economics as if People Mattered* (London: Vintage, 1973).

3 Timothy Miller, *How To Want What You Have* (New York: Avon Books, 1995).

4 Erich Fromm, *To Have Or To Be* (New York: Continuum Publishing, 1976). See also Paul L. Wachtel, *The Poverty of Affluence: A Psychological Portrait of the American Way of Life* (Philadelphia: New Society Publishers, 1989).

Chapter 4

1 The Harwood Group, *Yearning for Balance: Views of Americans on Consumption, Materialism, and the Environment* (Takoma Park: Merck Family Fund, 1995).

2 Jonathan Freedman quoted in Paul Wachtel, *Poverty of Affluence* Lester R. Brown quoted in *State of the World, 1991*, World Watch Institute (New York: W. W. Norton, 1991), p. 162.

3 Wendell Berry, "Does Community have Value?" in *Home Economics: Fourteen Essays by Wendell Berry* (San Francisco: North Point Press, 1987).

4 Berry, p. 183.

5 Wolfgang Sachs, in interview "Drowning in Stuff: Alternatives to Consumerism," Canadian Broadcasting Corporation, May 1999.

6 Margaret J. Wheatley, *Leadership and The New Science: Learning About Organization from an Orderly Universe* (San Francisco: Berrett-Koehler Publishers, 1996), pp. 24-45.

7 According to recent research, cars and light trucks have about three times the overall environmental impact per passenger mile as intercity rail, air, or bus travel. See Michael Brower and Warren Leon *The Consumer's Guide to Effective Environmental Choices* (New York: Three Rivers Press, 1999), p. 57.

8 William E. Rees, "Reducing the ecological footprint of consumption," A paper prepared for The Workshop on Policy Measures for Changing Consumption Patterns, Korea Environmental Technology Research Institute, Seoul, Korea, 1995, p. 3.

9 Paul Hawken, *The Ecology of Commerce: A Declaration of Sustainability* (New York: HarperCollins, 1993).

Chapter 5

1 Mark Burch, private communication to Internet discussion list, Positive Futures, 1997.

2 Mathis Wackernagel, and William Rees *Our Ecological Footprint: Reducing Human Impact on the Earth* (Gabriola Island: New Society Publishers, 1995).

3 Michael Brower and Warren Leon, *The Consumer's Guide to Effective Environmental Choices: Practical Advice From the Union of Concerned Scientists.* (New York: Three Rivers Press, 1999), p. 4.

4 Lester R. Brown and Hal Kane, *Full House: Reassessing The Earth's Population Carrying Capacity* (New York: W. W. Norton, 1994).

5 Paul Hawken, *The Ecology of Commerce: A Declaration of Sustainability* (New York: HarperCollins, 1994).

6 Steve Nadis and James J. MacKenzie, *Car Trouble* (Boston: Beacon Press, 1993).

7 Gregg Marland, Ph.D., Environmental Sciences Division, Oak Ridge National Laboratory, Oak Ridge, TN, (Private communication, 1998).

8 Campbell and Laherre, Petroconsultants Pty. Ltd., *World Oil Supply 1930-2050* (Privately commissioned study by the oil industry, 1995).

9 *The Winnipeg Free Press*, October 24, 1998, p. B24.

10 Paul Hawken, *The Ecology of Commerce*, p. 3.

11 David Pimentel, "Livestock Production: Energy Inputs and the Environment" (Private communication, 1999).

12 Lester R. Brown and Hal Kane, *Full House*, p. 168.

13 Alan Durning, *How Much Is Enough? The Consumer Society and the Future of the Earth* (New York: W. W. Norton, 1992), pp. 65-68.

14 R. Parson, *UV Radiation and its Effects*, Internet FAQ, 1994.

15 Colin Campbell, "The end of cheap oil." *Scientific American*, (1998), Vol. 279.

16 Alan Durning, Quoted in reference to "Escape From Affluenza", PBS Television, 1998.

17 Michael Brower and Warren Leon, p. 4.

Chapter 6

1 Mark Burch, spiritual diary, 1996.

2 Swamigal, *Dhammapada,* quoted by R. K. Aiyar, *The Call of the Jagadguru* in Goldian VandenBroeck, *Less Is More* (Rochester: Inner Traditions International, 1996), p. 102.

3 *Confucius,* XI. 15.

4 In Goldian VandenBroeck, p. 134.

5 Lin Yutang, ed & transl, *The Wisdom of Lao-Tse* (New York: Modern Library, 1976), p. 79.

6 David Cooper, *Silence, Simplicity and Solitude: A Guide for Spiritual Retreat* (New York: Bell Tower, 1992), p. 106.

7 Dom O. Rousseau, (OSB) "Poverty in the rule of St. Benedict" in Lancelot C. Sheppard, transl., *Religious Life IV: Poverty* (London: Blackfriars Publications, 1954).

8 Philip Kapleau, *The Three Pillars of Zen: Teaching, Practice, Enlightenment* (Boston: Beacon Press, 1965), p. 57.

Chapter 7

1 Charles T. Tart, *Living The Mindful Life: A Handbook for Living in the Present Moment* (Boston: Shambala Publications, 1994), p. 50.

2 Jon Kabat-Zinn, *Wherever You Are, There You Are: Mindfulness Meditation in Everyday Life* (New York: Hyperion, 1994), pp. 47, 58, 61.

3 Thich Nhat Hanh, *Being Peace* (Berkeley: Parallax Press, 1996), p. 61.

Chapter 8

1 Lin Yutang, ed. & transl., *The Wisdom of Lao-Tse* (New York: Modern Library, 1976), p. 176.

2 Timothy Miller, *How To Want What You Have* (New York: Avon, 1995).

3 Jay Hanson, "Neurological effects of television" (various sources cited) Internet discussion list, August 1996, sustainable development@civic.net

4 *Affluenza*, PBS Television, Nov. 1997.

5 E. F. Schumacher, *Small is Beautiful: A Study of Economics As If People Mattered* (London: Vintage, 1993), p. 42.

6 Joe Dominguez and Vicki Robin, *Your Money Or Your Life: Transforming Your Relationship with Money and Achieving Financial Independence* (New York: Penguin Books, 1992).

Chapter 9

1 The Harwood Group, *Yearning For Balance: Views of Americans on Consumption, Materialism, and the Environment* (Takoma Park: Merck Family Fund, 1995), p. 14.

2 Harvey Schachter, "The Hurrier I Go, The Behinder I Get" *The Globe and Mail,* 15 May 1999.

3 Jon Kabat-Zinn, *Wherever You Go, There You Are: Mindfulness Meditation in Everyday Life* (New York: Hyperion Books, 1994), p. 69.

4 Ira Progoff, *At A Journal Workshop* (New York: Dialogue House, 1975).

5 Joe Dominguez and Vicki Robin, *Your Money Or Your Life: Transforming Your Relationship with Money and Achieving Financial Independence* (New York: Penguin Books, 1992).

6 Alan Durning, *How Much Is Enough? The Consumer Society and the Future of the Earth* (New York: W. W. Norton, 1992).

Chapter 10

1 Ellen Goodman, *New Road Map Foundation Newsletter.*

2 Ira Progoff, *Depth Psychology and Modern Man* (New York: Dialogue House, 1959).

3 Charles Long, *How to Survive Without a Salary* (Toronto: Warwick Publishing, 1993).

4 Roy Morrison, *We Build The Road as We Travel* (Philadelphia: New Society Publishers, 1991).

5 Kathryn McCamant and Charles Durrett, *Co-housing: A Contemporary Approach to Housing Ourselves* (Berkely: Ten Speed Press, 1993) See also Connie McLaughlin and Gordon Davidson, *Builders of the Dawn: Community Lifestyles in a Changing World* (Seattle: Book Publishing Co., 1999).

6 Ken Norwood and Kathleen Smith, *Rebuilding Community in America: Housing for Ecological Living, Personal Empowerment, and the New Extended Family* (Berkely: Shared Living Resources, 1995). See also Robert and Diane Gilman, *Eco-villages And Sustainable Communities: A Report for Gaia Trust* (Langley: Context Institute, 1996).

7   Susan Meeker-Lowry, *Invested in the Common Good* (Gabriola Island: New Society Publishers, 1995), pp. 149-154. See also Nigel Leach and John and Mandy Winkworth, *Frequently Asked Questions About LETS, Version 1.0* (Manchester: LETSgo Manchester, 1996) (with contributions from Landsman Community Services Ltd.). From: mailbase-admin@mailbase.ac.uk.

8   Contact the E. F. Schumacher Society, 140 Jug End Road, Great Barrington, MA 01230; efssociety@aol.com

9   Francis Moore Lappé, *Diet For a Small Planet* (New York: Random House, 1982).

Chapter 11

1   Paul Hawken, *The Ecology of Commerce: A Declaration of Sustainability.* (New York: HarperCollins, 1994).

2   Wendell Berry, *Home Economics: Fourteen Essays by Wendell Berry* (San Francisco: North Point Press, 1987). See particularly his essays "Getting Along With Nature" and "Two Economies."

3   William James, *The Will To Believe* (New York: Dover Publications, 1956), pp. 1-2.

4   Daniel Quinn, *Ishmael* (New York: Bantam Books, 1992).

Chapter 12

1   *Affluenza* PBS Television, 1997.

2   Robert D. Kaplan, "The Coming Anarchy," *The Atlantic Monthly*, February 1994, pp. 44-76.

3   Mathis Wackernagel and William Rees, *Our Ecological Footprint: Reducing Human Impact on the Earth* (Gabriola Island: New Society Publishers, 1995).

4   William E. Rees, "Reducing the ecological footprint of consumption," A paper prepared for The Workshop on Policy Measures for Changing Consumption Patterns, Korea Environmental Technology Research Institute, Seoul, Korea, 1995, p. 3.

5   Wackernagel and Rees, p. 97.

6   Lester R. Brown and Hal Kane, *Full House: Reassessing the Earth's Population Carrying Capacity* (New York: W.W. Norton, 1994), pp. 46-47.

7   Peter Montague, "The major causes of illness," *Rachel's Environment & Health Weekly*, No. 584, (5 February 1998), p. 2.

Recommended Readings on
Voluntary Simplicity

Chapter 1

Bender, Sue. *Plain and Simple: A Woman's Journey to the Amish*. San Francisco: Harper, 1989. This is a lovely, honest, and deeply reflective book about one woman's emotional and spiritual dance with the Amish. It focuses on the fusion of homely arts like quilt-making with spirituality and simplicity. It quite wonderfully captures the airy, clean emotional overtones of simple living grounded in faith.

Elgin, Duane. *Voluntary Simplicity: Toward a Way of Life That is Outwardly Simple, Inwardly Rich*. New York: William Morrow, 1993. This was one of the first books on voluntary simplicity; it appeared at least a decade before the most recent spate of popular interest in the subject.

Shi, David E. *The Simple Life: Plain Living and High Thinking in American Culture*. New York: Oxford University Press, 1986. This is an excellent and highly readable, yet very scholarly survey of the role of simple living in American culture from colonial times to the 1960s counter-culture revolution. The book well describes the ambivalence surrounding simple living in the American psyche.

Thoreau, Henry David. *Walden and Other Writings*. New York: Bantam Books, 1989. This is a classic account of Thoreau's two years living by the banks of Walden Pond in 19th century New England. It is loaded with insightful critical observations of the vain strivings of ordinary mortals for peace through possessions and an unparalleled anthem to simple, self-reliant living.

VandenBroeck, Goldian. *Less Is More: The Art of Voluntary Poverty*. New York: Harper Colophon Books, 1978. This anthology is a wonderful collection of quotations spanning three millennia of mostly western philosophy and spirituality addressing the delights of simple living, as well as a spirited and often amusing critique of the "ways of the world."

Chapter 2

Sinetar, Marsha. *Do What You Love, The Money Will Follow*. Mahwah: Paulist Press, 1995. Marsha Sinetar is also author of *Monks and Mystics in Ordinary Life* and has a fine sense of how spirituality permeates the ordinary acts of living. In *Do What You Love* she zeroes in on one of the main principles of voluntary simplicity, namely that our lives gain coherence and meaning when we attend to our loves.

Culp, Stephanie. *Streamlining Your Life: A 5-Point Plan for Uncomplicated Living.* Cincinnati: Writer's Digest Books, 1991. This book has many tips about organizing our lives through reducing clutter and focusing on clear goals. It doesn't advocate voluntary simplicity so much as personal efficiency in applying effort. Nonetheless, for some people, the suggestions in this book may prove valuable.

Luhrs, Janet. *The Simple Living Guide.* New York: Broadway Books, 1997. A massive tome of reflections, stories, sources, advice, and exercises to promote your practice of voluntary simplicity. Janet Luhrs is editor of *Simple Living Quarterly*, a magazine about simple living.

McBride, Tracey. *Frugal Luxuries: Simple Pleasures to Enhance Your Life and Comfort Your Soul.* New York: Bantam Books, 1997. A beautiful book with a woman's touch and sensitivity to the sensuous delights of simple living with mindfulness and gratitude. Includes many suggestions on how to fill our lives with a sense of luxury on very slender means.

Chapter 4

Levering, Frank and Wanda Urbanska. *Simple Living: One Couple's Search for a Better Life.* New York: Penguin Books, 1992. A biographical account of a Los Angeles couple's search for the simple life in an apple orchard. This lighthearted book is written in the first person by both authors.

Nearing, Scott and Helen. *Living The Good Life.* This book helped launch the "back to the land" movement of the 1970s with the personal account of the Nearings, who left the city and returned to rural homesteading to discover a simple and satisfying life.

Shaffer, Carolyn R. and Kristin Anundson. *Creating Community Anywhere: Finding Support and Connection in a Fragmented World.* New York: Perigee Books, 1993.

Wachtel, Paul L. 1989. *The Poverty of Affluence.* Philadelphia: New Society Publishers, 1989. This book begins as a fairly incisive discussion of the psychological and social maladies related to affluence and the pursuit of affluence. It tends to digress a bit into discussions of the shortcomings of various explanations that have been offered of the damage caused by affluence, but also contains many useful insights.

Chapter 5

Brower, Michael and Warren Leon. *The Consumer's Guide to Effective Environmental Choices: Practical Advice From the Union of Concerned Scientists*. New York: Three Rivers Press, 1999. This is one of the best documented, most accessible, and "simplest" guidebooks for making strategic changes in consumption patterns that have maximum environmental benefit.

Durning, Alan. *How Much Is Enough? The Consumer Society and the Future of the Earth*. New York: W.W. Norton, 1992. Chronicles in detail the environmental impacts of the consumer society and the spread of the ideology of consumerism. If you ever had any doubt that consumerism was damaging to children and other living creatures, read this book.

Hawken, Paul. *The Ecology of Commerce: A Declaration of Sustainability*. New York: HarperCollins, 1994. This is a brilliant piece of work that insightfully identifies the sources of the socially and environmentally self-destructive behaviour of business and industry and makes many cogent proposals about how to move toward a "restorative economy," an economy that restores nature as it provides for human needs.

Chapter 6

Cooper, David A. *Silence, Simplicity and Solitude: A Guide for Spiritual Retreat*. New York: Bell Tower, 1992. David Cooper's book is one of my favourite source books; it deals very thoroughly with every aspect of retreat for spiritual and personal development. He covers such mundane things as considerations of setting and diet during retreat exercises, but also key aspects of meditation practice and the process of identifying spiritual "directors" to assist with personal growth during retreats.

Easwaran, Eknath. 1989. *The Compassionate Universe: The Power of The Individual to Heal the Environment*. Petaluma: Nilgiri Press, 1989. This is a beautiful book reflecting on how we can live from a spiritual perspective informed teachings of Mahatma Gandhi. The focus is upon everyday life and ways individuals can change their lives through the practice of mindful simplicity to help heal social injustice and environmental decay.

Moore, Thomas. *Care Of The Soul*. New York: HarperCollins, 1992. While this book is primarily a deep and sensitive exploration of the "matters of the soul," it focuses very well on the matters that for many people form the heart of simple living: valuing self and others, taking time to listen to one's own soul, and honouring its movements and needs.

Chapter 7

Tart, Charles T. *Living The Mindful Life: A Handbook for Living in the Present Moment.* Boston: Shambala Publications, 1994. This is a very "nitty-gritty" book about the practice of mindfulness meditation; it includes lots of questions and answers about common experiences and roadblocks that arise during meditation practice.

Kabat-Zinn, Jon. *Wherever You Are, There You Are: Mindfulness Meditation in Everyday Life.* New York: Hyperion, 1994. Also a how-to guide to mindfulness practice, Kabat-Zinn's book is the best, clearest, and most comprehensive single volume on meditation practice I have ever seen.

Chapter 8

Fromm, Erich. *To Have Or To Be?* New York: Continuum, 1997. A new release of a book originally published in the early '80s, Fromm's psychoanalytically based exploration of the acquisitive and the existential personality is as cogent now as when it was written.

Miller, Timothy. *How To Want What You Have.* New York: Avon Books, 1995. A fusion work of western cognitive psychology and a Buddhist perspective on life, Miller's book offers a lucid analysis of the origins and dynamics of as well as the alternatives to desire and the attempt to satisfy incessant desire as a way of achieving contentment and peace in life.

Chapter 9

Dominguez, Joe and Vicki Robin. 1992. *Your Money or Your Life: Transforming your Relationship with Money and Achieving Financial Independence.* New York: Penguin, 1992. Widely recognized as a major contribution to the literature on voluntary simplicity, though its principal focus is on money management and ways individuals can achieve financial independence.

Chapter 10

Fogler, Michael. *Un-Jobbing: The Adult Liberation Handbook.* Lexington: Free Choice Press, 1997. A practical guide that helps the reader evaluate the pros and cons of salaried full-time employment versus other options for making a living and/or reducing expenses.

Long, Charles. 1993. *How To Live Without a Salary.* Toronto: Warwick Publishing, 1993. A very witty introduction to breaking free of the 9-to-5 treadmill through savvy combinations of self-employment and bargain hunting. Packed with practical tips on where and how to find deals on everything and how to develop a more casual approach to earning a living.

Roberts, Wayne and Susan Brandum. *Get a Life!* Toronto: Get a Life Publishing, 1995. A highly readable and amusing compendium of anecdotes about the pioneers of what the authors consider a "new economy" of environmentally conscious and socially responsible entrepreneurs working at the margins of the consumer dinosaur to create business success stories that save the Earth, too.

Sinetar, Marsha. *Do What You Love, The Money Will Follow.* New York: Bantam Doubleday Dell, 1987. A detailed exploration of how to identify one's highest values in life and then shape a manner of living that expresses and honors them.

Chapter 13

Quinn, Daniel. *Ishmael.* New York: Bantam Books, 1992.

Index

About the Author

MARK BURCH is a freelance educator, writer and workshop facilitator. He currently teaches courses on voluntary simplicity as an adjunct faculty member of The University of Winnipeg and offers workshops on simpler living and adult environmental education across Canada. He has been a featured guest on CBC TV "Man Alive", CBC Radio "Ideas" and in the Knowledge Network documentary series "The Simpler Way". Mark Burch cultivates stillness, gathers Chi, and tends a garden in Prairie Canada.

If you have enjoyed *Stepping Lightly*, you might also enjoy other

BOOKS TO BUILD A NEW SOCIETY

New Society Publishers' mission is to publish books that contribute in fundamental ways to building an ecologically sustainable and just society, and to do so with the least possible impact on the environment, in a manner that models this vision.

Our books provide positive solutions for people
who want to make a difference.
We specialize in:

Sustainable Living
Ecological Design and Planning
Environment and Justice
New Forestry
Conscientious Commerce
Resistance and Community
Nonviolence
The Feminist Transformation
Progressive Leadership
Educational and Parenting Resources

For a full list of NSP's titles, please call 1-800-567-6772
or check out our web site at:
www.newsociety.com

NEW SOCIETY PUBLISHERS

NEW SOCIETY PUBLISHERS
P.O. Box 189
Gabriola Island, B.C.
V0R 1X0
CANADA

BOOKS TO BUILD A NEW SOCIETY

Our books provide positive solutions for people who want to make a difference.

❑ Please mail me a hard copy of your catalog.

Please notify me via email as new resources become available
in the following area/s of interest:

❑ Making a Difference
❑ Sustainable Living
❑ New Economics
❑ Conscientious Commerce
❑ ProgressiveLeadership
    • Organizational Devt.

❑ Ecological Design and Planning
❑ Sustainable Transportation
❑ New Forestry
❑ Educational & Parenting Resources
    • Education for Sustainability
❑ All of the above

Name_____

Address/City/Province_____

Postal Code/Zip_____Email Address_____

800-567-6772   **www.newsociety.com**

NEW SOCIETY PUBLISHERS